Original Cables from the Pearl Harbor Attack

Original Cables from the Pearl Harbor Attack

David Hurlburt's
War Comes to the U.S. – Dec. 7, 1941

Edited and Introduced by
Paul Rich

WESTPHALIA PRESS
An imprint of Policy Studies Organization

Original Cables from the Pearl Harbor Attack:
David Hurlburt's
War Comes to the U.S. – Dec. 7, 1941

All Rights Reserved © 2013 by Policy Studies Organization

Westphalia Press
An imprint of Policy Studies Organization
dgutierrezs@ipsonet.org

All rights reserved. No part of this book may be reproduced or transmitted in any form or by any means graphic, electronic, or mechanical, including photocopying, recording, taping, or by any information storage or retrieval system, without the permission in writing from the publisher.

For information:
Westphalia Press
1527 New Hampshire Ave., N.W.
Washington, D.C. 20036

ISBN-13: 978-0-944285-81-7
ISBN-10: 0944285813

Updated material and comments on this edition can be found at the Policy Studies Organization website:
http://www.ipsonet.org/

INTRODUCTION TO THIS EDITION

The first thirty hours of the start of World War II for the United States are documented in the carbons and mimeographs that compose a collection of cables from correspondents of the Time-Life-Fortune News Bureau. The numbering has been added for this edition.

This material came to the desk on what would otherwise have been a quiet Sunday of the then Bureau Chief David Hurlburt. The text can be disjointed and reflects the confusion of the two days as fifty reporters rushed to write the biggest stories of their careers. It is unedited except for deletions of a few references that might have been used by the enemy such as speculation about air strength of Japan and the damage done.

The first cable comes from Wilmott Ragsdale on Dec 7th from Washington, DC, who after the war became a distinguished professor at the University of Wisconsin, Madison. The last is from Charlton L. Whitehead, a local reporter in Norfolk, Virginia who on December 8th quotes the headline from the *Virginia Pilot*, PROCLAIM FACT AMERICA ENTERED WAR WITH CLEAN HANDS.

There are few sources for the initial reaction to Pearl Harbor, the "day that would live in infamy" that can have as much authenticity as the dispatches presented here. They offer a unique perspective.

Paul Rich

War Comes to the U.S. – Dec. 7, 1941

The First 30 Hours

as reported to the

TIME - LIFE - FORTUNE News Bureau

from the U.S. and abroad

WAR --- December 7, 1941

Each week the TIME - LIFE - FORTUNE News Bureau in New York receives scores of reports by phone, wire, cable, from its staff of close to 200 people all over the world.*

Running to tens of thousands of words each week, and ranging from special news dispatches to background and color stories, these News Bureau reports supply the editors of TIME, LIFE, FORTUNE, with exclusive stories and authentic documentation on the world's news.

The following 222 pages are the reports made to News Bureau Chief David Hulburd in New York by his Bureau Offices and Correspondents during the first 30 hours after the Japanese attack on Pearl Harbor.

Reports which might aid the enemy on subjects such as the relative air strength of Japan and the U. S., the extent of the damage at Pearl Harbor, and U. S. military and naval strategy, have been deleted. In cases where officials made "not for attribution" statements their names have been obliterated.

---

*The TIME - LIFE - FORTUNE News Bureau has permanent offices in: Atlanta, Cairo, Egypt, Buenos Aires, Chicago, Detroit, London, Los Angeles, Manila (temporarily closed), New Delhi, India, Rio de Janeiro, San Antonio, San Francisco, Washington. In addition it has full or part-time correspondents in 89 U. S. cities, 29 other cities throughout the world.

December 7, 1941

To: David Hulburd

From: Wilmott Ragsdale   Wire from WASHINGTON

1:00 Japan envoys asked appointment with Hull. It was scheduled for 1:45 p.m. 2:05 p.m. envoys arrived at the state department, twenty minutes late. They sat alone in the gloomy, diplomatic reception room under the portrait of Elihu Root. They were stared at from across the room by the cold bronze busts of Washington and Lafayette until:

2:20 p.m. they were led into Hull's office through the office of the Secretary's office force instead of directly through Hull's office door as usual. To a score of photographers and reporters, they nodded "yes" when asked whether they had asked to see Hull. At this time Hull must have known about the attack. The Japanese may not have known the exact time or at all.

2:26 p.m. the radio flash gave Roosevelt's statement that Pearl Harbor had been attacked. The Japs had handed Hull the reply to his "document" or principles presented last November 26. Hull "carefully read the statement ... turned to the Japanese ambassador and with the greatest indignation said: "...never seen a document more crowded with infamous falsehoods and distortions etc."

2:40 p.m. (about) two Japanese masks walked out of Hull's office, got their hats, and pushed through forty reporters to the elevator.

"Is this your last conference?" No reply.

"Have you any statement? Will there be a statement from the Embassy? No reply.

"Did you reply to Mr. Hull's document?" "Yes."

2:50 p.m. a telephone conversation with ███████████████ who said: NOT FOR ATTRIBUTION "Of course I can't tell the strategy but we will follow you

1.

immediately. We hope Russia will let us use Vladivostok, but we don't know. We will ask immediately. Of course we can't get there with ships, but we could fly in

3:10 p.m. DOS Chief of Information Michael McDermott came from Hull's office to the Press room and read the Secretary's statement on his meeting with the Japs. Forty British and American correspondents crowded around to get Mac's husky words. One Japanese correspondent for the Tokyo paper Asahi, Paul Abe, an American citizen and former student of Oregon State College wrote the statement down carefully presumably for dispatch to his paper. Chief Domei correspondent Cata was at the Embassy. He is a Jap citizen and will be held with another Jap reporter for exchange for the American newspaper men in Japan and occupied China. Abe and the other American correspondent for a Jap paper, Clark Kawakami are expected to stick in United States. Clark was married two months ago to a Japanese movie actress and had planned to send her back to Tokyo on the next boat. Another correspondent for the Tokyo Asahi, Nokamura, received the news first from a UP reporter. His face contorted, his hand went up to his shoulder, he said: "serious."

A reporter telephoned the Jap embassy and asked whether it would seek police protection. The spokesman replied: "No, we have great faith in the fairness of the American people."

3:38 p.m. ▮▮▮▮▮▮▮▮▮▮▮▮▮▮▮▮ called to see Sumner Welles. He said Welles may have been surprised by the character of the attack, "but you know Mr. Welles, he certainly didn't look it." ▮▮▮▮▮▮▮▮▮▮ said NOT FOR ATTRIBUTION "We will attack Japan with you. The Indies have been notified of the attack and are ready."

Upstairs in the Far East Division, the Foreign Service officers were gathered in the halls talking about the attack. There was criticism of the Navy. "Where were the patrols? How could they have let an aircraft carrier get so near the Islands. The carrier must have got within two hundred miles. Are they playboys or sailors?"

5:14 p.m. reporters were called into Howard Bucknell's office (assistant chief of information DOS). Before he read a statement, the crowd heard the radio flash from Tokyo that the Japs had declared a state of war. Bucknell's statement was that all official Japs and official Japanese establishments in U. S. territories would be accorded full protection."

The questions whether the U. S. can use Vladivostok -- the only near base to Japan -- is hot hot under the surface. Hull and Roosevelt may see Litvinoff tomorrow. Vladivostok is 600 miles, Manila 1,600 miles. Previous guesses of ▇▇▇▇▇▇▇▇▇▇▇▇▇▇ NOT FOR ATTRIBUTION have been that Russia would not let Vladivostok be used because of fighting one war in Europe. But ▇▇▇ NOT FOR ATTRIBUTION, said the Russians would let Vladivostok be used "if they think it is in their interest."

The Chinese in Washington were hilariously happy at having for fighting allies both Britain and U. S. People in corner drug stores were not excited by the news. Said one guard at the State Department: "We have been talking about this since I was a boy. I'm glad it's decided now."

The war with Japan means immediate "dislocation of vital supplies of tin, rubber, etc. from Malaysia, Dutch Indies, and India", according to ▇▇▇▇▇▇▇▇▇▇▇▇▇▇ NOT FOR ATTRIBUTION. He also said the Department has one report, not released, that the Japs have made a landing on the Thailand coast and that a Japanese submarine has been sighted 800 miles off the U. S. West Coast. Off the record this Jap landing on the Thai peninsula will be to cut the railroad from Singapore to Bangkok.

Subs and raiders will immediately begin attacking supply ships bringing vital materials from the foregoing three areas to the U. S. "It is our first worry. It all comes back like a nightmare to me now. How we plead on our bare knees four years ago, that the U. S. buy and stockpile these materials so the Navy could be free when this happened. We have been getting it fast these last three or four months, but before that we didn't get enough. The first thing Japan will do will be to dislocate these roots. Of course they can't cut off our supplies, but they can divert much of our Navy and cut some of them."

Thailand forces: From a military intelligence report, a State Department official told me these are the military forces of Thailand: 80,000 regulars and 300,000 reserves. The Thai minister told me several days ago, "Of course we have all our mechanized equipment on the French Indo-China border." The fellow giving me the Thai forces remarked, "Mechanized equipment means they have got spears."

There are 40,000 Japs in Peru. NOT FOR ATTRIBUTION ████████ fears they may attempt to blow up the Cerro de Pasco mine which is American owned and a big producer of copper and lead essential to U. S. defense.

Japan has been importing half the rice necessary for her city population from Formosa, and French Indo-China. The Navy may cut this.

DOS has no new figures on Japan's oil supplies. Last July the army military intelligence said Japan had enough oil for about a year of all-out war. Since the freezing order Japan has got not a drop of gasoline from the U. S., Netherlands Indies; has got small quantities from Sakhalin, the island they own half of with the Russians, directly north of Japan.

The Japs forced the American oil companies in Japan to acquire a six months advance supply back in 1934.

Kurusu, who was then director of the Foreign Office Economic Bureau was the Chief Negotiator with the American Embassy and oil companies in forcing the companies to store this oil.

(MORE COMING FROM ED LOCKETT)

December 7, 1941

To: David Hulburd

From: Ed Lockett

Wire from WASHINGTON

Tall, bald Eric Friedheim, INS roving newsman in Washington, was having a drink in the Press Club at 8:40 Saturday night. Just as he was finishing the Scotch and soda, someone came up to the bar beside him. He turned, recognized an acquaintance, small, brown-skinned, black-haired Masuo Kato, jovial little Washington correspondent of Japan's Domei News Agency. "Hi, Kato," said Eric, "did you hear about the President's message to the Emperor of Japan?"

"Good God, no," said Kato, "I just cabled the office: all quiet here tonight; no news."

If Kato is telling the truth, he was as unaware of Japan's plans to invade Hawaii and the Philippines on Sunday at Dawn as apparently was the U. S. Navy, the U. S. government at home, and, conceivably Japan's own Ambassador Nomura and Special Envoy Kurusu. This pair, and tall, courtly Secretary of State Cordell Hull were conferring on the "critical situation" obtaining in U.S.-Japanese relations "within an hour" of the time Nippon turned her war dogs loose on U. S. territory. Washington was recovering from Saturday night peacefully enough on Sunday when the news came. In the AP news room, on the third floor of the Washington Star Building, Bill Peacock, running the Sunday desk, was busily laying out the report for the wires. In the UP news room, black-haired, swarthy Arthur de Greve, veteran night wire top reporter was at his desk going over the big batch of handouts, culling the useless material from that which would go into the night report. Tall, lanky Arthur Hachten, INS oldster, was in the INS newsroom preparing for the work that would come a little later when the night wire opened at 3 p.m. Big, heavy Harold "Duke" Slater, running the Sunday day wire was reading the paper, his work nearly done. At approximately 2:20 the telephone rang in all these offices, and all three men picked them up. From the other end of the wire came these words: "This is Steve Early. I am calling from home. I have a statement here which the President has asked me to read." Then Early read to the three services the President's statement (pick up text from ticker) which told the U. S. that Hawaii was being bombed. He closed up the brief conversation with the observation that he was going directly to the White House, and "I will tell you more later."

Before Early could get out of his house, however, he had to make another telephone call to the Press associations - this time again on a three-way hookup, to advise at 2:36 that there had also been an attack on Manila.

Tall, lean Eddie Bomar, the AP's military analyst, was in the office at the time of the calls; he and John Lear and an AP feature writer, set out for the White House, were the first to get there, and were in the press room five or ten minutes before other newsmen turned up, learned from the police guards that Mr. Early had arrived, but wasn't quite ready to see them for a few moments. Meanwhile, the offices started mobilizing their staff. Stocky, black-haired, tacit Douglas Cornell, AP White House man, was painting a door in his basement when his wife called him to the telephone, and the office told him to get the hell over to the White house pronto. He got.

Heavy, jovial, fat newsman Mike Flynn of the Wall Street Journal, was getting ready to go to an oyster roast when his wife called him, just after his office called him. His oyster-roast host telephoned, asked him why he was late getting there. Mike said: "Sorry, but I'll see you after the war," and lit out for the White House.

Merriman Smith, small, black-moustached UP White House man, was shaving when his wife told him she had heard a radio announcement about the attack, and as he picked up the telephone to call the office, he found the office was calling him. He set out for the White House too.

Eric Friedheim was at the Redskins-Eagles football game as was his boss, bald William K. Hutchinson, INS Bureau Chief in Washington. "Hutch" knew where Eric was sitting, and after the boys in the press box got the news, passed it around, "Hutch" sought out Eric, sent him Whitehouseward. Half a dozen other reporters were in Griffith Stadium watching the ball game and didn't get into the busy scene of operations until afterwards. Hardly half a dozen reporters had got to the press room when the blue-coated policeman stuck his head in, announced: "Mr. Early will see you." The reporters filed into Steve's office found the red-faced secretary hunched behind his desk, looking very serious, unruffled. On his right sat his secretary, pretty, blonde, blue-sweatered Ruth Jane Rumelt, her notebook ready. "I have just a little additional information to give you, besides that I have already flashed to your offices," Steve began. "So far as is known now, the attacks on Hawaii and Manila were made wholly without warning - when both nations were at peace - and were delivered within an hour or so of the time the Japanese ambassador and special envoy Mr. Kurusu had gone to the State Department and handed to the Secretary of State the Japanese reply to the secretary's memorandum of November 26.

"As soon as information of the attack on Manila and Hawaii was received the War and Navy departments flashed it immediately to the President at the White House, thereupon and immediately the President directed the Army and Navy to execute all previously prepared orders looking to the defense of the U. S.

"The President is now with the Secretary of War and the Secretary of the Navy and steps are being taken to advise congressional leaders."

As reporters raced back to the press room, half a dozen late arrivals tagged at their heels, demanding a fill-in, and soon the press room was filling up.

At 3:23 p.m. Early's girl Friday popped her blonde head into the room, interrupted topspeed preparation of bulletins based on the opening press conference, reading from the shorthand in her notebook:

"So far as present information goes, and so far as we know at the moment, the attacks are still in progress. We don't know in other words that the Japanese have bombed and left. So far as we know both attacks are still in progress."

She had hardly gone before she was back again with another bulletin which she read from shorthand notes:

"The President has just received a dispatch from the War Department reporting the torpedoeing of an army transport, thirteen hundred miles west of San Francisco. Fortunately, the transport was carrying a cargo of lumber rather than personnel."

Back the reporters raced to their phones and by this time NBC had received permission from Steve Early to set up its microphone right in the press room. This had never been done before, but Steve said certainly and the electricians moved in and started setting up things.

At 4:09 p.m. and 50 seconds, Baukage of NBC was on the air, cut directly into the national network from the White House press room for the first time in history. Too late, CBS saw the NBC preparations under way, got permission from Early, and started setting up. CBS was more than two hours getting on the air direct from the White House.

Sharply at 3:35 p.m. Steve Early deserted his own office, walked into the press room himself, said he had an announcement: "The army has just received word and reported to the President signals of distress sent out by an American vessel believed to be an army cargo ship, seven hundred miles West of San Francisco. This concluded, he turned to go, then halted a moment to say: "So you can see that the Japanese submarines are well out in the Pacific."

This news threw the press room into another dither of flashes, and reporters were battling for the two booth telephones in the White House press room that are for public use. All of the press associations, many big newspapers, have direct telephones into the press room. Copy paper was getting scarce by a little after

4 p.m.; the news hawks used it up taking notes, and a few were writing. Mostly the news went out from the White House by telephone, however, and was rehandled in the newspaper offices.

At 3:57 Miss Rumelt brought word that Steve again wanted to see reporters, and they crowded into his office. Steve looked very serious. He was looking down at the floor intently as the newsmen crowded around his desk. He carefully waited for them all to get inside, had attendants close the door when the men were in, said:

"I have just called you in to bring you up to date on developments. The President now is with the Secretary of War and the Secretary of the Navy, and the Chief of staff, General Marshall. The President has just decided to call a cabinet meeting for eight-thirty this evening, and at nine o'clock to have the congressional leaders join with them in a joint meeting.

(Pick up conferees from ticker please)

Here a reporter inquired if the President intended to call in the leaders of both parties in Congress. Steve said yes and added: "I call your attention to the fact that is the same group he has been meeting with in the past. I say that, so you can give this an international meaning. He has not yet called in the chairmen of the military committees of Congress. You can also say that the President is assembling all the facts as rapidly as possible, and that, in all probability, he will as quickly as possible make a full report to the Congress. That's all I have, gentlemen."

At 5:58 came another call from Steve Early's office to the press room, and by this time the press room was packed with reporters, radiobroadcasters, and both CBS and NBC had set up microphones in the White House press room itself. With Baukage maning one; several CBS staffers handling the Columbia mike.

The press packed Early's office to the walls, and this time photographers, both stills and movies, were permitted to go in, and cameras ground as kleig lights turned the office into daylight, sent sweat streaming down the faces of tired newsmen.

"I call you in," Steve said, "to tell you that both the War and Navy, since the first report (of action in Manila) have been endeavoring to get in touch with commanding officers in Manila, and have been unable to do so. I suppose they are busy. Therefore, the President is now disposed to believe, and to hope, that the first report was an erroneous one.

"However, the President has just talked by telephone to Gov. Poindexter in Honolulu, and he confirms the report of heavy damages and loss of life there, including the city. He said that a second wave of planes was just then coming over."

Only a few minutes later, at 6:07 exactly, Early left his own office, came to the busy press room where reporters were still handling the bulletins from the latest press conference, and announced:

"The Navy has just reported a squadron of unidentified planes over Guam."

By this time, the photographers were taking pictures of the hot, busy, noisy and crowded press room itself. Some reporters had sent out for sandwiches and coffee. It looked like a long vigil.

At 6:24, blue-sweatered Miss Rumelt came back into the press room again, waved reporters to silence and attention, announced:

"The Navy just advised the President of dispatches that Guam has been attacked."

Again, at 6:54, Ruth Jane was back in the press room, and for the first time, her announcement after the press room snapped to attention was something of an anti-climax. She had come, merely, to say that the President had added white-haired Hiram Johnson to the list of congressional leaders invited to the White House tonight. She explained that Johnson was invited in his capacity as ranking minority member of the Senate Foreign Relations Committee.

By 7 p.m. the press room was a mess of torn papers, cigarette stubs littered the floor, the atmosphere was stuffy, hot, and reporters were growing very tired.

Glamorous Lee Carson of the INS was sitting at a typewriter, hammering out a night lead, her long bob, unusual dark coloring, and pretty gray suit much the most attractive spot in the room. Big, fat, Fulton Lewis got on deck about 6:45 in relieving his pretty secretary, Jean (koming); the Nelson Rockefeller office had its bald, blue-suited Robert McGill sitting in on the goings-on; Western Union had a flock of delivery boys popping in and out.

The White House boys got bits of developments in other departments by grapevine during the afternoon, and a small portable radio in the corner was running all afternoon. The folks in the White House press room learned, for instance, that speaker Sam Rayburn was out riding in his automobile when the news of the attack broke, that his frantic office was unable to get him and notify him until he returned to his home late in the afternoon.

Vice-president Wallace was in New York City, heard the news presumably over the radio, quickly got in touch with the White House by telephone.

The President was in his study most of the afternoon, close to the telephone, constantly in touch with the Army and Navy by telephone, an anxious listener who finally, dissatisfied with the reports he could get indirectly, put in a telephone call direct to Governor Poindexter in Honolulu.

Silently, during the afternoon, the secret mechanism always ready to swing into action for overall defense of the United States swung into action. Big, red-faced, tall, rugged Col. Ed Starling, White House Secret Service detail chief was quickly telephoned at his home after the news of the attack came; quickly came to the White House, started the process of calling in every one of the men assigned to the White House. The White House guard noticeably thickened; White House and capital police were stationed at every one of the entrances to the rolling White House grounds.

By 4 p.m., fully 500 persons had collected on Executive Avenue just outside the west side entrance to the Executive offices, attracted by the photographers' activities and the news they had heard over the radio. For a while they gathered around the southeast entrance to the State Department Building, across the street, but finally the activity around the executive offices drew them away and to the White House entrance.

Shortly before 7 p.m., Solicitor-General Charles Fahy slipped into the White House, probably through one of the living quarter entrances, was only discovered by reporters when he left at 7:09. He said he had been closeted with the President for only a few minutes, was very reluctant to talk at all. Finally, as reporters crowded around him when he was leaving, he thought a few moments, intently, announced in his whisperlike voice: "My visit had to do with the aliens--the Japanese--living in the United States."

It was just after this that the White House, fast coming all alert to the critical situation, clamped down a ban against any photographs in the White House grounds when George Dorsey (Identification later) one of the newsreel men, went into Steve's office, asked him what about pictures of the cabinet entering tonight, and the congressional leaders to come later.

"No, sir, no sir," Steve cracked. "We're not going to have the White House lit up tonight. Absolutely no pictures of the cabinet."

This was emphasized about ten minutes later when a Secret Serviceman called on the picture boys to halt as they started taking pictures of Fahy.

"No more pictures on the White House grounds," said Mike, and that was that.

Shortly after this Steven Early told a half dozen pressmen, for their own information and not for publication, that henceforth reporters could expect reports on developments following and concerning land-based operations, but that nothing could be expected from the Navy for obvious reasons.

"Every ship afloat has killed the radio, of course," he said. "We cannot expect to learn anything about sea engagements. About all you fellows can do now is clean up the story of land operations."

At 7:44 tall, graying Bill Hassett, Steve's assistant, came out into the lobby of the executive offices, gathered newsmen about him, and announced:

"The War Department has supplied the White House with a preliminary-- it is only preliminary--report on casualties. This report places the military dead at 104, and the military wounded at more than 300, on the island of Oahu alone. This is only a preliminary report, remember, and it gives no information whatever on civilian dead and wounded."

By 8:20 the press room was a complete wreck, with new telephone wires littering the place, tripping reporters up occasionally as they dashed about; all the radio networks had installed mikes by a little after 8, and each of the broadcasting announcers had little staffs of secretaries, researchers and reporters clustered about him.

Funniest diversion of the tense, wearing afternoon and evening was when slight, extremely comical Fred Paslay, crack reporter for the New York News, thought his telephone was installed. It looked very formidable and official, wearing a sort of skirt of wires around its base, and Fred picked it up to call the office. But no office did he get. Instead, as he put the receiver to his ear, the lilting, breezy tunes of a dance band came to his ears. Nothing else could he get, for half an hour. He tried innumerable times; each time he got an orchestra. Finally, one of the two dumb looking telephone company workers tangling up the wires in the room did some giggling, got the phone working right.

The Cabinet got to the White House right on time, for once-- although Secretary of the Navy Knox just got in under the wire at 8:30, the appointed time.

The first member of the Cabinet to arrive was big Jesse Jones, Secretary of Commerce, at exactly 8:20. Vigilant police carefully checked his big limousine through the Pennsylvania Avenue gate and into the grounds of the White House. In the order named, then came Wallace, Perkins, Ickes, Wickard, Morgenthau, Stimson --

tall and white-haired Hull, with two bodyguards; Biddle, and finally Knox. They entered the living quarters of the White House. (9:45 p.m. received)

To: David Hulburd
From: Felix Belair

Dec. 7, 1941
10:31 P.M.

Wire from WASHINGTON

Scene at Jap Embassy

Early in the afternoon the crowd began gathering across the street from the Japanese Embassy on Mass. Avenue. Occasionally, slant-eyed house boys could be seen peering out from behind drawn curtains. Police orders were enough to keep back the constantly growing crowd that kept on the look out for the story book smoke that always comes from the chimneys of foreign embassies of nations about to sever their diplomatic relations with their resident countries. The Japs had used more modern methods. Just before three o'clock in the afternoon a couple of lackies were seen by local reporters to carry out half a dozen square five gallon tins stuffed with papers over which they poured an unidentified liquid. There were a few whiffs of yellow smoke and, presumably, the papers were gone. Reporters were unable to go within fifty feet of the scene.

Around seven o'clock, Major Ed Kelly, Superintendent of Metropolitan Police, approached the Embassy gates but was refused admittance. He went around to the side door to the kitchen, emerged a few minutes later to say he had come to inquire how many policemen the Embassy required. (As if he didn't know) If he received any reply from the kitchen door, Kelly kept it to himself. Then he got into his car, blew the siren and moved down Mass. Ave.

To: David Hulburd
From Wilmott Ragsdale

Dec. 7, 1941
11:17 P. M.

Wire from WASHINGTON

A Japanese correspondent said upon leaving for his Embassy:

"Am I happy that Otto Tolischus and other American correspondent are in Tokyo."

To: David Hulburd
From: Wilmott Ragsdale

Dec. 7, 1941
10:32 P. M.

Wire from WASHINGTON

War caught approximately 200 United States Marines at post in North China. They are stationed in Peking, Tientsin and Ching Wang Tao.

Roughly, there are 5,000 Americans in Occupied China and 500 in Japan proper. Since last May, the number of Americans in Japan proper has dropped from 5,295 to 500. There have been several warnings from this Government that they should evacuate. The figure for Occupied China is about the same as it was last May.

To: David Hulburd
From: Jerry Greene

Dec. 7, 1941
9:50 P. M. -
10:25 P. M.

Wire from WASHINGTON

Washington Color:

Washington tonight is a city stunned, not afraid, not excited, but like a boxer who, after three rounds of sparring catches a fast hook to the jaw, rocks back, rolls with the punch. Tonight Washington is rolling back from the clout but in the rolling, sets itself grimly, solidly for the counterpunch.

Thin, sharp remnants of the afternoon's cold wind dither across bleak LaFayette Square directly in front of the White House tree limbs stick up bare and stark above the scant light of the posted lamps. Benches are deserted for the first night in weeks; two draftees hurry past the bronze of Andy Jackson in LaFayette Square the snap in their steps, the Square of their shoulders a sudden contrast to the demeanor of the draftee who slouched across the mall in early afternoon. Across the Square from the White House, the massive veterans' Administration Building remains one of the few in Washington without lights burning late into the night.

Pennsylvania Avenue is a mess for blocks on either side of the White House, traffic jammed, moving slowly with waits for from three to five light changes before cars can move a block. There is a silent deliberation in the movement of the cars. The driver, passengers in each turn their heads, stare with unmoving lips at the White House from the time they come within range until they are beyond.

Hundreds of pedestrians in a steady flow ease past the tall, iron picket fence separating the White House grounds from the Avenue. They are in groups of three to five. They move along quietly, talking if at all in whispers, subdued murmurs. Silence on the Avenue, despite the mob of cars, the mass of people, is apparent, deep enough to gnaw at the nerves.

Everybody, motorists, passengers, pedestrians alike, is watching the White House quietly, without noise, waiting, hoping somehow to see a visible sign of retaliation. Not even in mingling with the groups can one pick up enough audible conversation to catch the tenor of conversation.

Significantly, two fur-draped "chippies", passing up business opportunities, grasp the iron pickets, stare wide-eyed at the softly lighted white expanse of the executive mansion, mumble to themselves until the cops tell them to move along with the rest of the crowd. Even then the gaze of the girls turn backward toward the president's home, not toward business.

From outward appearances, there is little unusual going on in the White House. Across the leaf-littered lawn shine the soft beams of the great lamp hanging in the portico in front. A chandelier blazes from a thousand facets inside the main door. One cop walks his beat in measured steps directly underneath. Upstairs, deep inside are other burning lights clearly evident through uncurtained windows. A line of cars reaching almost from the brilliantly illuminated executive offices to the Pennsylvania Avenue Gate is first indication that business progresses. Further evidence is quickly apparent in the appearance of West Executive Avenue. Cars pack every parking space.

A stocky motorcycle cop, without his overcoat and sneezing frequently, blocks the entrance, permits only those cars which are on official business. Along the iron picket fence, an occasional cop keeps the crowd moving. But across West Executive Avenue, in front of the State Department, a mass of neck-stretchers fumbles around unmolested and unseeing.

East Executive Avenue is bare, deserted, despite the lone light burning over the East Portico of the White House.

One cop and three smutty red lanterns block traffic off East Executive Avenue at the Pennsylvania entrance. The traffic block extends over the entire White

House area. On 15th Street, at the west side, lanterns, cops, barricades have closed the entire elipse to traffic.

There are few cops, comparatively, around the White House itself. Patrolman Edward H. Ring of the 3rd Precinct, pacing back and forth before the Main Entrance Gate, on duty since 5 P.M., cold and nursing a pair of hurtful feet, had this explanation:

"They sent a bunch of us up here this afternoon but we had to break it up. You know how people are. This is the worst mess at the White House I have ever seen. I mean in the way of traffic. But let two cops get together and four people come up to see what's going on. Let 10 cops gather around and a hundred people come around. So that's why there are only a few of us here. Excuse me. You'll have to move along, there (to the crowds). Sorry, people, but move one way or the other.

"I hear the Army is coming up here tonight or tomorrow. Now don't quote me. That's just a rumor. But I guess they need it.

"I had a fine one while ago." A young draftee come along with his girl and asked me what all the fuss was about. I said, "Brother, you better take your girl home and get some sleep. You are in a war." He says, "You're nuts. What war?" So I told him and his girl turned pale and he give her the eye and they went off in a hurry. I guess it was the old last-chance game."

Strangely, there were few lights on in the State Department Building, but those few, on the East Side facing the White House, were staggered in the form of a rough "V", running from roof to basement.

At Treasury, as at State, there are more milling crowds, moving around slowly, aimlessly. Yellowish lights flicker out from scattered offices in the nation's counting house without pattern.

Down on Constitution, past the dark, empty elipse, there is a renewal of the same quiet, questioning, endless stream of automobiles all eyes turned toward the squat, trim Navy and Munitions Buildings. And there, Washington is seeing war close at home for the first time in a generation.

There aren't many lights on in either building, peculiarly. Navy flickers out at intervals like the orange spots on a new checkerboard. But there are more of the usual uniformed guards inside the brightly lighted entrance.

The cold steel of war shimmers icily along the front of the War Department Building. Troops in tin hats, with full equipment, packs, rifles, ammunition, fixed bayonets, stand stiffly before the entrances. The bayonets are like swift licks of flame in the moving, switching glow of a thousand automobile headlights. Faces under the tin hats are hard, lined, unsmiling. Before the main door of the Munitions Building one nonchalant husky eyes the mob, a submachine gun slung over right shoulder, close at hand.

There are more of these troops at the new War Department Building a few blocks to the north, where the engineers are hurrying in and out with more signs of hot activity than was seen at any other one spot.

But most significant of all was this: Of all the government Buildings seen in a quick survey of downtown Washington, in only one were all lights flaring, were all offices obviously occupied, with all help moving at top speed. That was the narrow, tall office building just to the north of the Munitions Building---the headquarters of Selective Service.

....

TO: DAVID HULBURD

FROM: FRANK MCNAUGHTON   W 12 - 4:30 Dec. 8, 1941

WHITE HOUSE CONFERENCE LAST NIGHT

"As you already know, Japan has attacked the U.S."

With these words, President Roosevelt, sitting in his big armchair behind his desk in the second-floor red room study at 8:45 last night, opened his conference with Congressional leaders -- the conference that led to Congress' all-time speed record for a declaration of war at 1:32 P.M. today, exactly 48 minutes less than 24 hours after the Japanese attack.

Congressmen were not caught by surprise. One leader, John W. McCormack of Mass., was unable to get back to Washington for the conference. Senate Majority Leader Alben W. Barkley flew in from Kentucky. Most of the others were in Washington.

They arrived at the White House singly and in pairs, were received by the usher and sent to the second floor. They were advised that the President would receive them in a few minutes. A cabinet session, grim and deadly, was still going on in the Red Room. Outside this room, the men who speak for all parties in Congress held an indignation meeting. Long, belligerent Senator Tom Connaly of Texas, Chairman of the Foreign Relations Committee, smoking a cigar violently, said the Japs had asked for it and they would get it. The talk turned to the thousand and one rumors that had swept Washington -- parachute troops landing in Hawaii, battleships sunk, Wake and Midway Islands captured.

A buzzer sounded, there was a scraping of feet and chairs inside the Red Room, and a girl announced that the Congressmen should enter. They filed up to the front of the room. The Cabinet discreetly moved to the back of the room, took other chairs and remained throughout the session.

The President was deadly serious; there were lines deeper than usual in his face; there was no smile, the switch to turn that on was dead. The President held a sheaf of papers, Navy reports, and his desk was piled with them.

Page 2 - To David Hulburd from Frank McNaughton - 4:30 Dec. 8.

He passed out cigars, Cuban Habanas dressed in the label of the Comision Nacional De Propaganda Defensa.

Then Mr. Roosevelt began reading the Navy reports to the Senators and House members. His tone was grave. He emphasized that the information he had received was spotty, and far from complete. Pointedly, Mr. Roosevelt reminded the Congressmen that while these attacks were under progress, the Japanese diplomats, Nomura and Kurusu were at the White House playing a game of diplomatic duplicity upon aged, sincere, peace-loving but now terribly enraged old Cordell Hull.

The President reviewed the major reports, said that they were still coming in at a very rapid rate and that no general overall picture could be formulated in detail. He said, however, that the Japanese had undoubtedly launched a craftily-planned "attack in force" upon every possession and strip of territory the U.S. had.

        More coming

12/8/41

To: David Hulburd

From: Felix Belair Jr.
Washington, D.C.

Subject: Roosevelt Goes to Congress

Grim determination was written on every line of his face as Franklin Roosevelt was wheeled out of the south door of the Executive Mansion and helped into his waiting limousine to begin what was to be his last journey to the Capitol until his State of the Union Address in January. His appearance had been awaited by a swarm of tense Secret Service men in plain clothes, who stood about in little groups on the south lawn. Ten highly polished black limousines bearing the seal of the President had been rolled into place. Up ahead and reaching nearly to the west gate the motorcycles of escorting police idled awaiting the signal from big Ed Starling to get rolling. More Secret Service men than had been assembled to protect the President even on the occasion of his three Inaugurals put their automatic riot guns into place, cocked and primed for any emergency. They wore no topcoats, these protectors of the President. Topcoats slow down the draw from the hip of the 38 service revolvers all carried.

Some said the President looked as mad as a wet hen. More probably he had been, but that was last night. Now he had a job to do. He was unsmiling as he sat back in the well-padded rear seat, adjusting his big dark Naval cape. His son, Captain Jimmy of the Marines, sat beside him, trying to express the seriousness that the occasion required. Slowly the Presidential motorcade circled the south lawn, spattering gravel from the driveway about the neatly trimmed grass. Past the east gate a fair-sized crowd cheered from either side of the street south of the Treasury Building. But here was no campaign parade and there were no campaign cheers. The President, however, was not too impressed with the solemnity of the occasion to fail to respond to the crowd. The smile and the wave of the hand was there, although the hand waving was a little less vigorous and the smile was not from ear to ear. The President's response each time was entirely in keeping with his silk hat and formal attire. It was a solemn obligation he was about to ask Congress to shoulder and it had best be done soberly. The President's mood was sobriety from start to finish. Probably never before during his life had the President been so completely protected. Although he rode in a closed car, a Secret Service man perched preciously on either running board. On either side his car was flanked by an open Secret Service car with three men on each of their running boards and four more inside cuddling up with their sawed-off riot guns. Another Secret Service car followed that of the President and ahead of him went "Big Bertha" or "the Queen Mary," a Rolling arsenal if ever there was one. If ever a President rode in a mechanized division it was Roosevelt today.

The Capitol grounds was alive with cops, Marines and plainclothesmen brought in from Baltimore, Richmond and Philadelphia. It would have been worth any man's life to try to break the lines. Reporters going to work as usual entered the House and Senate wing of the Capitol, found themselves confronted by Marines with fixed bayonets. A reporter tried to get into the House press gallery without showing his white card and was knocked back ten feet by the skinniest Secret Serviceman he ever saw. Another was absentmindedly entering the gallery with a rolled-up newspaper. It was snatched out of his hand so fast he scarcely noticed it. Washington cops and plainclothesmen discovered places around the Capitol grounds today they never knew existed. They were posted on both sides and behind the Capitol building, through the galleries and on the floor of the House. It was the same at the White House. They were on the roof of the Executive Office and patrolled the roof of both wings of the mansion itself.

In other words, the protection was more than ample and the day passed without incident.

#3
Washington

All over the White House establishment there was eloquent proof of the nation's peril. Reporters, radio commentators with their sound men, photographers and newsreel cameramen were falling over themselves. Appreciated only by the handful of reporters regularly assigned to cover the place in war and peace was the fact that a goodly number of the young men in the lobby and press room had no connection with the press or any other medium of public opinion. They were members of the White House Secret Service detail. An NBC technician discovered mumbling something over a microphone in his office downtown, almost had the same device shoved down his throat because of Steve Farly's notice earlier that there would be no more broadcasting from the press room. Telephone linemen we worked feverishly throughout the day installing phones for special newspaper bureaus to whom the idea had never occurred before.

But through all the bustle it was apparent that after hectic yesterday, the White House establishment was beginning to settle down. To /The White House establishment nothing could be worse than yesterday. Steve Early talked less excitedly to reporters at his morning press conference, weighed the few questions that followed his opening statement before answering. ▮▮▮
▮▮▮

Extra couches and overstuffed chairs were strewn about the lobby. Secretaries, stenographers and messengers moved a little more swiftly from office to office. Gone were the jitters of yesterday. Now war had become a reality, there was nothing to do but see it through. And this appreciation of the finality of the thing reached down to the last typist. All day long newsmen popped in and out of the Executive Office between visits to other departments and press conferences. At any moment a big story might break and it would be wise to be on hand for a first-hand version if possible.

(more coming later)

12/8/41

(by phone) 5:50 p.m.

To: David Hulburd

From: Felix Belair Jr.

Subject: Roosevelt Goes to Congress CONTINUED

The White House had become the funnel through which all news of Far Eastern operation must flow. At the Navy and War Departments old drinking companions of newsmen were saying: I'm still your friend but you'll have to get it from the White House or not at all. At the White House genial, ▓▓▓▓▓▓ Bill Hassett said it would take a few days for us to shake down and then there would be some thought of policy about communiques. He did not say who would issue them but if Steve Farly has his way he will not be the mouthpiece for the War Ministry.

All Washington was in the middle of a shakedown cruise and the White House was the focal point. Today the White House showed signs of settling down. Not far behind would come the rest of the capital. Once war came Washington started looking facts in the face. In a week or so Washington would begin to make sense.

Franklin Roosevelt has passed from reformer to emergency President to War President. From now on he would see none but those officials engaged in the conduct of the war abroad and home.

Wire from Jerry Greene, Washington, D.C. -- to David Hulburd, December 8, 1941 -
4:30 p.m.

Washington color:

Tight knots of people pressed smotheringly around half a dozen portable radio sets scattered through the crowd lining the sidewalks of the Capitol plaza. Minutes before, the Presidential caravan had swished up the drive, depositing the Roosevelt and Cabinet officers at the south entrance to the Capitol itself. Metallic voices from the radio speakers describing the scene inside the House Chamber were the only sound to rise above the heads of the tense, still spectators.

There was nothing to be seen except the hard, grey walls of the Capitol, bright and solid in the clear, pale noonday sun, except the dozens of policemen stalking about at every corner, in the street, along the sidewalk. Yet the face of every individual, the faces of all those huddled over the radios, were turned directly toward the towering pillars of the Capitol. There was a church-like hush, a sullen, angry silence. It would be ten minutes before President Roosevelt mounted the dais to ask recognition of the war by Congress. But those in the crowd outside who did speak, spoke in whispers.

What was the silence of shock last night, today was the cold, determined hatred of an outraged people. There was something of the tension of a lynching mob, a mob where there are no masks, where each individual is happy to be identified with the purpose of the assembly. A youngster barely above high school age, her bare legs tinged with purple from chill, above the anklet socks, clung tautly to the arm of her escort, a slight young lad in uniform of a Navy enlisted man, a youth whose jaw muscles rippled as he stared ahead stiffly through horn-rimmed glasses. "Gee," the girl whispered audibly, "Ain't there a way a woman can get into this thing?"

Fifty people were close enough to hear the remark but not a head turned in curiosity, not a smile cracked. The sailor did not answer. The girl chewed her lower lip.

There had been cheers when the President passed by; there were cheers when he left. There were more cheers after the message than before. But before the hurried glimpse of Roosevelt and afterward, there was quiet, quiet as if those who were watching realized that there was scant time for vocal demonstration.

All over downtown Washington those same knots of people ganged around parked automobiles which had radios, listening in the same unsmiling, intent seriousness. There were no wisecracks, there were few exchanges of remarks of any kind.

Washington was at work when the President went up to Capitol Hill, and, beyond a mob around the Treasury Department building, there were comparatively few lining Constitution Avenue to watch the procession.

Down Along the West End of Constitution Ave., more of the machine gun army guards, more of the stiff, tin-hatted troops with fixed bayonets stood at every door of the munitions building. Not yet were there more than the usual blue-uniformed cops at the Navy building.

But over under the shadow of the Lincoln Memorial, a tough, efficient squad lounged at easy alertness back of a drab, snub-nosed machine gun, set up to command the approach to the Memorial Bridge. Troops with fixed bayonets paced their beats at the bridge entrance. There was a duplication of this scene at the 14th Street bridgehead, except here those men not attending the gun warmed their hands before a small fire back at one side.

Without hysteria, without fuss, but with a solid, harsh determination, Washington went to war.

TO: David Hulburd (via telephone Dec. 8, 1941
                                   4:50 p.m.   - em)
From: Crosby Maynard

Add Washington scene during the President's speech.

25 officers, top men in the Navy's Bureau of Aeronautics, gathered a few moments before 12:30 p.m./today in the large corner office of their chief, Rear-Admiral Jack Towers. Towers was not present, was said to be with the Secretary at the Capitol.

Gray and white-haired four-stripers were very much in evidence; there were a few commanders, a very few of lesser rank. All were in uniform, all were serious, most were very calm, silent. The greetings exchanged were formal. Salutes, ranks were strictly observed.

They listened to the President in absolute silence. Cigarettes burned out. New ones were not lighted.

As the President finished, there followed the first bars of the Star Spangled Banner.

An unidentified officer said one word:

"Gentlemen!"

25 officers came to their feet at rigid attention.

As the last words died away there was a very short pause.

"Gentlemen, we have work to do".

The officers filed out.

- - - - -

December 8, 1941
7:40 p.m.

To: David Hulburd

From: Wilmott Ragsdale

ROOSEVELT:

FDR is standing up well under the pressure. He had only five hours sleep last night, looked fresh but grim today when he made his address to Congress.

During the afternoon he demonstrated once again his ability to snatch relaxation from heavy hours. After talking with Litvinof, he relaxed on his office sofa and slept soundly for an hour.

TO: DAVID HULBURD   5:05 P - 12-8

FROM: FRANK MCNAUGHTON   Wire from WASHINGTON

CHAMBER COLOR

The air was snappy, crisp. The atmosphere one of high-voltage tension ready to spark and bridge the gap to war at the slightest touch of the switch when Congress -- knowing war, thinking war, talking war, ready for war -- started streaming into the Capitol today.

There was not a man who did not know that before nightfall, the awful strength of America would be thrown into a struggle six thousand miles away that coiled and plunged its sting into even thick-hided isolationists, forced them to get their heads up and see what the world was about.

"Hell, it's the only thing to do. Shoot the God damned living Hell out of them," exploded isolationist Dewey Short of Missouri, Republican rable-rouser and bitter opponent of the President. There was only one cry -- war. There was only one question -- would it only be Japan, or Germany and Italy with her? No one knew. Everyone speculated that by laying off Germany and Italy, forcing them to take the initiative as Japan had taken it, the collective mind of America's millions could be solidified on anti-Axis war as it has become united, overnight, on a war with Japan.

Early this morning, a heavy guard of Marines was posted around the Capitol, more than 200 Secret Service men spread through the Capitol, searched even the Speaker's office. Fully 400 policemen were lined up at the south side of the Capitol, reviewed, and then stationed in and around the building.

The Speaker's office was a madhouse. Egg-bald little Sam was seeing Army men, Navy men, telephoning frantically for late news, pulling legislative wires, conferring with Majority Leader McCormack, Minority Leader Joe Martin,

Page 2 - To: David Hulburd
From: Frank McNaughton   5:05 P - 12 - 8

Foreign Affairs Leader Sol Bloom, greasing the skids for the war resolution. A similar scene was going on in the Senate Foreign Relations Committee room over at the other end of the Capitol where Barkley, Tom Connally, Vice-President Henry Agard Wallace were meshing the gears for a quick take-off to war.

Down on the first floor, on the House side of the Capitol, the staff of aged house chief doorkeeper Joe Sinnott were going crazy. Tickets for the galleries were being dispensed there - one for each Congressman. The Senators tickets had been sent to Barkley's office.

(more coming)

Second Take - Chamber Color - From McNaughton 12-8

Dozens of Congressmen wanted one-two-three tickets: They get one. A messenger from the office of Admiral Harold R. Stark, Chief of Naval Operations, waited for an hour in the line outside Sinnott's door. It became a jam, a crush, as the hour neared for the President's address. The House was to meet at 12 Noon, but it was 12:5 before bald, raspy-voiced little Speaker Sam Rayburn whanged his heavy gavel - he keeps two handy, a light and a heavy - called the House to order, then ordered "all unauthorized" persons who had cadged seats at the rear of the chamber, to clear out. There was a bustling, scraping of chairs, and dozens of gate crashers moved back behind the iron and bronze railing in the chamber. Most members of Congress, heeding Rayburn's orders telephoned night-long last night, were in their seats by noon.

Tall, toothy majority leader John W. McCormack, a Massachusetts Irishman to the core, his iron-grey hair flying wildly, his black suit flecked with cigar ashes, hot-footed it to the rostrum, whispered in Rayburn's ear. Little Sam, in a freshly-pressed blue business suit, nodded vigorously, his pince-nez glasses bobbing on his nose.

McCormack scrammed back to the two desks on the Democratic side, in the middle of the chamber, took a seat behind the House microphone, pushed slightly at the broadcasting mikes placed in front of him. Minority Leader Joseph W. Martin of Mass. - hitherto voting isolationist with the majority of his Party - rushed about conferring with the Republicans, patting them on the shoulders, pulled out his written speech, gave it a glance, shoved it back into his pocket.

Doorkeeper Sinnott announced a message from the Senate. It was the passage of House Concurrent Resolution 61, agreeing to a joint session. Three minutes after the House met, the Senate was filing into the chamber. Vice President Wallace helped along octogenarian, fiery old Carter Glass of Virginia; the Republican and Democratic leaders, McNary and Barkley walked arm in arm; aged, infirm Republican

isolationist Hiram Johnson of California linked arms with tall, silver-haired Elmer Thomas, Oklahoma Democrat. It was arranged as a demonstration of solidarity, politics out, a Democrat and a Republican in many cases marching along together.

(more coming)

Third Take - Chamber Color - From McNaughton 12-8 5:55P

Up in the Executive Gallery, Mrs. Eleanor Roosevelt, in black hat, black suit, wearing a silver fox fur, peeked from behind one of the tall, upright girders installed a year ago to keep the house roof from falling in. She had one of the poorest seats in the House.

Sinnott announced the Supreme Court, and they marched in, Chief Justice Harlan F. Stone's bulldog jaw set in hard lines.

Old isolationist, British hating Republican representative, George Holden Tinkham of Massachusetts waddled around the wall of the House, his beard freshly combed, wearing a freshly-pressed blue suit in strange contrast to his usually disheveled garb. He hauled up a chair close to the left of the speaker's rostrum, bowed, sat down.

Secretary Hull led in the Cabinet, and he looked almost like a ghost risen for the occasion. Tall, slightly stooped, he seemed almost exhausted. His face was deeply lined, sad. His white hair was neatly brushed, set off by his blue suit, black tie and white soft-collar shirt.

One Missouri Congressman, carrying a check for $3,000, vainly tried to buy Defense Stamps at the Capitol post office, finally wound up investing in National Defense Bonds.

In full uniform, Admiral Stark, General George C. Marshall, Brig. Gen. Henry H. Arnod talked earnestly together on the House floor, finally took seats over at the left of the Chamber, in front of the diplomatic corps from which the Axis diplomats, to a man, were missing. Cadaverous, tall Lord Halifax leaned over, whispered long and fervently to Admiral Stark, checking up on the latest information for Britain, too, was fighting at Hong Kong and Singapore.

Joe Martin pointed a stubby forefinger at the chest of isolationist Ham Fish, lectured him, and Fish nodded vigorous agreement. A dozen children were on the floo

Page 2 - Third Take - Chamber Color - From McNaughton 12-8

sitting in their parents' laps. Back at the rear of the Republican side of the Chamber, delegate Sam King from Hawaii talked with round-headed, bald and bitter Harold Knutson, only man now in the House who voted against war in 1917, ▮▮▮▮▮▮▮▮▮▮▮▮▮▮▮▮▮▮▮▮▮▮▮▮▮▮▮▮▮▮▮▮▮▮▮▮▮▮▮ -- talked with first one member, then another.

The President got 1-1/2 minute ovation when he hobbled up the ramp to the speaker's dias on the arm of son James who was in his Marine uniform.

For the first time in eight or nine years Republicans generally applauded Franklin D. Roosevelt. Only a few sat on their hands -- Hiram Johnson of California William Lambertson of Kansas, Ulysses S. Guyer of Kansas.

(More coming)

TO: DAVID HULBURD

FROM: FRANK MCNAUGHTON

12-8 6:05P

Fourth Take - Chamber Color

It was the first time the Republican Party, in bulk, en block ever gave Franklin D. Roosevelt anything but the silent treatment.

The President, in formal morning attire, took a firm grip on the reading clerk's stand, flipped open his black, looseleaf notebook like every schoolchild uses, adjusted his glasses, took a long, steady look at Congress and began to read.

The hum and overtones which had rumbled through the galleries, across the floor for an hour, died out instantly. The Chamber was brilliantly lighted, and as the President read, he gazed almost directly into a battery of floodlights which had been arranged for the photographers. A thousand people were behind the rails, another two thousand in the galleries. The press gallery was jammed to brimming, a hundred reporters tried to peer through the doors.

Speaker Rayburn, introducing the President, made it snappy: "Senators and Representatives, I have the distinguished honor of presenting the President of the United States."

It was Roosevelt at his best; an hour later, the House at its best.

A year ago, Franklin Roosevelt trembled as he adjusted his nose pincers to read his annual message to Congress, a message condemning the Axis. He almost dropped his glasses that day. Today, that tremor was gone. His hand was firm, its muscles bulging as he gripped the desk, as he thumbed the five pages of big print. His face was grim; a wisp of iron-grey hair hung slantwise along his forehead. But the main thing -- the hand was firm, the voice steely, brittle with determination.

When he said America would remember "this onslaught," Republicans and Democrats broke into applause. In a front row seat, Chief Justice Stone, whose legal precepts have struck hard for freedom, nodded his approval. Again, when Mr. Roosevelt said "righteous might" will win through, the Congress, the Supreme Court, the Diplomatic

Page 2 - Fourth take - Chamber Color - From McNaughton

Corps leaped to their feet, gave a full minute of wild applause ... "We will gain the inevitable triumph -- so help us God." Again Congress applauded. The Roosevelt jaw was thrust out, there was no show of weakness, no lack of confidence. It was an almost brutal display of the will to win. Then -- up with his right hand, a determined smile, a wave to Congress and to the galleries. Again wildness.

It had taken exactly 10 minutes -- undoubtedly, according to Congressmen, the shortest war message ever delivered to an American Congress.

Speaker Rayburn congratulated the President, accepted a copy of the address; Wallace congratulated him. Rayburn proclaimed the joint session ended.

The phrase is McCormack's - "The President at his best; the House at its best."

(more coming)

TO: DAVID HULBURD

FROM: FRANK MCNAUGHTON   6:18 P 12-8

Fifth Take - Chamber Color

Immediately, McCormack moved to send the President's message to the Foreign Affairs Committee, have it printed, Rayburn declared the motion adopted, then McCormack waved a sheet of white paper, said he had sent the resolution to the Clerk's desk, moved to suspend the House rules and pass it immediately.

Aged, grey-haired, ill House reading clerk, Alney E. Chaffee, read the resolution, House Joint Resolution 254, declaring war on Japan. Rayburn asked if a second were demanded. Joe Martin said a second was requested. Vainly, Jeanette Rankin, at the rear of the Chamber, leaped up to her pipestem legs, protested shrilly, sought to lodge an objection. Rayburn almost brutally ruled that an objection could not be entertained, that no unanimous consent request had been propounded. McCormack used just 20 seconds to defend his motion, said Japan had attacked, moved its adoption. Joe Martin followed, reading his prepared speech that he had written out painstakingly in his hotel room at nearly 3 o'clock this morning. It was a plea for all-out unity, no more strikes, full prosecution of the war. The members leaped up, cheered little Joe, rushed over to congratulate him.

There were yells of "vote, vote, vote," from the democratic side. Rayburn, pounding like a piledriver, shouted, "It won't be long," and pleaded, "Let us maintain order at this time particularly."

Little Sam's voice was almost reverent. Then Ham Fish said his piece, rather rea it from a crumpled sheet of onion skin paper, in a high singsong voice and with apparent nervousness. He would, at the proper time, he said, seek an assignment with a combat unit "preferably colored," as he did in the world war.

Again Jeanette Rankin flounced to her feet. "Sit down, sister," yelled short, thin John M. Dingell of Michigan.

Page 2 - Fifth take - Chamber Color - From McNaughton

Rayburn recognized Chairman Sol Bloom. Bloom hunched over the microphone, like a brown teddy bear in his brown suit, and said one short mouthful: "Speedy action, not words, should be the order of the day." Then little bantam-like Luther Johnson of Texas demanded war, immediately. McCormack slipped over to the Republican side, whispered in Joe Martin's ear, patted Joe affectionately on the arm. Politics was adjourned.

Grey-haired, ex-war nurse Edith Nourse Rogers of Massachusetts said Japan had "stabbed us in the back." The President used the same term against Mussolini in his Charlottesville speech in the summer of 1940. Black-haired, pretty, Mrs. Katharine Byron of Maryland, mother of five sons, widow of a Congressman, said her husband served in the world war, said she was "willing to give my sons if necessary," said she favored war. So did black-haired, formerly oppositionist Joseph E. Casey, Massachusetts Irishman.

(more coming)

TO: DAVID HULBURD

FROM: FRANK MCNAUGHTON   6:42 P 12-8

Sixth Take - Chamber Color

The House was getting restless. Speaker Rayburn called on Republican, white-haired, swarthy-faced, bulky Charles A. Eaton of New Jersey, one of the few Republicans who, years ago, was declaring that aggression was a plot of world conquest, and who, when Japanese were stripping English women in Tientsin, pleaded for a strong American course; told Congress "there are some things a man had better die against than submit to once."

An orator of the Old school, Eaton shunned the microphone, boomed in a loud roar that America had met "the call to unity . . . the call to courage . . . the call to victory." It would be necessary to kill this accursed monster of tyranny and slavery," . . . it would "be a long battle," but America would not stop short of victory.

At 1:04P, Rayburn ordered the roll call. Again Jeanette Rankin tried to interrupt proceedings, and stop the roll call. She was again brutally thrust off by Rayburn. She sat down in a back row seat, drummed her fingers on the arms of the seat, smiled in a bemused manner.

Down the line, without a break, the isolationists voted for war. Even Tinkham, pointing his beart at a rakish angle, bellowed his "aye" vote. Fish of New York, Knutson of Minnesota, Ludlow of Indiana, Mundt of South Dakota, Peterson of Georgia, Rabaut of Michigan, holding his little daughter in his lap, Rankin of Mississippi, Vorys of Indiana and dozens of others who have been the House core of ostricism. The clerk reading the roll call, Irving Swanson, called, "Rankin of Montana."

"No," Jeanette Rankin smiled. "SSSSSSSS." The hisses echoed through the House Chamber, and Rayburn violently pounded the gavel, until the razzing subsided. Swanson proceeded with his roll call.

Jeanette Rankin still smiled. A dozen Republican Congressmen rushed back to the rear of the Chamber, ganged up and sought to change her vote -- Everett M. Dirksen of Illinois, Francis D. Culkin of New York, Forrest A. Harness of Indiana, Harold Knutson of Minnesota, white-haired Democrat isolationist, James F. O'Connor of Montana, Bulky George H. Bender of Ohio, Karl Stefan of Nebraska, curly-haired James Van Zandt of Pennsylvania, Baldish blocky Karl Mundt of South Dakota, tall George Dondero of Michigan, big-raw-boned Paul W. Shafer of Michigan, and James W. Mott of Oregon.

She smiled, argued, refused. What did she tell them? That it might all be a mistake, it might be propaganda. How did Congress know for sure that Hawaii had been attacked? It might be another Presidential ruse. There was so much propaganda nowadays. Look at the Kearney and some of those other incidents. It might turn out to be nothing more than propaganda. No, she wouldn't change her vote. ███

(more coming)

TO: DAVID HULBURD

FROM: FRANK MCNAUGHTON   6:58 P - 12-8

Seventh Take - Chamber Color

There was no weeping in the galleries, or on the floor when the house voted. It was a grim resolve to go to war. There was another burst of cheering when, at 1:26 P.M. Sam Rayburn whammed the gavel, announced the vote as 388 Aye, one No. Immediately thereafter, the house indulged in another spree of cheering. The Senate sent in its Senate Joint Resolution 116 - identical to the comma with McCormack's Resolution. Quick as a flash, McCormack was on his feet and asked unanimous consent to "take from the speaker's table" the senate resolution and pass it.

"Without objection, the joint resolution is read a third time and passed," Rayburn yelled. Then the proceedings by which the House had passed its own resolution were "vacated."

At 1:32 P.M., eight minutes short of an hour after the President finished, Congress had voted war against Japan. There were no tears. The tension was not as dramatic as when the House passed the amendments to the Neutrality Act. Why? Because this time, America had been attacked, and Congress' will was not to be doubted. Its will was to declare war, fight like Hell, and as the resolution stated, "All of the resources of the country are hereby pledged by the Congress of the U. S. all in for an all-out war, nothing less.

The Senate scene was somewhat the same. Tom Connally plunged in with his resolution. Short discussion by Connally, by Arthur H. Vandenberg. No disagreement. Then the roll call. Two names stood out above the rest in that roll call. Little squint-eyed Gerald P. Nye, who has been the darling of the American Quislings, intimate of Charles A. Lindbergh. He couldn't muster the guts for a No. He voted Aye.

(more coming)

TO: DAVID HULBURD

FROM: FRANK MCNAUGHTON   7:07 P 12-8

Eighth & Last Take - Chamber Color

Robert M. LaFollette, Jr., voted Aye. Venerable old George W. Norris of Nebraska also voted Aye. There was not a dissent, 82 to nothing, a complete shutout of America First, a route of isolationism beyond even the expectations of the President's advisers. Japan accomplished what the emergency, what the eloquence of the President couldn't budge.

The Senate passed its resolution at the chime of 1 P.M.

Again there were no tears.

It was an almost anti-climax in the House and in the Senate. There was no prayerful silence such as when the roll was called on amending the Neutrality Law, no days of debate, no squabbling, no backbiting. It was just the American Congress, its neck bowed, its back arched, and itself buckled down to the job of giving "blood, sweat and tears" in any volume necessary to defeat the most audacious attack of the aggressors.

End.

To: David Hulburd
From: Crosby Maynard

Dec. 7, 1941
11:05 P.M.

Wire from WASHINGTON

Army Statement on Censorship

"Gentlemen, I need not tell you that the United States is at war. You all know that. I have no additional news for you, now. I have called this conference so that we can have a clear understanding of the position of the U.S. Army in the future, as concerns the news which will be released and which you can print."

The speaker was long, lean, hook-nosed Brigadier General Alexander D. Surles, Chief of the Army's Press Relations Section. The occasion was an emergency meeting the Army and the Press held in the untidy press room of Washington's Munitions Building at 7:30 tonight, scarcely five hours after the announcement of the bombardment of Pearl Harbor.

More than 50 reporters were crowded in the small room a few minutes before General Surles arrived. Many of them were White House correspondents, comparative strangers to the War Department, seeking an additional shred of news. Most were in evil temper, because getting into the Munitions Building had suddenly become very difficult. The mild mannered police who had patroled the building on Saturday afternoon had been replaced with regular Army men, in full equipment, gas masks, fixed bayonets, their rifle loaded with live cartridges. The soldiers had orders to exclude all who did not have full War Department credentials and were doing so very effectively.

Throughout the afternoon the radio had issued frequent bulletins telling all officers on active duty to report for work tomorrow in uniform. Most of those at the Department tonight had put away civilian clothes. General Surles was in mufti, apologized, said he hadn't had time to change.

He came to his point immediately. After emphasizing the gravity of the occasion, he said:

"I know there will be questions you will want to ask. I am here to answer them, so far as I am able. But first, let me say this. Our relations in the past have been very pleasant. Now, we reach a new phase in those relations. All irresponsibility must stop.

"I shall do my best to keep you informed of all events that concern me and would be of interest to you. But the time has now come when any failure to protect any information which comes to your possession can mean the loss of American lives.

"So, it has become necessary for the War Department to invoke the act of April 16, 1918 (50 U.S. Code 34). It is a somewhat detailed act but, as it concerns you immediately, I emphasize these points. You and your papers cannot print any reference in any way to troop movements, disposition, location, designation, components or strength outside of the continental U.S. No references can be printed to the movements of troop transports, even if they are in the waters of the continental United States. That is about all. Are there any questions?"

General Surles was asked almost at once to define irresponsibility, in the sense which he intended it to be taken.

"I mean," said Surles," that in the past, certain information has been printed by certain publications which must have given considerable comfort to potential enemies. Now, all loose observation of our regulations must cease. I don't want, even now, for the word 'censorship' to be used, unless it becomes absolutely necessary. Restrictions are necessary. Restrictions are what we are imposing tonight. They must be observed and I am sure that they will be."

He added that there would be no relaxation of the restrictions until conditions warranted, but that when, and if conditions changed, the regulations might be modified.

Surles was not prepared to say tonight what the penalty would be for violation of the April 1918 regulations. The statute provides for fine and imprisonment but the severity of the penalty varies, depending on war footing. Presumably, the more severe penalties will be meted to convicted violators but Surles said that was entirely a matter for the courts and not for him to say.

As Surles was finishing, an aide brought him a note, and he announced that orders had been dispatched to Hawaii and Panama authorizing the immediate arrest, by the Army and the FBI, of suspicious aliens.

Finally, as an after thought, General Surles said that Secretary of War Stimson, Assistant Secretary McCloy and General Marshall had been at their desks when the news broke and, as he was going out the door, he said in answer to a question that he did not believe Christmas leaves would be cancelled.

December 8, 1941
7:43 P.M.

To: David Hulburd

From: Wilmott Ragsdale

Wire from WASHINGTON

Kurt Sell, DNB correspondent and well-known figure around Washington for more than ten years, arrived at the White House to turn in his building pass. "Do you want my card?" "Yes" was the emphatic reply of the first guard, who grabbed it.

Meanwhile FBI men went to Sell's office and collected all U. S. Government identification cards which would permit him into federal buildings.

There are no longer any Italian correspondents in the U. S. Sell was the last German correspondent in Washington.

(Washington - by phone)   12/8/41

To: David Hulburd

From: Robert Sherrod

    For N.A.

Specific paragraph of 1917 Espionage Act is No. 32. But War Department is invoking much broader powers in announcement expected momentarily, covering legal restriction of all information concerning routes, schedules and troop movement, and of transports within or without the U.S. Under act of 1898 as amended 1918. Casualties will be announced but names of unit will not be. Navy also invoking Espionage Act forbidding publication of news considered "of value to the enemy."

TO: DAVID HULBURD

FROM: WILMOTT RAGSDALE

7:35 P 12-8

There is increasing evidence that nobody in Washington was prepared for the attack Sunday.

When a reporter went to the Navy Department at 4 P.M. Admiral Blandy, Chief of Ordnance, was in line to get in and had difficulty because he had no pass. He got in on a driver's license. He had been to the Redskin Football Game. The Navy was letting odd assortments of people in who did not have passes. In the press room the reporter found half a dozen people with no passes at all.

Meanwhile the War Department was so strict that nobody without a special Sunday pass was allowed entrance. When the guards were stationed around the Department later, they were asked whether their rifles were the new Garands or Springfield. "Neither," they replied, "they're shotguns."

End.

From: Washington (by phone)　　　　　　　　　　　　　　　　　12/8/41

To: David Hulburd

From: Jerry Greene

Subject: Economic Defense Board and Your Query

　　Hector Lazo, son of a former Minister to the U.S. from Guatemala and now executive director of the District Stores, a nationwide cooperative chain, today was picked as head of EDB's new European division, will assume his duties this week. Lazo's headquarters are in XXX Washington. He attracted attention of EDB's executive director Milo Perkins because of both his executive ability and his knowledge of Europe.

　　His appointment rounds out the geographical expansion and reorganization of EDB.

　　Colonel Royal XXXXXXX Lord of EDB said approximately 100 men were transferred when Carl Spaeth from the Rockefeller committee to EDB.

　　EDB today cleared x a way last of its red tape, will begin actual requisitioning of inactive stockpiles tomorrow with tin seizures. Formal clearance is expected from OPM tomorrow for seizure of tinplate now lying in seaboard freight-yards, formerly consigned to Europe.

(Washington - by phone)   12/8/41 - 6:40 p.m.

To: David Hulburd for Business

From: John Crider

Subject: Far East Metals

From ████████████████████████ not for attribution to him:

Metals most affected by the war are tungsten, chrome, mica, and graphite. About 25% of our next year's supply of tungsten was to come from China via the Burma Road. The Government has about 7,000 tons of tungsten stocks, of which 5,000 are tightly locked up by Treasury procurement for release only on Army or Navy orders.

We were getting about 30 to 35% of our chrome from the Philippines and New Caledonia. Government stocks hold about 400,000 tons of chrome, which is about a five-months supply. Turkey is one of our other sources of chrome, but we may still be able to get this.

The only source of high-grade mica splittings in the world is India. This type of mica is indispensable in electrical equipment. We use about eight or nine million pounds of this a year, and virtually all is going into defense. The procurement division has some secret stocks of this stuff, and industry also probably has some stocks.

Ceylon is the only producer of a certain grade of graphite. The Government has no stocks of this, but industry probably has some. Other types of graphite come from Madagascar and Mexico.

Since June the U.S. and Britain have taken the entire output of the commodities named above from the sources indicated, with small quantities going to Russia.

If Singapore holds out we will probably continue to get material from southeast Asia, but it is a certainty that most of the shipping from Asia will now be routed around Cape of Good Hope.

Wire from Robert Sherrod to D. Hulburd - Dec. 8, 1941 (Washington)

A Congressional leader who has access to reports from the Pacific (off record: ████████ told a reporter: "This is the blackest day in American military history since 1812." This might tie in with Congressman Dingell's demand for court martial of five army and navy leaders, including Admiral Kimmel and General Hap Arnold. (See press dispatches).

(Washington - by phone) 12/8/41 6:10 p.m.

To: David Hulburd

From: Robert Sherrod

Reliable sources say they know definitely the U.S. had not reached an agreement with Russia by Dec. 1 on what Russia would do if the U.S. and Japan went to war. One source says there is much gnashing of teeth around the State Department because a quid pro quo was not reached at the time we agreed to send Lend-Lease material to Russia. He doubts that an agreement has been reached in the past week.

TO: DAVID HULBURD 　　　　Wire from WASHINGTON

FROM: WILMOTT RAGSDALE 　　7:17 P 12-8

STATEMENT BY EX-AMBASSADOR DAVIES

The following statement on the Russian position in the Far East hostilities was prepared by Joseph Davies, former Ambassador to the Soviet Union, at the request of TIME. It may be quoted directly.

"The question of an attack from Vladivostok or from American Air Bases in Siberia upon Japan's wooden cities, is one for the Military High Commands and the Governments of Britain, the Soviet Union and the U.S. Japan's infamous attack provided unity not only in the U.S. but assured a united front on the world battle lines. Japan has a non-aggression pact with the Soviet Union and Japan is in deadly fear of bombing from the air because of her wooden cities. Japan would undoubtedly desire to try to keep the Soviet Union out of the fight. Hitler's interest might be to have the Soviet Union attacked on two fronts. If the mobilization of Japan's troops in Manchukuo means an attack upon the Red Banner Army on the East, it is certain that she will be gravely menaced by bombattacks from Vladivostok.

"The next few days ought to throw some light upon what the plan is. If Japan, as now seems indicated, wishes to take advantage of the non-aggression pact with the Soviet Union, the Allied Commands will have to determine their policy with long-range consideration as to which would be best; whether to run the risk of a pincer German movement against the Soviet Union or to bomb Japan from the air. There is always the question involved of winning a battle and possibly delaying victory. As long as the Government of the Soviet Union maintains its entity and the Red Army remains intact, Hitler will never feel secure on the land. Britain and the U.S. control the seas and have enormous supplies of man power and industrial production. The Soviet Union has proven its great effectiveness. It may be a long haul but ultimate victory is certain."

　　　　　　　　　　　　　　　End.

(Washington - by phone)   5:50 p.m.   12/8/41

To: David Hulburd

From: John Crider

Economic Action

U.S. business found itself submitting this week to the necessity for tightened Government control. The smoke hardly cleared from Japan's first treacherous attack on Hawaii when long-readied economic machinery started moving in Washington:

Using his customs and asset-freezing mechanism, Secretary Morgenthau loosed some 4,000 Treasury agents to forcibly cover all economic ties between Japan and the U.S. Every Japanese bank or business concern in the U.S. was visited, taken over.

The economic defense board invoked a "total embargo" on shipments of every kind to Japan or its occupied territory.

President Roosevelt, meeting with heads of Government financial agencies, decided to keep the securities, bond and commodity exchanges open unless some chaotic uncontrollable condition developed. However, the commodity exchange administration on Tuesday innovated by freezing futures in soybeans, wheat, butter, eggs and flaxseed at the Monday level.

Invoking the trading with the enemy act, Morgenthau closed the borders to Japanese or their agents, and declared it illegal to transact business with Japanese.

Plans were immediately announced for putting the defense industry of the nation on as nearly a continuous operating basis as may be possible.

The time had arrived for formalizing control in certain areas such as in fuels, transportation and capital issues which, until Monday, had been supervised by loose cooperative arrangements between Government agencies. While something

#2.
Economic Action

along the lines of the capital issues committee of World War I was forecast, Morgenthau said he preferred the informal cooperative method if it continued feasible. Capital issues will be controlled.

Price control automatically got a new set of teeth with the declaration of war. Lawyers disputed the expense of price Tsar Henderson's legal powers in the absence of a precise legislative definition, but no one doubted that from Dec. 8 Henderson would no longer have to rely upon "jawbone control." The necessity for administration's much-chastised price-control bill became academic. In any event, Henderson will need, and probably will employ, greater power than that bill contains.

Morgenthau, as yet unrelenting in his demand for a limitation of corporate profits to 6%, said higher taxes proportionate to the greater war expenditures now needed, would be required; that the public would be more willing to pay in a state of declared war.

The President and Vice President of the New York Federal Reserve Bank stayed at their posts all night Sunday with beds handy in case they got time for a nap.

Morgenthau said the Government did not enter the bond market to support prices when war was declared on Monday. He found the price drop in Government bonds on that day most gratifying.

Fighting a war of great distances, Washington immediately turned its attention to tighten up domestic consumption of fuel needed by the Navy and Air Corps.

LONDON CABLE Unnumbered

From Mary Welsh to David Hulburd -- December 8, 1941

Herewith Britain's reactions, including Commons: Public reactions: excepting newsmen only the fewest Britons heard the news until BBC's nine p.m. news (the week's widest audienced program), when cool, pedagogue-voiced Alvar Liddell led off the news with "President Roosevelt has announced that the Japanese have bombed the Hawaiian base of the United States fleet at Pearl Harbor." In the West End Restaurants, bars, hotel lobbies, the news spread like fire in heather, but in the average, especially lower class, English home the news which was so undramatized by BBC carried little significance. No news was flashed on movie screens as in the United States and no further BBC bulletins until midnight, and the average Britisher went to bed before that, mildly remembering Hawaii was somewhere in the Pacific and wondering what the bombing meant -- little more.

But among politicians, diplomats, United States and British journalists, there was wild excitement with offices frantically trying to reach country week-enders, embassy phones and Western Union head office snowed under. There were no crowds at Whitehall or the American Embassy where Marine Guard strength was doubled. The embassy was a beehive bedlam all night, with everybody rushing to duty, sending out for food and drink, including Champagne, for, like most Americans in London, the Embassy wanted to drink privately and unofficially, not to death and destruction but in relief and to the clarification of the morass of academic issue-dodging.

Winant, who had been week-ending in the country with Churchill, conferred with Churchill until 2 a.m., then had a long conference with Biddle, and was working again by 8 a.m. Today the embassy is still a minor bedlam, but the average Britisher is still calm though sympathetically. This morning seven British friends telephoned me offering sincere and still surprised condolences, such as "Terrible to think it's spread even to you." And "So sorry about your fleet losses." But "Too bad for you, but I'm feeling a slight sadistic pleasure that the war has caught

page 2 -- unnumbered London cable from Mary Welsh, Dec.8,1941

up with our people who rushed over to your country." (There's always been resentment of Britishers who escaped the war to America.)

When questioned on their apathy, bookkeeper, barman, secretaries, elevator men explain: "It's a long way away." And "Won't it stop lend-lease things coming here?" And (cockney) "Thar's a certain amant of excitement abaht it I suppose."

Certainly primary reactions of the British mind, as evidenced by Public, Commons and the press, are firstly the war's effect on lend-lease, secondly worry over Pearl Harbor fleet losses, thirdly that the U.S. won't declare war on Germany. Few, even politicians, seem to grasp the enormous reorientation of war strategy now necessary. They are still thinking of Britain's front line, not perceiving that British and United States are chiefly factories delivering goods to action via whichever route is most sensible. Housewives even mention they are afraid Britain will get no more lend-lease food. Certainly the average Briton doesn't see the declaration's production impetus and therefore is unable to weigh it against naval losses and lend-lease holdups.

There's evidence that the sentimentally, illogically Britons in their secret hearts are slightly sorry they no longer stand alone. Old soldier who remembers how he earned a shilling daily in the last war and could buy fried eggs and french fried for ninepence at Passchaendale, and how at the Yankees arrival the same dish shot up to two shillings sixpence. He's worried the Yanks will say they won this war, too.

Herewith Commons: Since Commons customarily doesn't meet on Mondays, many M.P.'s started out at the crack of dawn to reach Commons on time, found no trains, thumbed lifts, arrived breathless. Commons' catering manager Robert Bradley, whose staff is ordinarily off duty, rushed out to markets, started fires himself, then found the staff turning up voluntarily, and lunch buns, sausages, cakes were ready on time. By 2:45 crowds were standing at the members' gate giving their

page 3 -- unnumbered London cable from Mary Welsh, Dec.8,1941

usual little cheers for their favorite ministers, and the central lobby was jammed with MPs and friends, especially Americans hoping to gain last minute entrance to the House. Lady Astor telling a friend "I simply can't believe it" was interrupted by a Russian haltingly asking her to find some MP friend of his, and Astor replied "Certainly will. I don't like your politics, but you're great fighters."

Mobs pushing into the Chamber were suddenly shoved aside making room for Churchill and his wife, Churchill looking tired eyed but amused at the crush, and Clemmie smiling, wearing her most informal hair scarf, sports fur coat, flat heels. (Flash: We've just heard a rebroadcast of Roosevelt's declaration and now comprehend Churchill's amazing gravity and general Common's solemnity, which obviously grows out of the fact that the United States didn't declare war on Germany, which all but the pessimists here were hoping and expecting.)

Commons was nothing like the broadcast of the joint House session in the United States. There was only a mild ripple of cheering a couple of times, once at Churchill's "The Japanese began a landing in northern Malaya ... and they were immediately engaged by our forces which were ready." And "The root of the evil and its branch must be extirpated together." Churchill with typed quarto-page notes on a new (since the bombing) black leather dispatch box, read his speech using black-horn rimmed glasses. He didn't produce any usual dramatics, telling inflections or brilliant pauses, didn't give the final sentence about light any of his usual oratorical mastery.

Although the MPs and the gallery didn't know his now obvious reason for restraint, they followed his lead, responded in minor note, causing the Herald Tribune's Joe Evans when exiting to say: "Don't know why I came ... wasn't hardly worth it."

Undoubtedly Roosevelt's declaration will be a bitter disappointment here. The narrow Commons balconies held an array of Ambassadors, including Polish, Brazilian, Turkish, Chinese, also Canadian High Commissioner Massey, United States Naval Attache Vice-Admiral Robert L. Ghormley and temporary Air Attache (in Lee's absence) Colonel Arthur McChrystal, both for the first time in uniform. The only empty seats on the Commons floor were Conservative back-benches where sit various MPs now with the forces abroad, etc.

Clemmie sat among the diplomats and RAF in the right balcony, Lords and other diplomats in the left balcony (both have only one row of seats), Pamela Churchill was among the press who were noisy, running to the telephone.

Lobby conversations afterwards were amazingly noncommittal, everybody wanting more news and wondering about Germany. Press reaction was general and interpretative rather than exciting, with Mirror's Cassandre saying: "It would not have been commensurate with Nipponese dignity to have kept silence at a batch of awkward questions put to them by paleskinned foreigners .... Mr. Kurusu has blandly denied ... the effect of this soothing syrup has been rather similar to a fireball being tossed into a gunpowder factory. The morality of the New Order, both eastern and western brands, is such that the sound of a dove cooing is a signal to take cover. The olive branch has become a lethal weapon."

Following from Osborne: Winant, looking no more cavern-eyed than usual, had an off the record press conference with U.S. reporters this afternoon. U.S. Marines with sidearms were stationed today at the previously unguarded Embassy, questioning all comers, including Winant himself. Officials here generally are in a position of "You know more than I do if you read the papers", and awaiting specific information from Washington. There was greatest interest this afternoon in the President's speech which was rebroadcast here at six thirty London time. The weather almost forced BBC to cancel the rebroadcast.

page 5 -- Unnumbered London cable from Mary Welsh - Dec.8,1941

You can assume Americans in the Dorchester, Savoy, Cumberland lounges tensely listening.

Hundreds of the 25,000 Americans in theBritish and Canadian forces, especially air, are already beseiging the Embassy and military super-wigs for transfer to U.S. forces. No specific information on Washington policy and no arrangements for such transfers yet. Also none for U.S. civilians here who want to enlist. These arrangements will be made but, of course, depend somewhat on the President's speech. Chicago Tribune's pale, pudgy veteran Larry Rue is taking a merciless kidding for the Trib's recent exploit. Nearly all Americans I've talked to today and tonight had a sudden overwhelming feeling that they belonged at home. Sketchy available news reports leave everybody tense, uncertain, hungry for more American news. Newswise there's also a keen interest but no specific information yet on what, if any, information and censorship facilities the U.S. will establish here and how they will be keyed with the British.

LONDON CABLE No. 3432

From Walter Graebner to David Hulburd, December 8, 1941

Re 949, from Vaidya:

It is too early yet to give a birds-eye view of Colonial reception but significant developments are already occurring in India which now obtains a key position in the war set-up.

Gandhis has requested the recently released Congress present in Moulana, Abdul, Kalam, Azad, to convene at meetings with a working committee and all-India Congress Committee "at an early date" and has made a further friendly gesture by suspending civil disobedience pending the meeting's decision and thereby presumably/having given Britain the opportunity to revise the attitude to India.

Indians in Britain who share the Congress viewpoint opine thusly: It's no good for Britain to continue to portray India as a "difficult" problem, as if it is some jigsaw puzzle for British statesmen to solve as a peacetime hobby. India's tremendous manpower and abundant natural resources must be made use of now by accepting India as a free, friendly partner in the allied setup and thus make the Allied Front overwhelming against the Fascist front. The Indian Nationalists' non-violence principle can go overboard over-night as most Congressmen accepted it as a matter of necessity. Actually, India can start with a certain advantages, such as through 20 years of political agitation she is morally mobilized while for military purposes there is a good, drilled force numbering several hundred thousand composed of Congress militia and Moslem League Volunteer Corps. Incidentally, these are/the only two Indian political parties which count, although and though on internal matters they may differ, they are united in the demand for India's independence. The time has long past for Britain and the Indians to quibble over formulas for a constitution, the Indians will be satisfied if given control of all portfolios including

London Cable No. 3432, Dec. 8, 1941   Page 2

defence, finance, foreign relations, etc., though they are willing to take Anglo-American aid for the interim period. In return for such a liberal gesture on the part of the Allies, particularly Britain, India is capable of putting at least 10 million soldiers (this figure is based on Indians' minimum manpower resources) in the field within 2 years while India can be turned into an allied arsenal for defence between the Pacific and the Mediterranean by gearing up her industrial potential with allied technical aid.

Some British publicists claim India's war efforts are progressing but that isn't so; in more than two years Britain's been able to raise only an army of 750,000, viz. the size of the Rumanian Army, while regarding war production, India in spite of her resources is unable to produce tanks, planes, motors or battleships.

In fighting Japan, Anglo-Americans must reckon to face a force of anything up to 10 millions. The American contribution can be chiefly naval and even if America has enough troops for Malaya, they will have to be carried across a wide ocean which is infested with hostile craft. Britain can muster 5 million soldiers of which a large proportion will have to remain in Britain against threat invasion and for possible counter-invasion in Europe.

She has in addition a garrison in Africa and the Middleast and only the remainder can go to Malaya. As regards Australia, her army will always remain in the vicinity of half a million because of her limited population, and in addition nearly half the Anzacs are already engaged in the Middleast.

From where, then, can the Allies secure numerical strength and armaments for defence of the south Pacific or Middleast, which according to reports last week, the Nazis soon intend invading by air, except from India? India was never pro-Fascist and is willing to throw in her lot with anti-Fascist forces provided she ~~has~~ is accepted as a free and equal partner in the allied fold. There is no need to question Indians' fighting qualities, they have proved it in Libya, Abyssinia and Iraq.

LONDON CABLE NO. 3433

From Jeffrey Mark to D. Hulburd - Dec. 8, 1941.

Regarding the Jap war, I feel sure London reaction is much less intense than you'd imagine. Frankly, the man in the street has as yet no conception of the real implications. He has talked about it at lunch today but reverted to other subjects. Similarly, there's no overwhelming preoccupation in this morning's newspapers. For instance, last night in a pub just after the/nine o'clock news, I heard a party saying the Japs had bombed Hawaii. The most serious observation I heard was, "Hitler has been trying to make a Pacific diversion for a long time."

It is important to realize that to Britishers, Hawaii is not a naval base but a South Sea island with a Hollywood ukulele and hula hula trimmings. The feeling now is that Uncle Sam has been caught with his pants down. The first thought is that it's a good thing as it will get America seriously going but it is qualified by the thought that America will now attend to her own defense needs frantically and tend to neglect British and Russian lease-lend. Secondly, it is thought that she'll remove much of her Atlantic patrol to the Pacific and that this, with increased British naval concentrations at Singapore, will thin out the vital Atlantic life-line precariously.

Regarding the dominions, it's too early yet for any reasoned summary but here's what's available:

Prime Minister John Curtin announced today that "Australian troops are at their battle stations," while Army Minister Forde announced that all forces' Christmas leave was cancelled. The Commonwealth War Cabinet is expected to make a war declaration against Japan later today with Curtin saying, "This is the gravest hour in our history." The only other significant likely internal development is a crackdown on Aussie middleeast troop shipments with renewed agitation for the return of a large proportion of those already there on the "Australia First" slogan.

Page 2 -- London cable no. 3433

There's no official pronouncement of any sort from New Zealand yet but London New Zealander's reaction is almost exactly the same as the British outlined above.

Ottawa cables say the Dominion forces were instructed to engage the Jap enemy wherever found and submission to His Majesty the King for formal war declaration is due later today. Canada also announced that Pacific coast defenses are out on full war footing and a new chain of air bases on the American Alaska border are equipped with radio guide equipment and now in operation. Canadians' reaction here is that the Jap menace is not regarded so formidable at it was regarded a year ago. They are also glad it will quell American isolationism which latterly has been particularly irritating to them.

The South African general reaction is the same as London's and I expect they'll move directly behind the Commonwealth. Also that it will minimize internal disputes and throw dissentients more directly behind Smuts. Most significant reaction is that with the Mediterranean closed to shipping, the Cape route has become of paramount importance. Hitherto, this was not seriously menaced but Jap entry may do so and so bring South Africa nearer the war center.

Meanwhile, the Canadian Royal mounted police are now rounding up Canada's 23,000 Japs which are mostly concentrated in British Columbia. It is further estimated that there's 8,000 Japs in British Borneo Straits and Malay, about 3500 round in Sydney and 2600 in British India and Ceylon. There are no Japs to speak of in South Africa as the immigration law is closed to the entry of Japs and Chinks. It is estimated that there are about 500 Japs in Britain. Apparently the war declaration completely surprised the Jap embassy here from Charge d'Affaires Kaminura down. Says press-secretary Matsui, "We have heard nothing at all from Tokyo. We will have to go back, but how? Everywhere is a battlefield and it's going to be very difficult to get back."

The Netherlands East Indies, after the war declaration announced "A state of danger from air attack" and invited the RAF to station aircraft at points supporting the NEI airforce at Ambon and Kupang on Timor Island to assist the NEI aircraft and observe air approaches which also concern Australia.

LONDON CABLE NO. 3434

From S. Laird to D. Hulburd - Dec. 8, 1941

Immediately after the clear reception of Roosevelt's speech, the BBC announcer said, "I think you would now like to hear 'Ballad for Americans'". Then they played a Paul Robeson recording.

LONDON CABLE No. 3435

From Stephen Laird to David Hulburd -- December 8, 1941

Herewith review of local lead editorials today: Best was young Michael Foot's in the Evening Standard: "The whole world is in flames. A battle rages across the seven seas, and every great nation is at war for its life. No corner of this planet remains immune. Perfidy stripped of the thinnest disguise has decreed that no single home and no single human being shall escape the scorchings of this conflict .... The early contest will not be easy for our Allies. The generous material aid which they have given us will be required partly now to save America's existence. A huge fresh strain will be imposed on our sailors and our ships. The next six months will be hard. We shall need all the Dunkirk spirit and more ... The biggest battle is still the battle in Russia for the simple reason that Berlin is still the first lair of this beast which is unloosed among men .... The world is one and the war is one. All the hopes, and now all the energies of the vast majority of the human race, are securely attached to our cause. Believe that the ambitions of young America, that the sacrifice of Soviet Russia, that the long agony of China, that the courage of conquered Europe, that the will of Britain which for one whole year held the pass of freedom, believe that all these great facts can be set at nought by this latest shallow piece of trickery, and you may believe too that the pillared firmament is rottenness and earth's base is built on stubble."

Says the News Chronicle: "If it were not that Japan were the pioneer among aggressors we would say that the Emperor had learnt his part from the Fuehrer to perfection. No one can welcome the extension of indiscriminate slaughter to another wide area of this suffering globe. But if it had to happen it could have happened in several ways less favorable to allied interests. If Japan had struck at Siberia she might have put just that extra strain on the Russian war machine that would have broken it. If she had struck at Britain the free nations would have waited in

page 2 -- London Cable No. 3435

suspense to learn America's verdict. But Japan has struck at America direct. America is in the war ... All the doubts and questionings that have assailed the government and people of the United States these past protracted months are swept away. The question is resolved for them. They are in the war -- and the war is indivisible .... From today onward such a combination of industrial output and moral determination is forged as makes certain the complete destruction of the aggressors."

The <u>Daily Mirror</u> says: "Hitler's pressure, Hitler difficulties have convinced them (the Japanese) that it is now or never in the division of loot and the search for living space. Were the Axis to be destroyed the Japanese vision of imperialistic expansion must vanish forever. The Axis is suffering severely. Japan is called up in hope of righting the balance. No doubt this last of the hungry jackals is only too willing to support the other robbers. Yet her plunge is a signal of despair as well as a symptom of madness...."

<u>Daily Mails</u>: "...Hitler's methods of unprovoked aggression have been not merely copied, even to the timing of a weekend spring. They have been improved upon with a devilish malignity ... Isolationism dies in the waters of Honolulu. The war which its exponents sought to avoid leaps at America's frontiers .... The Axis powers now dare the might, the resolve, the resources, and the valour of the most powerful nations in the world. In such an array of forces there can be but one decision, long and bitter though the pathway to it may be .... All doubts resolved, all pettiness swept aside, they (Americans) will now find, as we did ourselves in such a crisis, the essential greatness of soul of a people determined to be free."

The <u>Times</u> editorial was dull plodding resume of portents pointing toward the Pacific war, finally rouses itself to say; "....Japan has decided upon war, and she now finds herself faced with forces which, in the long run, she will be powerless to resist ...."

<u>Daily Herald</u> foresees: ".... The Japanese attack will have the effect of

page 3 -- London Cable No. 3435

pushing American production to the peak much more rapidly than would otherwise have been the case. But it will also require yet a further diversion of supplies which were destined for Britain ... Greater than ever, therefore, is Britain's need to organize her own production without delay to the limit of efficiency ..."

Daily Express on the whole was most pessimistic, concludes with "... America is fighting for her own life. Arms workers of Britain and Russia must be ready to provide from their own factories some of the weapons they had expected from America...

The Telegraph's dull, on the lines of the Times, includes this interesting phraseology: "Now the die is cast and the United States is compelled to take action as a belligerent."

The Daily Sketch outlined the formidableness of the opponent, including: "... Japan is no mean antagonist. Her people can easily be whipped up into a fanatical hatred of the white man and to a frenzy which will make them exceedingly difficult to defeat..."

LONDON CABLE NO. 3436

From Lael Laird and Dennis Scanlan to D. Hulburd - Dec. 8, 1941.

Re Allied governments and U. S.-Japanese war:

Short, goat-bearded Polish Information Minister, Prof. Stankslav Stronski, stated early to a TIME reporter, "Today when the war which Germany started against Poland in September 1939 has become a world war in the fullest sense of the word, there is no one among the Poles who does not realize the importance of that fact which has now assumed such proportions that the problem of the independence and freedom of Poland is not an isolated question but it is the same problem of the freedom of mankind against the forces of aggression, plunder and slavery. ... Poland took up today a position together with all her allies against Japan as she before took up the position against all the allies of Germany ...(recapitulation of German defeats in Russia and Libya) ...it was Germany who has put to Japan the demand 'now or never'.

"Although we are very far away from the theatre of war in the Pacific, we realize that the war in the Pacific is the result of Germany's failures and I think that the cause for which we fight which is common to us and to the Americans has gained a mighty ally who will decide the war in victory for us."

- - -

Here is the TIME exclusive message from DeGaulle:

"To the people of the United States: France, the real France, will fight alongside the great American republic, the British empire, and their allies, against their new enemy who, with the help of treason, has already taken Indo-China. The French Pacific Possessions New Caledonia, Tahiti, New Hebrides, who have already joined Free France, place all they possess at the common disposal in this war for liberty."

(For the colonies mentioned, see LIFE packet 717, TIME packet 366, also LIFE

Page 2 -- London cable no. 3436

packet 688 for pictures and notes on Dargenlieu who is "Free French High Commissioner for the Pacific Possessions" and is ex-provincial of French Carmelite order. Dargenlieu was a naval officer in the last war, became a Carmelite monk after the war, then at the armistice, joined DeGaulle.)

The following is not for publication before Wednesday:

The Free French will declare war on Japan tomorrow following a National Council conference this afternoon.

For New Caledonia: Inhabitants have formed their own home guard called "La Milice Civique de la France Libre" and Australia has helped to fortify the new harbor defense works including giving heavy coastal defense battery whose New Caledonian gunners were trained in Australia.

- - -

Norway held no special cabinet meeting. Foreign Minister Trygve Lie gave TIME the following exclusive statement, "The Norwegian government and the Norwegian people fully share the indignation of the American people aroused by the Japanese aggression. We are convinced that the great American democracy will come out of the war victorious and that Japan together with the other militant aggression states will suffer a final and decisive defeat. The fight the U.S. has now entered upon constitutes one of the most important links in the common fight of the democracies against fascism and barbarism and the victory of the U.S. will also mean victory for all other free peoples. We Norwegians feel a deep sense of gratitude for the sympathy which the American president and the American people have shown for our fight for freedom. We are convinced that the common fight and the common sacrifices will strengthen the friendship between all free peoples and form a basis for international cooperation after the war."

- - -

Yugoslavia's young King Peter heard the news of the war over the radio in his room at Clare College Cambridge, hot footed to London this morning to keep in touch.

Yugoslavia's short, grayish Foreign Minister Dr. Momcilo Nincic stated for the press, "The War with Japan represents one logical step in this conflict between the two worlds which are waging an eternal struggle: the world of force and barbarism created by evil forces and the world which believes in good and is working for the progress of humanity and for the equality of men and all the peoples."

"The way in which Japan has committed brutal aggression shows her up as a worthy ally of Germany and Italy and does not surprise anyone. It represents yet another proof of how important and urgent it is to destroy those regimes whose aims and methods are barbarous.

"But the latest aggression of Japan will only result in arousing the American people, I am convinced, and uniting them so that their inexhaustible resources will be mobilized to the fullest extent and will make possible the victory of civilization over barbarism." This message and more will be broadcast by Yugoslavian representative over BBC to Jugoslavia at 9:15 this evening.

- - -

The Belgians held no cabinet meeting as the procedure for this contingency was entirely outlined in advance. The Belgian government has told its Tokyo ambassador to leave Tokyo with the British and American.

- - -

The Netherlands' Queen Wilhelmina's declaration of war will be broadcast over the Radio Orange to the Dutch people by Prime Minister Gerbrandy at 7:45 tonight. The announcement of the state of war, following the cabinet meeting at 1:30 this morning, was "Not formal" as the formal declaration is awaiting the Queen's proclamation.

LONDON CABLE No. 3427

From Stephen Laird to David Hulburd -- December 8, 1941

If you are shifting the cover to Grew: last October Grew (off the record) told me something like this: "My mission here is ended. The military group taking power here speak a language all their own and argue from premises impossible to comprehend. It is my belief Japan is completely capable of national Hara-kiri, that is, rather than be defeated in a ten years' war of attrition with China, rather than turn north and chance defeat by the despised Communists I think Japan may prefer attacking the greatest powers in the World, Britain and America. Britain and America have always been thought of by the Japanese as great and powerful countries. The Japanese military mind would consider defeat by these powers glorious and honorable."

For Grew finding a fake airbomb in his swimming pool, see our letter from Japan to Mr. Hulburd last October.

LONDON CABLE No. 3429

From John Osborne to David Hulburd -- December 8, 1941

U. S. Naval officers here under Vice-Admiral Ghormley shifted from mufti to uniforms today. Army officially hasn't shifted yet, but some individual officers are in uniforms. Baggy-eyed Ghormley, who is former chief of Navy's warplans division, didn't sleep all night, worked through today with a weary staff.

The Embassy and other U.S. military offices were buzzing all night behind blacked-out windows. Most of the activity was just officers who wanted to know what's what. So far there's been no rush of orders to home.

FYI: General Lee, U.S. Chief Military attache here, will be glad to see you in New York or Washington, but hopes his Christmas visit won't be publicized as he wants to rest privately with his family.

The only direct effect, aside from navy uniforms, against U.S. militarists here so far is the receipt of certain orders to carry out pre-planned administrative procedures regarding information, communications, etc.

Unnumbered London Cable

From John Osborne to David Hulburd -- December 8, 1941

In the Savoy, Dorchester, pink-walled Suivis, and other spots where Americans enjoy expense accounts, they are playing and singing "Over There" tonight. Also Tipperary, There's a Long, Long Trail, etc. Britishers were vastly pleased at first, but today, especially after Roosevelt speech not mentioning Germany, Churchill's with a minimum mention of the U.S., and his and London press reminders that the U.S. now must supply itself, there's a dark undercurrent of apprehension for effects on Britain, Russia and the Battle of the Atlantic. Churchill noticeably was not smooth, not happy when he referred to the "gap" looming in U.S. aid to Britain. Indications already are that this has been a subject of high quarters' discussion.

Graebner feels that with all regard to America's pressing present need we should point out that only balanced perspective and careful joint weighing of each comparative need can prevent the Jap war from immeasurably aiding Hitler. No official decision is known yet on readjusting lend-lease flow, but it is assumed that aircraft and vital ordnance items will almost, or entirely, cease to arrive here for a while.

MANILA CABLE

From Melville Jacoby to David Hulburd -- December 8, 1941

Press Wireless lost contact with the United States.

War feeling hit the populace about noon time when there were full runs on banks, grocery stores, gas stations. All taxis and garage cars were taken by the military, clogging transport systems. Our own planes overhead are drawing thousand of eyes now, while they didn't earlier this morning. The High Commissioners office still holding hurried meetings, while Mrs. Sayre's Emergency Sewing Circle called off this morning's session.

Downtown were building managers' daylight meetings to make basement shelters hurriedly. They found an acute shortage of sandbags over all Manila while Quezon's palace bought the remaining supply of 20,000 bags to reinforce Malacanang shelter. There was a frantic rush this morning to tape all shop windows in town for the first time.

Philippine scouts, riding in big, special orange buses, fully equipped with new packs and uniforms, rounded up a majority of Jap nationals. They took 500 Nips from Yokohama Specie bank and countless others to concentration camps after surprise raids.

Soldiers raiding the Nippon Bazaar in the center of Manila found twelve Japs barricaded inside. They broke down the glass doors, capturing them, found a thirteenth Jap hiding under the counter.

Police inspecting Jap nationals, many of whom appeared with knapsacks packed with tinned goods, etc., found large rolls of bills in the sacks, also a few fire-arms. Jap women, though not wanted, came with their husbands. Police found one old, but much used set of harbor charts in a Jap building searched.

The general military situation is still flexible, hard to analyze. You have press association reports which are all available until this evening.

Shipping from Manila has been halted. The French steamer Marechal Joffre, in the harbor, will probably be taken.

Reportedly the U.S. legation in Peking has been taken by the Nipponese.

MANILA CABLE

From Melville Jacoby to David Hulburd, December 8, 1941

<u>10 a.m.</u>

Manila has not yet digested the fact of war. Balloon and toy salesmen and vendors on the streets with extra editions are just appearing as fully equipped soldiers are appearing. Small groups of women in hotel lobbies are beginning to collect children at their sides. All this is happening, simultaneously taxi drivers comment: "Not serious--not the Japanese Government's doings -- only the Japanese Military's small mistake in Hawaii."

It is confirmed now that Davao was bombed at six thirty this morning, also Forthay and Baguio where all civilian emergency officials are remaining, also TA.

MacArthur's headquarters were the grimmest place at dawn this morning when the staff was aroused to face war, send troops to their battle stations. Extra headquarters guards arrived around 9 a.m. as officers began donning helmets, and gas masks while grabbing hurried gulps of coffee and sandwiches.

Newsmen were waiting around headquarters deluging the press office. Hart's headquarters were quiet. Airforce headquarters were the scene of most bustling, helmeted men poring over maps, occasionally peering out windows to the sky.

There has been no air alarm in Manila City yet but it is expected by the minute. Rumors are flying very thickly everywhere. It is nearly impossible to get an operator on telephone calls. The High Commissioner's office is blocked off by military police. The whole thing has busted here like one bombshell, though, as previous cables showed the military has been alert over the week.

There is no censorship as yet but the voluntary basis is adhered to.

Rumors are flying very thickly even among informed people. Attacks and defense have not yet taken a definite pattern, however, the Davo bombing possibly signalizing a blitz landing attack.

The Bangkok's radio silence and lack of reports are leaving us cut off from action anywhere else in the Far East.

MANILA CABLE

From Melville Jacoby to David Hulburd, December 9, 1941

The Philippines overnight assumed a war basis with censorships, round-ups/of aliens, rationing, continual blackouts, evacuation of populated areas. There is a feeling among the populace that there is a long siege in view. The appearances of ack-acks on the parkways, wardens, Red Crossers, brought real live war to Manila. The Filipino and American general populace are just getting the experience of war, far behind even the Chinese children in Chungking, who can distinguish bomber and pursuit sounds, and well know the difference between flash of ack-acks and searchlights. However, in a few days more at this rate, the locals will soon become seasoned veterans of bombings and automatically go for cover instead of watching the "show."

Bleary-eyed Americans are still jovial. It is an oddity to see horse-drawn calashes with Americans rolling in front of the swank Manila Hotel, while all taxis are requisitioned for military usage and gas stations are closed temporarily following yesterday's rush. Life is going on surprisingly normally in the daytime considering the frequent wailing of loud sirens which are still not familiar to the populace. There is a terrific run on groceries and other supplies, especially good concentrates, bandages, iodine, flashlights, kotex. Many stores with bare shelves are closed. All Japanese shops are closed while the Chinese are labeling their shops with signboards reading "Chinese."

The military have already effected a carefully aforeplotted scheme of requisitioning all essentials, even film.

Optimistic signs of the formerly lax Civilian Emergency Administrations are the air wardens helping to direct traffic and avoid panic, cooperating under "advice" from MacArthur's headquarters. Though people are still numbed by the actual attack by the Japs on American soil, they are slowly coming out with grim

Manila, Dec. 9, 1941   Page Two

determination. The smoothness of the Japanese blitz tactics in the air still amaze even
informed people. Though it is militarily unwise to give out detailed information, the Japanese, despite attacks ranging from Thailand to Honolulu, are managing to concentrate their superior aerial forces against the Philippine strategic points. It is obviously a Japanese plan to cripple our striking power, eventually landing according to blitz plans as accomplished in the Far East very recently.

Though the constant unconfirmable rumors persist that the Japanese are landing hither and yon, there is still no real indication of where they will strike hardest. However, my previous messages point out one very likely spot.

It is the United States' policy, despite reported temporary losses of the island linking the Philippines with Hawaii, to hold out in the Far East to the last man, meanwhile striking harder and harder against Japanese bases with material at hand. It is already critically obvious that the entire ABCD strategy leading to the Philippines defense must depend on new and stronger Pacific supply lines. It is foolish to draw over-early conclusions. However, continual daily and nightly exchange visits between Hart, Sayre, and MacArthur, point out the seriousness of our position. Incidentally, Hart and MacArthur are in closest cooperation. When Hart left MacArthur's office this morning, MacArthur escorted him arm in arm to his car. Hart commented on the large passageway under the old wall in MacArthur's office, joked that it is better than anything he has to go in during raids.

Due to lack of adequate communication with other Far East points being blitzed, the U. S. Far East Command is treating the Philippines as a separate defense problem momentarily while U.S. Naval forces alone, but undoubtedly also with the British, are striking powerful blows in the vicinity of the Gulf of Siam.

Naval and military activity are a very close military secret now, even aerial losses from yesterday's and today's battles, one of which was seen over Manila, were not revealed. It is reliably known that Japanese planes shot down over the Philippines have been from air-craft carriers, also from Formosan bases. Some observers, impressed with the Japs' excellent tactics, accuracy, etc., suspect not only Nazi planning, but possibly Nazi planes of Heinckel type and pilots. The foregoing, however, is absolutely unconfirmed.

The Japs have mixed high altitude bombing, dive bombing and strafing round in all major attacks.

Wire from Wm. S. Howland, Nashville, Tenn. to D. Hulburd - Dec. 7, 1941.

The news came first to Nashville by radio. All three stations, WSM, WLAC and WSIX had flash bulletins of the first attacks. All three have been breaking all programs all afternoon for bulletins.

Most Nashvillians were at dinner when the news came. Many heard it by radio on autos. Because many did not hear it as apparently dead listening time just after church, there was not a big rush on phones then. The Tennessean came out with a swell extra at 4:30 standard time.

The general reaction when people first heard the news was "What are we going to do about it?" That was heard on every side. There was not much indication of amazement that Japan had attacked but everyone was asking what the American Navy was doing. I have some more good quotes which will send shortly.

I honestly believe that Tennesseans generally are greatly aroused. They always have been among the first to fight for the country and I heard no pacifistic comment tonight. Indication of how seriously people are aroused is that recruiting stations in Nashville have been jammed with call for men wanting to enlist.

Also the Union station was jammed with soldiers who had been on weekend leave rushing to get back to their post at Camp Forrest. All were vigorously expressing eagerness to get at the Japs. Some quotes on this coming later.

When the news came, Nashville and the middle Tennessees were enjoying a brisk, sunny Sunday. Churches were well filled. Most people were on the way home. Sunday dinner was what most were looking forward to. There were no football games and movies do not open until mid-afternoon.

Conversation at all dinner tables centered on the news. Again, general reaction was what America was going to do about it. Tennessean slammed a hot editorial and cartoon in the first edition from which quotes are coming as follows:

"Like a gangster whose ego has broken all bounds, the Japanese have decided to stake all in a desperate challenge to the U. S.

"The Rising Sun they hope is to shine over the teeming millions of the Asiatic world and even beyond. But in reality that sun is destined to set. The war that Japan has started will be ended by the U. S. on its own terms.

"There can be no compromise with the Japanese. They have staked their own fate on the sword and the sequel must be victory or Hari kari.

"And though we shall win we may as well understand at the beginning that it will not be an easy way. But we can say here and now that the sun of Nippon has reached its height and will rise no more."

Wire from Wm. S. Howland, Atlanta, Ga., to David Hulburd, December 8, 1941

Atlanta was just getting up from Sunday dinner to make the most of a sunny, warm afternoon following a cold Saturday, when the radio broke the news of the Jap war. The big station, WSB, jumped out first with a flash from the AP at 2:30 Eastern Standard Time. The flash came at a station announcement time just before the Chicago Round Table program opened. This was broken later by NBC for more bulletins. WSB cancelled the Tony Wand (Wons ?) show and also its transcribed Chilean Nitrate program to give war bulletins. The station immediately went on a 24-hour basis. Another big station, WGST, broke the news on CBS World Today program. The CBS program, Spirit of '41, was on when the flash came from AP but the station waited for CBS to break the news. The other two stations came in with the news shortly thereafter.

The Atlanta JOURNAL came out first with an extra at 4:40 P. M. The CONSTITUTION also extraed a few minutes later. Both were somewhat caught with their pants down but kept running extras to meet demands from nearby towns. Both said it was one of the heaviest runs in history.

Telephones were more jammed here than in Nashville, probably because of the time difference making the people here through with dinner. The phone company had to call in extra operators for both local and long distance.

All the movies broke their programs to make announcements of the war and to allow Army officers to call soldiers to their Post. The biggest picture showing was "Two-Faced Woman" at Loew's. Also showing were "Birth of the Blues" at Paramount, and "International Squadron" at the Roxy, which had a good many soldiers in the audience.

General public attitude was surprise at the manner of attack, followed by what the Atlanta JOURNAL aptly describes as "quietly infuriated." Some quotes following:

End

Wire from W. S. Howland, Atlanta, to David Hulburd, Dec. 8, 1941-2:50 P.M.

SECOND ADD ATLANTA WAR REACTION.

Most spectacular single incident of Atlanta war reaction was closing last night of famed Wisteria Garden Restaurant on Peachtree Street in center of downtown shopping area. Following orders issued by Lindley Camp, head of State Defense Corps, and of Mayor Roy LeCraw that all Japanese nationals must go to residences and remain there, the restaurant closed. Its proprietor is Sada Yoshinuma, a Japanese who has contributed to China relief funds, was perplexed. Said he "I was advised to close and that's all there is to it. I want to cooperate." Many Atlantans, coming downtown for justly famed steak dinners at Wisteria Garden, were perplexed by sign Closed Today which hung on door. The few who were in the restaurant early quickly ate and left.

Closing of this restaurant caused more comment than any other local reaction, as in Nashville, soldiers on leave in Atlanta appeared to welcome news that there was something to prepare for. This was very noticeable at the movies. For example, at Rialto one soldier shouted "Oh boy, this is it," when announcement of war came; and a sailor said "That's what we've been waiting for."

One Atlantan, Sydney H. Banes, whose son in law is Navy officer at Wake Island wired Knox "Allow me to suggest that special Ambassador Kurusu be held in custody until all officers and men of our Navy now at Wake are released."

Following are brief quotes from newspaper editorials:

The Chattanooga Times headed its editorial "WE ARE ATTACKED."

From Times editorial: "The Japanese could have had peace. It is doubtful if any American desires war with Japan. We shall have unity now. The America First Committee will speedily undergo an amazing metamorphosis. It is a terrible thing to be at war again. Now that it has come, we can be glad that we have the chance

Page 2 -- Howland ADD Atlanta War Reaction - Dec. 8, 1941

the men and women in 1917 and 1918 gave us -- the chance to preserve for ourselves and for others what they helped preserve for us, a free people and a Free country. God grant that this time we can win both the war and the peace that comes after it."

Ralph McGill in his One Word More column in the Atlanta Constitution "It is important to keep in mind that war is for the purpose of hurting the other nation, if we don't take off the gloves, if we don't begin to kill as many Japanese as we can, the war will be fumbled and drawn out. It is inconceivable that we should have been caught so asleep. The scrap iron, the oil, the gasoline and the materials we sold Japan in an effort to appease her out of the European war are coming home and killing American citizens, soldiers and sailors."

The American Journal editorial says "War having come to America, we have no other course and no other will but to meet it unflinchingly and to wage it to such a conclusion that the aggressor never again can menace the kind of world we stand for and on which our security depends. We are now one people with one faith, one hope and one baptism of danger and devotion to our dear country's cause."

Those are main points of reaction and newspaper editorializing. As indication of desire of soldiers to get back to posts, Dixie Limited train on which I returned from Nashville, was one hour late account putting on extra cars to handle soldiers from Nashville to Camp Forrest.

Checking further and standing by. Want any reaction to President's speech?

Wire from Wm. S. Howland, Atlanta, Ga., to David Hulburd, December 8, 1941

Add Atlanta war reaction.

Here are some sample quotes:

John Tyler, student, said, "Undoubtedly the Germans prompted the Japs, but I think we should go after Japan and whip her as soon as possible. I only wish I were 20 years old. I'd join the Air Corps so quick it would make your head swim."

John T. Akin, druggist, said: "I think we ought to give 'em everything we've got and clean 'em up quick."

Ralph Tilly, YMCA clerk, said: "I don't like it. I think it's dirty. The Japs pretended to be here on peace missions and stabbed us in the back."

Miss Jo Compton, a stenographer, said: "I want to know what Lewis and Lindbergh think now."

Danny Zell, student, said: "The Japs were damned fools."

Luther Singleton, famed dirt track auto racer, said: "It's like taking a dose of salts. We knew we had to do it but kept putting it off. Now let's get it down and over with. It won't be so bad after all."

Dorris Greene, aviation cadet from Rhode Island, said: "We ought to hop right to it and knock Hell out of them."

Negro population displayed particularly strong unity. A sample of the following quote from O. C. Moore, "Colored folks are good fighters when you get 'em stirred up. Maybe the little yellow men don't know that but they are going to find out."

Generally, quotes were of the same tenor as those in Nashville. More coming.

End.

Wire from Bill Howland, Atlanta - to David Hulburd - December 8, 1941

Add to war reaction:

As details of damage to the Navy were revealed, the general public reaction here in addition to the mountain of anger against the Japs, is the question of how the Navy got caught with its pants down so badly. I heard that on all sides on the street during lunch hour. The stores were practically deserted while the President spoke.

Wire from Bill Howland, Atlanta - to David Hulburd - Dec. 8, 1941

Add to war reactions:

Here is a quote from Sergeant Alvin Cullom York at his Tennessee Mountain home, as reported by the Chattanooga Times: "We got to put up a united front and give those folks a lickin' right away. We should take care of the Japs first and then take on the Germans."

The Nashville Tennessean quotes him in an obviously ghost-written story as follows: "I say, on to Victory America. With Senator Wheeler and all Americans, I say, 'Give Them Almighty Hell!'"

First to declare war on Japan in the south was Local Union No. 1442, United Brotherhood of Carpenters and Joiners at Chattanooga which Sunday night issued an official declaration of war "on the Japanese Government and any other Government that may be allied with her against the United States."

All over Atlanta in business offices, groups gathered to hear the Roosevelt speech. Business was practically suspended during that time.

To David Hulburd
From: William S. Howland, Atlanta

Dec. 8, 1941
4:12 A.M.

Following additional info reaction to war. Checkup radio stations shows that WLAC broke in on CBS Philharmonic Orchestra program with first United Press bulletin at one twenty nine Central Standard Time. WSB broke in on NBC University of Chicago Roundtable about same time with flash, WSIX broke in on MBS Fort Dix program with Trans-Radio flash at one thirty six P. M. Central Standard Time.

All three stations said tonight they had been deluged with phone calls all afternoon and night.

WSB said it had interrupted its own programs at least one hundred times with flashes and that NBC had been also breaking in frequently. Further check shows telephone company pretty well deluged with local calls. Heavy jams on long distance calls to St. Louis and Chicago. One hour delays were reported on calls to Chicago. A good many calls were placed to San Francisco which almost made it impossible to get through. Also there were numerous calls to Honolulu and Manila, which the phone company could not get through, presumably because of official jams, but no censorship on calls yet.

Western Union reported deluge of cables to Honolulu and Manila, which accepted for delivery if and when. Also jammed with hysterical wires to boys in camps, asking if any danger of them being transferred to Oriental front.

As wired previously, immediate reaction was what was the U. S. Navy doing.

Here are some quotes:

Mayor Thomas L. Cummings: "Those dirty b-----s over here with an olive branch in one hand and a dagger in the other."

John I. Suzuki, a Japanese graduate student at Vanderbilt University and former squadron leader of the Japanese Air Force against the Chinese: "If possible, I will not go back to Japan. I will stick to my religion and principles. I have been a Christian several years. I will not carry arms for page 2

my own or any other country for my life."

Of twelve other Japanese students at Madison College, which is seventh day adventist institution here, only two want to go back. Names available if want. Other ten say America is their home.

Private Estel Berry of Cody, Wyoming, 168th Field Artillery at Camp Forrest: "I'm eager and ready to go any time Uncle Sam sends me."

Sergeant Kennet Nelson, 129th Infantry at Camp Forrest: "We'll wipe 'em off the map in quick time, if the Army will send us over immediately. I'd rather be in Japan fighting than spend another 18 months in camp doing nothing."

Corporal William Quinn, of Illinois, in 124th Field Artillery at Camp Forrest: "This is something we'd like to tackle."

Leon Smithson, a cab driver: "We ought to go over there and wipe them off the map."

Assistant Attorney General Frank H. Taylor of Tennessee: "My stomach had a hollow feeling after I heard the news broadcast. I guess the best thing for us to do is to get into it immediately and wipe them out."

Congressman Atbert Gore was at a family reunion far up in the hills when political reporter Joe Hatcher of the Tennessean telephoned him the news. Gore hastened to Nashville, bulldozed American Airlines into putting him on the early morning plane to Washington. Said he: "There is no question but that Congress will act at once and I think the vote will be unanimous."

Grim realism added to Nashville reaction when radio and movie theatres broke programs to issue call for men of the 4th Depot Group of Army Air Corps, homeward bound from maneuvers to Patterson Field, supposedly camping overnight in the suburbs, call was for them to report at once for immediate departure on forced journey with no stops except for gas.

As wired, further check shows most dramatic and important local incident

was jamming of Union Passenger Terminal and bus stations with soldiers from big Camp Forrest, seventy five miles distant, hurrying to report back to post without getting orders. All seemed in excited mood, anxious for action against Japs.

City is in an excited mood tonight, but actually appears relaxation of tension of past few days and apparent relief that now the U. S. has an objective for all its military preparation.

Leaving for Atlanta where will begin checking reaction upon arrival and wire by mid morning.

Wire from Fill Calhoun, Chicago, Ill, to David Hulburd -- December 7, 1941

The Sun at 7 p.m. came out with a "War Extra No. 2" which was virtually the same as No. 1 except for fresh bulletins and a new banner "Japan War on U.S." The thought occurs that inasmuch as the Herald American ran the first Hawaii attack news as a regular peach edition and without the "extra slug, the Sun in one way can claim, in its first week of existence, having beaten all other Chicago papers with an "extra" in the biggest story yet. The Tribune for reasons I wish I knew, held up their plans for an extra and didn't come out until the regular time at 7 p.m. with a "Metropolitan" edition of tomorrow's paper. The Tribune bannered "Japan attack U.S." and above a column of war bulletins ran the following editorial:

"War has been forced on America by an insane clique of Japanese militarists who apparently see the desperate conflict into which they have led their country as the only thing that can prolong their power.

"Thus the thing that we all feared, that so many of us have worked with all our hearts to avert has happened. That is all that counts. It has happened. America faces war through no volition of any American.

"Recriminations are useless, and we doubt that they will be indulged in, certainly not by us. All that matters today is that we are in the war and the nation must face that simple fact. All of us, from this day forth, have but one task. That is to strike with all our might to protect and preserve the American freedom that we all hold dear."

Incidentally, note the Tribune's big scoop about U. S. war plans followed the Tribune's previous blasts about Roosevelt and his map of Nazi plans which the Tribune poopooed because any country naturally has war plans. Now where is the Tribune again?

The radio definitely broke the war news to Chicago as it was more than two hours before the first war paper, the Herald American, hit the streets. Off the record,

Chicago, Dec. 7, 1941 -- Calhoun -- page 2

Chicago Times men listening to the radio, also watching the press association tickers after the first flash, report that the radio was 20 minutes ahead of virtually every bulletin. C.B.S. which may have been beaten by the N.B.C. first flash, says New York will have to announce times and programs CBS interrupted, but I was listening to the Chicago Round Table when the argument over Canada's war effort was snapped and a brief flash read of the Hawaii and Manila Bombings. Thereafter on the next program, New York Philharmonic, was broken up, one time by an announcer so excited or inept that he twice pronounced Philharmonic as Philharminic, apologizing only for the first slip. There was an added rush of telephone calls as friends called friends, but no jam up of lines.

The first flash came just as Chicago home dwellers and suburbanites were digesting the roast beef and mashed potatoes of Sunday dinner which traditionally starts at one p.m. Many cancelled visits and plans to go to the movies to sit by their radios awaiting later bulletins. It seemed to me the radio took an unearthly time getting background together and any color into its news casts, but it was the retelling the people long before the newspapers.

First comments almost invariably were: "Well, it's here, or "Those Japs must be crazy."

Typical comment from a formerly Isolationist mother was: "If Hitler had just let the Japs alone this would never have happened. How terrible for the Japanese -- it's mass suicide."

Another mother, interrupted by the news while playing rummy, said: "We're in it and we'll just have to make the best of it." From younger men generally came this comment: "Well, we've got to whip the whole world -- and we can do it." What I'm trying to drive home is that no where did you hear comments about the possibility of anything but a U.S. victory. Some said "What an insult to the President when he was trying so hard to get things settled peacefully."

And many were the comments here, as probably different from those on the West Coast, that "it really is too bad for the Japanese people." Whether rightly or wrongly, people seem to believe all the so-called experts' claims that Japan has only two bath tubs in the navy, no money, no oil and all Japanese fliers are so cross-eyed they couldn't hit lake Michigan with a bomb.

Another lovely comment which also indicates how the war news first came to those who bought newspapers, was a fat woman at Michigan and Randolph. She approached a newsstand where the boy was shouting inaccurately "U.S. declares war on Japan," and apparently paid no attention to what he was saying. "What's this" she asked when she saw the big headlines. We're at war, lady, for crying out loud." "Well, she said, what do you think -- who with."

From all sides one first comment was: "This may be just what we needed to get us together and stop all these strikes and funny business." No matter what drivel they have been fed the people occasionally seem to hit down to fundamentals as exampled by comments such as: "Now we'll start turning out something.... Watch us go now. We'll turn out planes now or by God we'll know the reason why."

The Midwest, in my opinion, has known very well that they weren't doing half enough and that we were playing at business-as-usual.

Summing up comments and what they mean comes three main points: 1) Japanese attack has got people mad because they think this is a dirty deal pulled while the U.S. was trying all peaceful ways for a settlement, 2) they don't blame the Japanese people so much as they do "them warlords" and the Nazis egging them on, 3) they are glad in many ways that a break came the way it did because now we have God and everybody on our side and boy, just watch us go. The city, as such, was just getting ready for a good after dinner belch when the war news came. The temperature was 37 above, nippy and overcast with threat of snow that is now falling tonight. The usual wind was revealing legs in silk and nylon on Michigan Boulevard, torn up Loop Streets were beginning to fill with window-shoppers

Chicago, Dec. 7, 1941 -- Calhoun -- Page 4

and matinee crowds. Newspapermen were spreading rumors about what was going to happen with the new Sun cutting into Chicago circulation and advertising. Copies were tweeting their strangely shrill whistles, bookies were wishing the newest gambling investigation would get over with, drunks were beginning to show up on South State Street and on North Clark where there is one place which advertises: "2 Big Shots of Whiskey and a Cold Bottle of Beer - 10 cents".

Chicago, the Godless and ungoverned had finished dinner and was wondering what the (censored) to do with itself when the news came. There was a pro-football game between the Chicago Bears and Chicago Cardinals, where, before the game, the orchestra played the "Star Spangled Banner" and the audience, as usual, rose and actually sang it. By half-time the Herald American's extra was out and there was a rush from the stands to buy it with word spreading through the whole place that "The Japs are raising hell and attacking Hawaii." The audience buzzed and papers passed along the rows. It was like Podunk High Schools suddenly walking on to the field to play the Bears. Theatres, having no sense of the theatrical here, interrupted no programs and matinee crowds learned about the news when they came onto the darkened streets.

The biggest single development here is, of course, that the Tribune has pulled in its horns and that for all intents and purposes Isolationism and America Firstism is deader than a bombed soldier at Hickman Field. I tried to reach General Wood 15 minutes after the first flash but his telephone is "temporarily disconnected." I presume he'll come out with a statement tomorrow a la Wheelers. The Jap attack was all that was needed to cut the ground from under America First's feet. It will be ridiculous to talk Isolationism in the next few days, dangerous to your own health in a few more after that. Some one just phoned to say the Tribune has a banner reading "My country, right or wrong."

Wire from Sidney James, Los Angeles, to David Hulburd --
December 8, 1941 -- 6:21 a.m.

When the newspapers finally took up the play it was a hey day for them too. On the third floor of the imposing stone pile in downtown Los Angeles that is the Times office, AP man Ted Gill was settling down to another routine Sunday of work when the bell of the printer rang its frantic flash warning at 11:30. He ran across the room with word of "the news" to News Editor Nick Williams, who immediately called Managing Editor L.D. ("LD") Hotchkiss. Hotchkiss, entertaining guests in the suburban quiet of his home at La Canada, ordered an extra. An hour later Times and Hearst's Examiner waived an agreement not to hit the street downtown on Sunday before 3:15 with the first Sunday edition. The Times hit the street downtown at 2:10 with four inch block letters screaming "War". The Examiner beat it to the streets with "U.S. at War", by a few minutes.

Commented news editor Gill, remembering that last emergency extra in Los Angeles announced the fall of France on a Sunday, "If it's real big it always happens on Sunday. Ordinarily the Times would have printed 25,000 copies in its first edition, but up to five o'clock its succession of extras had totalled 150,000, and they went like hot cakes. Its normal daily circulation is only 220,000. As night fell the editorial writers of the Times and Examiner came on and caught up with events. Under a head of "Death Sentence of a Mad Dog" the Roosevelt hating reactionary Times began "Japan has asked for it. Now she is going to get it". It ended with: "This is a time for every American to show his colors. It is a time for coolness and courage. It is a time to sink without trace not only the enemy abroad, but the enemies within. Let there be an end of internal dissension, and end to the foolish if well-meant isolationist obstructionists, above all, an end to the efforts of disloyal self-seeking labor misleaders to hamstring our arms program."

He interrupted the speech and made dramatic announcements. "I have just received word that Japan, who only yesterday announced its peaceful motives, has bombed the harbor at Manila." Governor Murray D. Pat Van Wagoner and Detroits young Mayor Edward Jeffries were with Biddle. Virtually every newspaper man in town was attending the Newspaper Guild's annual bingo party at the Book Cadillac Hotel. Shortly after 3 o'clock messages for various ones to report to their offices began coming in and most of the working newsmen among the 1,000 people present left. The Detroit Free Press was the only paper to extra tonight, however, and the Free Press as a morning paper had little difficulty in hitting the streets at 6:45 and again at 8:40. The Detroit News and the Detroit Times both plan to have extras out tomorrow morning around 7:30, but they couldn't round up printers etc. Sunday afternoon.

The Chinese Merchants Association went into meeting tonight. They were trying to find out why. There are at a least thousand Chinese here, but almost no Japanese. Hotel lobbies tonight are strangely deserted, and managers guess everyone has his ear glued to the radio. The radio stations are breaking in often with bulletins and with messages for all soldiers and sailors to report to their stations. This seemed to bring the gravity of the situation home to the listeners. There are no editorials yet. The most important immediate reaction here will be a redoubled precaution against sabotage defense plants.

Wire from Strother(Detroit) to D. Hulburd - December 7, 1941

The news that war was on, reached Detroit via radio. CBS had a flash at 2:29 and then led off The World Today with a Washington announcement at 2:31. An NBC flash broke the Chicago Round Table of the Air. The reaction was an unsurprised "Well, there it goes". It was a clear crisp day after a succession of murky ones, and an unusually large number of people were out riding with car radios turned on. Many of them caught the tail end of the bulletin or oblique references later, and newspapers and radio stations had a flood of calls between 2:30 and 4 o'clock. Movie houses were playing to capacity crowds, including many workmen with pockets bulging with cash from paychecks fattened by defense overtime. The Michigan Theatre was playing Fibber and Molly in "Look Who's Laughing" and had a long queue in front of the box office. Theatres didn't announce the outbreak, but new arrivals brought the word, and it spread swiftly. Many outgoing patrons stopped at the office to ask if the news was true. Station WJR in the Fisher Building has a big bulletin board in the lobby. A throng gathered at once and the concensus was "Well, I hoped it wouldn't come, but they asked for it and now they're blankety-blank well going to get it."

Men who called newspapers were generally both angry and cheerful. "Here we go. Happy landings", one said when told the news was true. One fellow was good and mad. "Why those Japs." Sitting down in Washington talking terms and then -- whambo! Some women callers burst into tears when the news was confirmed. "Oh gee, gee now he will probably get shot", one said as she hung up. Several men asked newspaper switchboards where they could join the navy. A large proportion of callers wanted to know if the U.S. had also declared war on Japan. Some asked how far it was from Los Angeles to Hawaii and others how many ships in the Japanese Navy.

Attorney General Francis Biddle was addressing 1,200 Americans of Slavic extraction at a metting of the Slav-American Defense Savings Committee in the Masonic Temple.

Wire from Sidney James, Los Angeles, to David Hulburd --
December 8, 1941 -- 6:21 a.m.

Hearst's <u>Examiner</u>, which is anti-Roosevelt and has also fought the U.S. foreign policy said: "The U.S. is at war with Japan, and will conduct the war with every resource at its command and with the grim determination and unswerving loyalty of the American people. "This conflict is of course undesired and unwelcome." "But it is accepted with complete confidence of ultimate victory." "And it is entered with complete national unity."

We'll send along tomorrow the editorial comment of the <u>Daily News</u> which didn't get out an extra. more coming.

-end-

Wire from James (Los Angeles) - 12/7/41 - rec. 12:34 a.m.

Southern California never awoke to a less war-like day Before noon the thermometer climbed to eighty, and a fickle, caressing breeze played up and down the coast, moving now from the North, now from the Southwest, and even at times from the direction of Japan. It was as handsome a day as any day in June ever was. It was perfect for swimming in the Pacific, for golf, for riding, for picnicking or for any midsummer Sunday recreation. The "Little Worlds Championship" between the Hollywood Bears and the Columbus Bulls professional football teams at Gilmore Stadium in Los Angeles seemed singularly out of tune with the lazy weather. It wasn't a day for physical combat even on the field of sport. The talk until "the news" came was mostly about how the UCLA Bruins had managed a surprise 7-7 tie in their traditional game against the Trojans of USC the day before, and the incredible shellacking the Texas Longhorns had given to the Oregon Webfoots. The front pages of the morning papers had suggested no better topic for discussion among sports-loving Southern Californians: "Roosevelt Sends Note to Mikado","San Quentin called hotbed of reds," "Belgians' Leopold weds commoner," "Finnish ships in U.S. ports taken over," "Litvinov vows Russians will continue battle," "U.S. stalling, says Toyko." The more devout were at their places of prayer while "the news" was being made across the Pacific. At Temple Baptist Church they were hearing bespectacled Dr. "Dad" Brougher discuss "The Power of Personal Influence." At First Congregational Church energetic Dr. James W. Fifield Jr. was preaching the truth that "Waters Find their Levels." At Angelus Temple Aimee McPherson was singing through a production called "One Foot in Heaven." At First Methodist Dr. Donald H. Tippett was talking about "The Bright and Morning Star." The Rev. McKinley Walker at the Annandale Methodist Church was taking his theme from the single word "Courage"

(End first take, more coming)

James (Los Angeles) - 12/7/41 -5:38 p.m.

War Add:

The sum total of immediate reaction in Los Angeles was highlighted by the exclamation that was uttered in various forms and added up to what one householder reduced to: "Why the dumb bastards" such was the overall feeling. The action itself seemed incredible but what it meant--war with Japan-- had long been taken for granted. More than one person was heard to say with resignation and a kind of finalty: "Well, this is it". To continue with the thread of "the news" coming to Los Angeles, the point must be made that the radio was the Paul Revere in the picture. After the immediate facts of assault were broadcast it was radio that saddled the ether waves and gave the door to door call to arms. Typical, from that point on is the KNX log of broadcasts for local consumption. Broadcasts were sandwiched in between the newsbreaks which filled most of the air time. At 12:38 KNX broadcast that all army and navy furloughs had been cancelled, and all were urged to report back to their posts immediately. At 12:50 the San Pedro Naval Base announced cancellation of all leaves, at 1:22 the sixth California State Guard was called to immediate duty. At 2:31 all city policemen and firemen off duty were called to work. At 3:30 the public was urged to stay away from aircraft plants and flying fields. At 5:54 all civilian and military personnel of the Fourth Air Corps headquarters at March Field were ordered to report immediately to their duty stations. Interspersed were such announcements as these: motorists were asked to assist men in uniform returning from leaves to Camp Roberts. All members of the Sheriff's emergency reserve were asked to report to the Royal Palms Hotel, 360 Westlake Avenue, Los Angeles. In San Diego all plant special police were called to duty at Consolidated's 40 million dollar plant, and all unofficial traffic was diverted away from the plant. All personnel of Navy recruiting stations were called to duty. All offices will be open continuously. Unlimited war time recruiting. All male citizens over 21 were asked to report to

James (Los Angeles) - page 2 (5:38 p.m. take)

their nearest fire or police station to volunteer for aid in an emergency. All city firemen and policemen who were off duty were ordered to report for emergency duty. All firemen and policemen are placed on two-platoon duty. All aircraft warning stations ordered fully manned for 24 hour duty. Col. Charles Branshaw, Chief West Coast procurement officer, ordered the public to stay away from the defense plants, asked citizens to stay at home unless it was necessary for them to be out, since traffic officers were needed for duty elsewhere. Governor Olson called all members of the California State Council for defense to meet with him at the State Building in Los Angeles Monday. And so it went. Radio station switchboards were lit up like Christmas trees without a break. A check with the three networks revealed that 95 per cent of those calls were from unexcited citizens who merely wanted to know when their favorite commentator could be heard again. One hysterical woman screamed over the telephone to a KNX operator that "your station ought to be ashamed of itself broadcasting all this terrible war news" but those calls were few and far between. There was some trouble early in the day from small fry municipal executives requesting the stations to make hysterical warning announcements. For instance, an unidentified man at the harbormaster's office called KNX telling them that "you better broadcast all over town that the Navy is going to blast the hell out of every boat they see, large or small, in the harbor". These calls were checked immediately with the Army and Navy who squelched them. Donald W. Thornburg, CBS vice president in charge of West Coast operations rushed back from a week end in Delmonte; Fox Case, in charge of special events broadcasts for the Columbia Pacific network was hustled out of town mysteriously late this afternoon to set up supplementary listening posts up and down the coast. CBS fervidly trying to make arrangements with the military authorities to get two announcers to Honolulu immediately. CBS sent a special policemen to their transmitter building at nearby Torrance.

James (Los Angeles) - page 3 (5:38 p.m. take)

A special guard, one man, was placed outside the master control room in the CBS building. Those, however, were the only precautions they took. Visitors were allowed to crowd through the lobby and gawk at the Christmas display and "the news" apparently didn't bother audience-show addicts who swarmed into the several CBS radio theatres for Sunday night feature shows. At NBC's pale green Hollywood Radio City, separated from the CBS building only by the Palladium, popular jitterbug haunt doing good business as usual, it was a different story. They took "the news" more seriously. They supplemented their normal special police force with hastily called Pinkerton men, Los Angeles policemen and two FBI agents. All tourists were barred from the building after 2:00 p.m. The master control room guard in the main lobby was boarded off. A special guard was placed around their far eastern listening post in North Hollywood. A NBC engineer, came face to face with the barrel of a policeman's gun when he tried to report to work at the Engineering Room at 4 p.m. had to be identified before he could get in. But there was no evidence that NBC had any more cause than other stations for alarm. Even a small band of IATSE workers who have been picketing the Radio City building for a year because NBC wouldn't recognize their maintenance man's union, called off their picketing for the first time today. So it wasn't strange that the NBC publicity department looked pretty silly when they issued the following statement about 7:30 pm: "It ("The News") was a great shock to our stars (Jack Benny, Victor McLaglen, Edmund Lowe, Basil Rathbone, Nigel Bruce, Irene Rich, Edgar Bergen, all Sunday night features) they all went on without a break." Generally speaking people went about their usual Sunday night routines without outward evidence that "The News" had overwhelmed them. As a wiseacre reported in a gossip column some months back, "If Los Angeles ever had an air raid the people probably wouldn't pay any attention to it. They'd think it was just another Hollywood preview."

James (Los Angeles) - page 4 (5:38 p.m. take)

But they weren't just being blase, they were simply gradually accepting a fact that they had been long expecting--only they had never expected it to become a fact on so fine a Sunday. (More coming)

(end)

Wire from Sidney James, Los Angeles, Calif.
        to David Hulburd -- December 7, 1941

Add War:

At Hollywood's El Capitan Theatre skittish Edward Everett Horton played to a full house matinee in a revival of "Springtime for Henry." At the Music Box, Hollywood's new, review "They can't Get you Down" entertained a sizeable "bargain" matinee crowd. At the Theatre Mart "The Drunkard" hooted and slapsticked its way well into a ninth year of entertaining Los Angeles audiences. And the movie audiences turned out normally for a Sunday afternoon of Cinema entertainment. "Citizen Kane" went into its eighth week at The Hawaii. "One Foot in Heaven" was at Warner's Hollywood. Abbott and Costello in "Keep 'Em Flying" played at the Hollywood Pantages and the RKO Hill Street (downtown) theatres. The big elaborate Paramount Theatre in downtown Los Angeles, showed Charles Boyer and Margaret Sullavan in "Appointment for Love", while on the stage, a road show of the musical comedy "Meet the People" entertained customers. And at Grauman's Chinese Theatre in Hollywood, the morbidly curious, tipped off by the Legion of Decency's campaign against it, crowded in to see Greta Garbo and Melvin Douglas in "Two Faced Woman."

When "the news" did come it didn't hit Los Angeles with a bang. It leaked in to the super-curious and the shut-ins, who even on a perfect day can stay by their radios. It got around at first almost by word of mouth. "Did you hear the news?" neighbor asked of neighbor. It spread limpingly, not like a fall brush fire in the Hollywood hills. There was no hue and cry on the public streets where the outdoor loving were bound for their Sunday pleasures. It moved through backyard gardens, across golf courses, into bars where more convivial citizens were braving some more of the same to rehabilitate themselves from the rigors of the night before, and finally to the beaches of the fateful Pacific. Typical was the way it came to a group of paunchy Hollywood newsgatherers and press agents:

A pint-sized moppet, proud of a piece of news he didn't understand completely, page 2 -- Sidney James, Los Angeles, December 7, 1941

stepped up to the sidelines and said "hey, did you fellas hear about U.S. and Japan?" The goings on in Herbert's drive-in bar in the San Fernando Valley was typical of the casual acceptance of "the news" by the run of the mine Angelenos two hours after it was out. As bulletin after bulletin broke into the regular broadcasts, a Franck Symphony, a sermon, a swing fest, the occupants of the small barroom fell into a jocular mood. "You guys with the Japanese gardeners, how do you feel now"? cracked one. A stocky, medium-sized blond youth and his taller companion became the butt of numerous bad jokes. It was apparent that the blond youth was about to be drafted and that the other recently had been released from army service under the new draft law, but was subject to recall. There was a resounding guffaw when the already flash-tortured Franck Symphony ended and a saccarine-voiced announcer blurted: "Do your Christmas shopping early." Then an over-painted female, slightly in her cups, sitting at the end of the bar, giving no sign she had the slightest idea of what the hell was going on, told (loudly) the story about the "destitute prostitute". At a booth, five men played hearts, talked vaguely about the war situation. Brightest remark from this group: "Do you suppose Hitler had anything to do with this".

Typical of the small working man's reaction is the remark of a waiter at Romanoff's restaurant, in the middle of the afternoon. "I don't want to think about it. It's too hard to believe". Even the theoretically more-informed classes were apparently lacking in any real comprehension of what the hell it meant. Charles Einfeld, vice president and head of all advertising and publicity at Warner Brothers, hearing the news as he came in off the Hill Crest Golf course at 2:00 p.m. had only this to say; "I'm dazed".

The Los Angeles rich play-girls and play-boys week-ending at Palm Springs, hearing the news by accident in mid-afternoon (because of magnetic disturbances caused by the surrounding mountains it is impossible to get radio programs in Palm Springs until well after dark) were blase. A young aviation officer from March Field spending the weekend at the Springs' El Mirador Hotel, got a hurry call from Headquarters to report back for duty. He had to cancel his dates in town and so the word spread through, leaked slowly by telephone gossip until nightfall when people began to gather at bars. Not singular were the remarks of one pretty, black-haired socialite resort girl when she heard the news. "Everybody knew this was going to happen, so why spoil a perfectly good Sunday afternoon worrying about it." A little later she remarked, "They couldn't have bombed Pearl Harbor. That Admiral I met in Coronado is in charge and he is a perfectly lovely person".

For the first few hours after "the news" broke you couldn't raise long distance or the telegraph services. By early evening the Southern California Telephone Co. asked all radio stations to ask civilians not to make any unnecessary or purely social calls because all telephone facilities were needed for military and municipal purposes. By mid-afternoon, the outlets for the major radio chains were fully staffed and humming. Mutual's KHJ broke into "Hollywood Whisperings", a Hollywood gossip program, at 11:45 to break "the news" to their listeners. "The news" came to CBS listeners at 11:30 over local KNX during Columbia's European Roundup "The World Today". NBC listeners here, tuned to local KECA, heard the news about the same time when the University of Chicago Round Table Program was interrupted for the Flash. More coming.

-- end --

Wire from Sidney James, Los Angeles, Calif.
        to David Hulburd -- December 7, 1941 (12:34 p.m.)

War Fourth Add:

After all these excited local break-ins--for now every Radio in the City was turned on -- it is no wonder that by evening there was evidence of hysteria. By this time movie theatres were breaking in for flash news on the screen and newsboys were hawking extras everywhere. Finally every radio station began broadcasting intermittantly at the request of the Chief of Police and the Sheriff who had been swamped with calls from hysterical citizens: "There is no immediate cause for alarm."

Wire from Sidney James to David Hulburd, Los Angeles, Calif.
December 7, 1941 -- rec'd 7:47 a.m.

We are breaking in here to give you a cogent observation from LIFE's Peter Stackpole who spent some time in Hawaii on assignment recently. Having recently returned from a month's cruise with the U.S. Fleet in Hawaiian waters, I returned to the mainland with the opinion that I had just seen one of the world's best protected bases. I had believed the encouraging boast of navy personnel that, due to certain devices for detecting the presence of enemy ships and planes, no enemy craft could approach the Oahu area without first being detected and intercepted before it ever reached the shore line. Tonight when I hear reports of heavy damage to Hickman Field, Ford Island, and the possible sinking of two battleships in Pearl Harbor, I can begin to realize a few of the possible reasons for our force's apparent failure to meet the attack quickly.

The fact that a second wave of Japanese planes was able to reach the base confirms the fact that damage must have been heavy and the job of mustering flying personnel and getting them out to the air bases must have taken hours. Saturday night in Honolulu is not unlike that in any large American town. Sailors and officers usually enjoy a weekend shore leave. Officers include most of the flying personnel and they are allowed the whole weekend ashore without having to report back to the ships at Pearl Harbor until early Monday morning.

This means that though many of the ships were well manned with sailors, large numbers of officers and fliers were still ashore. Because of a decided housing shortage, the whole Honolulu-Waikiki-Pearl Harbor area is jammed with defense workers, sailors and soldiers, who, due to the regions bad transportation have relied on old rattle trap cars for which they have paid a high price. Oahu's undersized highways have thus become jammed with cars, serious traffic problems have developed. To make matters worse, the average officer prefers to spend his weekends in Waiki, which is about 20 miles from Pearl Harbor, separated by downtown Honolulu.

page 2 -- Sidney James, Los Angeles, Dec.7, 1941 (7:47 a.m.)

To cover this short distance one can usually expect to remain in transit from an hour to an hour and a half, whether he takes a crowded bus, a taxi or his own car. The latter would be quickest. Sunday mornings were the only periods when I don't recollect having heard the constant drone of planes overhead from army, navy and marine bases. Ironically enough, the only plane which actually met the attacking Japanese when they came in was a private ship whom the Japanese didn't bother to shoot down.

Taking for granted that the Island's defense system was taken by surprise, possibly because of an over-confident feeling among its defenders, we can best judge the extent of military damage by coming reports of how many Japanese planes and ships our forces were able to sink during this fateful Sunday. The fact is that it is traditional in the service to get blind drunk on Saturday night. The Japs must have been counting on this, apparently they were right. End Stackpole. More coming.

-- end --

Wire from Sid James, Los Angeles, to D. Hulburd - Dec. 8, 1941.

7TH ADD

The hottest spot in this area is Los Angeles harbor and specifically, Terminal Island. Earliest radio broadcasts told of the rounding up of all this area's some 3,000 Japanese. Despite repeated instructions to all civilians to keep away, many carloads of curiosity seekers headed down Sepulveda Blvd. for the harbor. On their way, they saw the huge B-19 at Mines Field, probably wished it was in Hawaii with a load of bombs. As they passed through Hermosa Beach, they saw visible evidence of preparedness: camouflaged anti-aircraft guns manned by alert gunners. When they approached the harbor, they were politely but firmly turned back by a swarming force of policemen and soldiers. No one was allowed near the Point Fermin area where the army's concealed coast artillery is placed. Even residents of that area were escorted home and practically put to bed by soldiers.

Unable to get near the harbor, many inquisitive drivers went up the steep hill west of San Pedro, got a good look at the harbor. The whole area was quiet and motionless. Below them the red tile roofed barracks of Ft. MacArthur reflected the setting sun. The only sound came from the loud speaker of the football game at the fort. The only moving objects in the harbor were a few odd sailboats and the returning Catalina Island boat loaded with weekenders.

Earlier in the day, all the vessels had been ordered away from the pier and by this time all the big ships and commercial boats were at anchorage. Across the inlet from San Pedro, Terminal Island's huge refinery tanks stood out against the low, brown shacks of the Japanese fisherman behind Terminal Island was a huge backdrop of Long Beach buildings and behind this the dome-shaped signal hill oil field whose crowded derricks made it look like a huge pin cushion. Down at the Terminal Island ferry landing, two busy army intelligence men, supported by policemen and armed soldiers were busy searching every car for alien Japs.

Already that day they had interned over 300. Each boat-load brought a few more. The bewildered Japs were placed in a makeshift chicken wire detention camp near the entrance to the ferry. Self-conscious rookies occasionally followed the giggling Japanese across the RR tracks to the lavatory. A young Jap boy was making a steady journey between the pay phone and his parents inside the detention station. An elderly Jap complained bitterly when the officers took his new Buick and placed him in the camp.

But there was no violence. Across the inlet on Terminal Island, everything was almost too quiet. Soldiers patrolled the streets in pairs. The main street of Fish Harbor usually very gay on Sunday night, was almost dark. One Jap restaurant was open. In there, an old bald Jap was screaming to anyone who would listen that he has been in the U.S. since 1906. His three children were working quietly. Occasionally they would interpret his jumbled remarks.

A one-armed sailor was making sweeping statements about the harbor's defense. An American commercial fisherman was complaining because the Navy had kept him from going out of the harbor that morning. "How do they expect us to make a living? I'd sneak my boat out but they've got enough dynamite in that harbor to blow the whole Jap navy to bits. Hell, I wouldn't try to get a canoe through that net." It all seemed calm and quiet but these 3,000 Japanese are sitting right in the middle of our biggest west coast harbor. There Japs could drop a match and set a million dollars worth of gasoline on fire. And another match would take care of three or four shipbuilding plants. Japanese district of Los Angeles, largest colony of Japanese outside Asia, loosely called "Little Tokyo" looks almost as vulnerable to fire bombs. It lies just a few blocks from the Civic center, is bordered on other sides by skid rows and factory districts. There live about 3,800 of Southern California's approximately 60,000(to be checked) Japanese. Of these, about 2/3 (more rather than less) are Nisei -- born in America.

Page 3 -- James - Los Angeles - 7th Add

If you had happened to wander down into little Tokyo today that is what you might have seen. You would (if you came from the better part of town) have passed the civic center, there seen policy officers, sheriff's officers, recruiting station men from army, navy and marine corps (they were all ordered to their posts for the duration over radio in apparent expectation of sudden large enlistments), just plain citizens in as busy a mob (on Sunday) as the center sees on the busiest weekday.

You wander down into the Japanese section and note that workmen are busy on tall ladders, growing out of a truck, raising Christmas garlands (with a gay Santa Claus) across First Street, near Los Angeles St. You might notice that the Christmas decorations extend from near the entrance to the Yokohama Specie Bank to the Tojito Trading Co (with its window filled with Christmas gifts). You might also notice that both Los Angeles St. and First St. were filled with double lines of traffic each way, that on each corner were two policemen. If you were aware of things as they used to be you would know that policemen work in pairs only when there is imminent danger, that traffic is thick on weekends and week days in that part of town.

You might talk to one pair of cops. He says: "The God damn fools. I've worked in this district for years. I like these nice clean people. They're a damn sight cleaner than those lousy wops and spiks cafes a few blocks from here. But these damn fools Sunday drivers have to come down here to have a look at it. Maybe they expect a bomb or some Jap to cut his guts out in the middle of First St. They are the same guys who would drop their water if a single bomb dropped, but would come out later to look at the hole without sense enough to worry about when the next bomb was going to drop. And the same guys would help lynch a poor bastard Japanese who might be trying to earn a living down here selling his countrymen's junk. We gotta protect the Japs against the Americans, not the other way around.

But FBI and Naval Intelligence (who for years have had dossiers on every Japanese in the district) are picking up some 14 of them, herding some 300 more into a corrall at Terminal Island. If you chance to take a cab the driver might tell you, "I

Page 4 -- James, Los Angeles - 7th Add

live next door to a Japanese family -- nice people too. Hell they're said to give more tips than any white man."

Easily the most intelligent source of Japanese information in Southern California is the Los Angeles Daily News, of which Neisi Togo Tanaka is the English Language editor. So if you had a chance to walk into the editorial rooms of the Daily News tonight (between English Linotype and ending cases of Japanese characters, among which soft-slippered, slick-fingered Japanese character-slinked) you would have walked immediately into a tiny room which looked as though it couldn't hold all it held. Here where all the leaders of Japanese thought in Southern California, ready and willing to agree with anything which would "please" allow them to go on living life they had been living. If you were lucky you would have chance to overhear the whole group (representing every honest Americanized Japanese group) vote to accept a statement phoned from San Francisco by Saburo Kido, national president of the Japanese American citizen League (leading patriotic Japanese group). The statement read:

"The National J.A.C.L. has offered the facilities of its entire organization to the government in this great crisis. We are pledged to an unequivocal repudiation of Japan and bend our energies now to the common objective of an American victory and a defeat of Japan. I am confident that Americans of Japanese ancestry will respond with true loyalty to America and that we shall have cause to be proud of their record. I am also confident that all their parents, who are non-citizens, because the naturalization laws have prevented from becoming citizens, will stand by us and faithfully abide by the laws of good Americans.

"We recognize the need for unity and are confident of our usefulness to America to this common defense of our shores.

"This sort of statement does not necessarily represent the entire Japanese colony in Southern California.

You might remember that some 600 representatives of Japanese business were here (such business at Matsui, Matsubishi) that the less than 1/3 of the others were born across the Pacific, that, after all, these people believe in their country, might want to support it, that they might be forced into action by threats against their relatives in Japan.

"You might also talk to them and learn they are almost more American (again the 2/3 we can account for) than most of your own ilk. Typical of them is young Joe Masaoka who has a horribly flattened nose, low-growing black hair, slant eyes. He also has an honest face, a perfect English accent, a college education (Utah), a fear of occidental "hoodlums" who might choose to attack his kind.

"Masaoka and I watched the family Sunday, radio-listening cars go by all day by his people's stores whose owners only wanted to sell their goods in order to buy an American sort of Christmas for their children. Most of them were sensation seekers or the type of skid-row people whose only boast is they have a Caucasian face.

"This guy Joe (and he is typical of a dozen) said: "Look, you Americans have among you Irish faces, German faces (and I understand Germans fought with you against Germans in the last war, just as brother fought against brother in your own civil war) Italian faces. What's wrong with Japanese faces? I know what you say: we are Oriental faces, we can't integrate, but why not? My best girl friend went to Japan five years ago to learn dancing. You know what happened to her? She was arrested on the street for wearing too much lip-stick. She's back here now and she's going to stay. And the rest of us. I have enough money to own a car. Don't you think I like that, do you think I'd change that? That is something no one of my generation and breeding could do over there ever. Over there I'd be a coolie. Over here I can talk to you. Over here, by God, we'd fight our own nation and that isn't being unethical because really we think they are just trying to get for themselves something we (as citizens of America) have already got. We believe enough in that so we'd fight Japan.

"Off to some sort of war this week went some 2500 (local estimate of number of Japanese in the U. S. army). This figure should be checked, but according to local sources represents highest proportionate representation (by two and ½ times) of any racial group in the U. S. and according to local knowledge, not one has/ever been guilty of major infraction of army rules. The navy will not take Japanese. Only this morning ten huge army trucks went to the center and posed for pictures while Japanese members of the Japanese shrubbery Association loaded them with shrubs they were donating to Camp Roberts."

Hollywood note: By the time a bright three quarter moon was high in one of Los Angeles' better Chamber of Commerce heavens, they had accepted the fact. "New news" was driven home by things like an early evening report on movie boxoffices throughout the country. The report said revenue had dropped from 15 to 50% with the hinterlands and neighborhood houses reporting biggest slumps. Apparently the working masses, accustomed to Sunday night escape at the movies before "blue Monday" chose to stay at home with their ears glued to the radio.

Things like Producer Joe Pasternack's Japanese gardner walking into the Pasternack living room at 6 p.m. announcing flatly: "I no work anymore." FBI agents stating a preliminary investigation of Hollywood shenanagins, as an aftermath of the Bioff trial, got orders to forget about glamorland for the moment, were all over the country over 40 trunk lines reserved exclusively for their use. At Ciro's, Hollywood's top night spot, usually pack-jammed on a sunday night because of a weekly charity show, attendance was half of normal. For the first time, the evening opened with a rendition of "The Star Spangled Banner". On a half dozen tables in the gaudy, green and red draped cafe, portable radios had at least one ear of the diners. Ciro's charity supporters sat on their hands when Noel Crorath, a dark, sloe-eyed entertainer sang a song entitled, "I'm an International Spy", didn't crack a smile when he said, "Here's one written in B. H. (before Hitler)."

Page 7 James -- Los Angeles - 7th Add

One note at least warmed their hearts. Comedian Bert Wheeler announced that he wished to sing a song, written this afternoon by musician Lew Pollack and lyricist Ned Washington. He explained he had been driving up Sepulveda Blvd. just after two o'clock when Washington overtook him in his car, hailed him to the curb, said he had an inspiration, was about to jell it at Pollack's house. The inspiration, which Wheeler sang for the Ciro audience: "It's here at last -- the die is cast -- America.

	The flag flies high -- so do or die -- America
	Let's stand together today in that old American way
	Get in this fight with all your might and make those
Chorus	cowards pay.
	Oh, we didn't want to do it, but they're asking for it now.
	So we'll knock the Japs right into the laps of the Nazis.
	When they hop on Honolulu that's a thing we won't allow.
	So we'll knock the Japs right into the laps of the Nazis.
	Every man will do all he can to knock every soldier of Japan into kingdom come, things'll hum.
	They'll hear the beat of a million feet of people who'd rather fight than eat.
	And here we come, here we come.
	I'd hate to be in Yokahama when our bombers make a bow.
	For we'll knock the Japs right into the laps of the Nazis."

Earlier in the evening, army MP's scoured the town, let it be known flatly to all restauranteurs that no drinks were to be served to men in uniform. And to cap off Ciro's charity evening, a blonde, blushing lieutenant of the 364th infantry mounted the podium and boyishly asked all military men to report to duty at once, assured the patrons, "We have the situation well in hand. It is up to you people to protect the civilian front." He promptly sat down amid hearty applause and ordered a drink.

Wire from Holland McCombs, San Antonio, to J. McConaughy -- Dec. 8, 1941

First take:

The day was coolish and switched from gray to clear. People were lounging around homes and apartments. Some were nursing hangovers from Saturday's football games and Saturday night's jamboreeing. And their gals were cleaning up after picnics in Brackenridge Park, getting ready to visit the zoo and "take pictures." The smart set was getting in naps before later cocktailing. Some were headed for a polo game, others for rides in park and country. Many had gone to ranches and ranch parties for the weekend. Downtown streets were quietly full of ambling salesmen, soldiers, girls, school kids. Lines were beginning to form in front of picture shows. Out in wooded Brackenridge Park, kids were riding the ferris wheel and flying jenny, babies were being held in swings, miniature trains were tooting and whistling as kids were whirled by adoring parents. Other kids were riding ponies around a little sawdust circular ring. Still others were riding burrows (free) down fenced lanes in the park. Here and there down the downtown streets among San Antonio's polyglot population you'd see a carload of Japs, Chinese, Negroes, Mexicans, Italians, Germans, Bohemians, Poles, even Hungarians. The main streets were pretty full of wistful-eyed window shoppers. Some of the folks at home were eating, lounging, listening to the University of Chicago Round Table Discussion. These were the first to hear a cut in. It was a flash from WOAI newsroom. This was about 1:35. Into Batkxk Batcherlor House stormed a member who had just heard the flash on his car radio: "Those s.o.b.'s have done it." This man was getting ready to go hunting, and blurted: "To H. with hunting quail, I got a notion to go out and hunt Japs." Another man at home had just finished a quarrel with his wife, though he had gone to lie down on the couch and pout. She went in another room and pouted. Then Kaltenborn came on. This was the first news in that home. After the first few statements, the quarrel was forgotten, both joined in listening, commenting with force, even held hands in excitement, began calling friends, jabbering, cussing.

Men in the San Antonio Light heard it over the radio at 1:45, called the AP Bureau at Dallas who had not heard about it, "We woke them up," say Light men. The Light had an extra on the street at 2:15 and kept crews on hand all Sunday. The San Antonio Express (morning) had to round up a crew, got out an extra at 5:00 p.m. Folks weren't so surprised that happened. But they were completely flabbergasted at the way it happened. One guy called me and exclaimed: "Are the bums crazy? Do they think they can make a frontal attack on the U.S.?" Another said: "There's something behind all this we don't know about. If we were so much on the alert as they claim we are out there, how in H. did they get in to bomb Pearl Harbor? It's the most fantastic thing I every heard of."

Except for my friend going hunting, folks didn't seem mad until later when reports came about specific loss of life. Some people heard it at one-thirty over the World Today, cut in for a newsflash, program. Others listening to small stations had record-programs interrupted.

Wire from Holland McCoombs, San Antonio - to J. McConaughy, Dec. 8, 1941

Second Take:

We went downtown at 5:30 Sunday p.m. The streets were crowded with soldiers and civilians but except for an occasional "Damn those Japs," and newsboy cries of "War Extry" things were pretty calm. Soldiers seemed more interested whether they are to get Xmas leave than anything else. In front of the Majestic Theatre where they are playing "Skylark" with Claudette Colbert, was a long line of soldiers and civilians. Just in front of us was a pretty, calm, self-sufficient young Japanese woman with a cute little 2-year-old girl. Folks didn't seem to mind and she was perfectly at ease while newsboys kept shouting right in front of her face, "War Extry!" "Japs Attack U.S.!" etc. She bought her ticket right in front of me, walked into the show which was constantly interrupted with announced flashes and when a newspix of Kurusu flashed on the screen and the audience hissed him heartily, she actually cheered news announcements of Japs attacking Pearl Harbor. By this time folks were getting a bit war-feverish. By nightfall San Antonio police had begun rounding up Japs, investigating them and have already outlined their behavior, requiring them to report to the police regularly.

Corpus Christi Naval Air Training Station was the first military post in this territory to order all men to their posts. Third Army Headquarters ordered all men to war uniforms, to report to their commanders. M.P.s flocked downtown, joined forces with the police on rounding up anybody who looked suspicious. Extra guards were thrown around San Antonio's great army supply depots, airfields, machine shops, etc. Telephones to all army posts around here were jammed. If the Japs were coming across the Rio Grande it wouldn't be possible to advise some army posts by phone. Phone service in these posts is always lousy, now there just ain't any. Officers were stationed at the home of the Jap consul in Houston. The San Antonio Light ran a sort of full page call to arms, headed "United Nation Marches to Victory."

Filipinos in Dallas were afraid to go out on the streets, asked Dallas people to please learn "differences in our races." They say they are being mistaken for Japs. As the President's speech comes on here in San Antonio, 10 women are now standing in the rain on the streets weeping because of the loss of American lives. / One of the Things that got me most when news was coming in on the radio, was how we'd listen to this world-stirring drama, then be switched back to Bulldog Drummond, The Shadow Face, etc. and were we supposed to shudder? We felt a bit disgusted at the attempt of fear through the sugared, hush voices. Then when we got a newsflash of the bombing of the Hickman barracks with the loss of lives, we were (switched) to Catholic Hour dedicated to and talking about Peace. We felt like saying, my God, if that's a recording, take it off, simply out of respect for the times; if it's spot stuff, why don't somebody tell the Reverend what' has and is happening. This morning there were larger crowds at mass than usual. At one six o'clock mass were dozens of officers in uniform. People were renting and buying radios. One radio shop reported it rented out fifteen receiving sets last night.

(More Coming)

End

Wire from Holland McCombs, San Antonio, Texas to James McConaughy - 12-8

Add Jap War (Third Take)

The spotter we have in headquarters third army (lodged in a downtown office building) just called and reports that guards have been placed on all floors, even in elevators. A tunnel between that office building and downtown hotel have been closed.

In Orange, Texas, K. Suski, representative of Jap Steamship Lines for 16 years, offered to surrender to police. So did Jap K. Kishi, 35-year resident of Orange.

Officers of Third Army headquarters hurrying from office to office with grim expressions and working under tense pressure. Firemen and police leaves cancelled Sunday. This morning San Antonio arsenal (containing tanks, guns, ammunition) correlated its radio with that of San Antonio police and doubled guards. This morning's San Antonio EXPRESS carried an editorial headed: "Stand by the Nation." First sentence: "Treachery has been characterized as the most infamous and detestable of all the vices to which human nature is subject." Further: "From out of a smokegascreen of Japanese treachery -- laid in this nation's capital during the two weeks past -- emerges war upon the U.S. . . . The U.S. is at war with the Axis partner of Hitler and Mussolini -- as Nazi Germany had schemed and desired. Stand by the Nation."

Deserter, Jap soldier, in 45 Division is being held in Camp Barkeley stockade and refuses to tell court martial where he has been for the past two months of A.W.O.L... more

End

Wire from Holland McCombs, San Antonio, Tex.
      to James McConaughy -- December 8, 1941

Add war (fourth take): Dallas police picked up six Japs, say they are now holding them for immigration. El Paso has sworn in a hundred deputies to augment the police force. Border Patrol reports adding men, increasing vigilance along the border. Home Defense Guard at El Paso is furnishing patrols for bridges and other vital points along the border and guarding 100 miles of Southern Pacific Railroad.

Recruiting offices opened in San Antonio at eight this morning, were swamped with young men wanting to enlist. The attitude of soldiers this morning is roughly expressed by the observation of one Texas private: "Well, let's have a war." A soldier draftee from New York says he was out playing football with the men of his company when he first got the news. The game didn't even stop. He said: "The Texas boys seemed to be happy about it. The Eastern boys were more concerned."

Two officers and two privates when asked: "Well, what are we going to do now" gave exactly the same answer: "We'll whip 'em." Out at Fort Sam Houston enlisted men in all shapes of dress and undress gathered in the "day rooms" to hear the President's message, seemed to realize what might mean to them, were cool, collected and so far there's been very little conversation between them about the war or its portent. This afternoon's San Antonio Evening News editorialized:

"An act of basest treachery unworthy of a nation calling itself civilized and has all the earmarks of having been Made in Berlin ... The amazing and almost incredible fact was that the American defenders were taken by surprise and allowed the raiders to get within bombing distance..."

This nation is shocked, certainly; but in coming out of the impacts of the first shock, it is rising up in wrath to strike back... Looking ahead even for a day, what could the Japanese have expected to gain from that initial advantage? They must have gone mad. This is an act of desperation -- a way to commit national suicide (this is also the opinion of lots of people we've seen and talked to today)...

"Orders have gone out to army personnel that they are not to make any comments whatsoever and everything in this area is to be released directly from the office of the Commander of the Third Army.

Most significant evidence of war here is the general tightening up on the whole army front from headquarters of the Third Army on down. Officers must wear uniform on all occasions. Young Lieutenant just in office is griping about having bought a new civilian suit, and now wants to sell it, says, "It'll be a h. of a long time before I'll wear that suit."

This is the end of the first spurt, but will keep on the lookout for anything specially worthy and will wire when we come across it.

Wire from Holland McCombs, San Antonio, Tex., to James McConaughy 12-8

Add Jap War:

Radio Station KTSA has put up a bulletin board in the lobby of the Gunter Hotel as people are crowding around reading bulletins as they are posted. Now since things have sort of simmered down, people seem to be glad that a definite break has been made and that we have good "causus belli." There seems to be a general toughening up of sentiment. Majority figure Japan is in for destruction or some such, and that Well, they asked for it."

End.

Wire from Hammond (San Francisco) to D. Hulburd - December 8, 1941

Herewith answers to your questions. More to come on 1) developments on both sides of the bay and outlying counties where many war industries are located 2) color, San Francisco and Transbay and country. 3) General roundup unduplicated by wire services.

1) How news came to San Francisco: The radio was the first to announce with KSFO (Columbia) and KFRC (Mutual) coming on about the same time with a first one-line flash that Honolulu and Manila were being bombed, Manila bombing unconfirmed. KSFO was tuned into CBS coast-to-coast hook-up on "The World Today," a ~~drinks~~ roundup of ~~drink~~ world's capitals. New York interrupted "shortly after" program began at 11:30 A.M. KFRC got a phone flash from the local AP at 11:32, read the same one-line flash over the air at 11:44, interrupting "Strings In Swingtime"..sustaining musical program from Hollywood.

NBC stations KGO and KPO were cut in on by New York sometime after 11 but did not log time.

Telephones were taxed by innumerable calls everywhere. Lyle Brown, Division Manager of the Pacific Tel & Tel, says long distance facilities were particularly taxed. He is requesting the public to refrain from making anything but the most urgent long distance calls. Radio station switchboards were flooded with people asking for more info, asking if they'd heard aright.

KSNO went on the air after an hour or so asking the public not to phone in, that news would be broadcast as soon as they got it. NBC and CBS each estimate that they received "Several thousand" calls between noon and 8 P.M.

Newspapers: The Chronicle newsroom received the first flash at 11:29 A.M., which would be a phone call from the AP downstairs.

The first papers hit the street at 2 P.M. with the presses running steadily since. The Examiner got the flash between 11 and 11:30. Oscar Gardiner, Ass't. City Circulation Manager, says the Examiner hit the street at 12:45 with the first Steve Early flash. Ed McQuaide, Ass't. City Editor, however, says the first edition was at 2:09. No one on either paper has any circulation figures. People are gobbling them up as fast as they roll however. The Chronicle carried a topline of four-inch letters WAR:

2) It was like a rubber band breaking, a rubber band which had been stretched out for a long time," said Benjamin Fox, special officer, who stood on Market St., San Francisco's main drag from noon to eight P.M. "Ever since I was a kid, we've been expecting something like this. Now it's come and it's a good thing and I think almost everybody thinks so."

"I think Japan had m Goddam well struck her neck out a little bit too far this time," said E. W. Mallery.

"That's my honest opinion and I think that Japan's neck is going to get nipped off."

Generally the reaction in San Francisco, most Japanese-fearing city in the United States was first: surprise, stunned surprise. Then indignation. Then a smiling sense of relief, confidence that the Navy which has been itching to get at Japan for many years, would take over and "Blast/goddam that country off the map."

Although local defense councils were flustered into action finally, there was no fear that bombs would start dropping on the coast. Most people viewed the war as a naval engagement, nothing to touch the home shores. Officialdom, however, rushed to man the barricades, special guards were ordered for defense plants and special anti-sabotage patrols were instituted or supplemented.

A sum-up of attitude would be "They've got a lot of guts. They're asking for it and now they're going to get it, really."

A service-station man, "Boy, this is important to me. It means maybe I go to war. I used to be a marine."

A motorist in the service station: "I just heard about it. Down the street

I almost ran over a ~~xxx~~ Jap on a motorcycle. Maybe I should have hit him. That would be my contribution.

3) Will be covered in supplemental material following immediately.

4) Mayor Angello J. Rossi proclaimed a state of emergency for the city, setting aside emergency funds to pay for civilian defense directors, calling on employee, employer groups to "Forthwith terminate their existing differences during the present emergency and end all disputes so that San Francisco may present a united front and so that every citizen may work for the one end, the safety of our country."

Previous to the Mayor's proclamation, ~~xxxxx~~ John F. Shelly, President of the San Francisco Labor Council (AFL) and State Senator had announced a meeting of all AFL striking unions to compose differences with employers. Strikes current in San Francisco: 16 hotels picketed in strike against 26 members of the San Francisco Hotel Association; The Department Store Employes Union is picketing three stores, including the city's largest, The Emporium. Berkeley workers in the park, street, corporation yard and garbage departments had scheduled a 240 hour work stoppage for Monday; welders, (CQ) cutters and helpers union (independent) seeking a breakaway from AFL crafts, had threatened a nation-wide strike on the basis of four grievances of San Francisco ship yards. Berkeley, opening wedge in CIO's national drive for organization of municipal workers, was called off. So was the welders strike. Rossi called the Monday meeting unions, employers in local strikes, to seek a settlement. Important development: A terrific civilian response to a hitherto lagging drive for 25,000 volunteers 12,500 air raid wardens, 10,000 auxiliary firemen and 2500 auxiliary cops. In the last two weeks of registration of the drive only 3200 people signed up. Tonight no one knows the exact total on the day's registration but Civil Defense Headquarters estimate conservatively at least 1500 signed up, probably more. An operator on 24 trunk lines at the

Fire Department Headquarters said she had handled 3000-4000 calls herself. Many are just fearful and asking for miscellaneous information, but many are asking imperatively where and how to sign up for civil defense work. The swamped operator wailed: "I hadda call for help". Sampling of 54 fire stations and 10 district police headquarters, which are the registration points, reveals 49 persons signing up at one fire station in an hour, 60 at another. Consensus is that on an average 60 to 70 persons signed up at each registration place. That would mean better than 4000 people-and they're still queued up all over town waiting to sign up.

Unable to get a 24-hour total until 9 Monday morning when Fire houses and police stations tabulate and report to headquarters. The registration was held up to an average in the Japanese section where there are a lot of Negroes, poor white people; in the North Beach which is the Italian section and in the Potrero district which has a heavy settlement of white Russians.

5) Editorials San Francisco Examiner: With the nation at war every industry becomes a defense industry. There is no room for strikes. Both for the good of the labor movement and as a patriotic gesture, the hotel and store unions should call off their strikes. Anything that hampers business, hampers the nation in its defense and San Francisco has now become a key point in the war. This is no time for debates about the open or closed shop: no time for pickets to be parading the sidewalks when Americans are being killed by bombs. There couldn't be a better time or a better reason for calling off the strikes. San Francisco Chronicle Editorial "By the act on Japan, America is at war. Time for debate has passed and the time for action has come. That action must be united and unanimous. 'Politics is adjourned'. Whether between parties, faction or economic groups. From now on America is an army with every man, woman and child a soldier in it all joined to the one end of victory. If war had to come, it is perhaps well

that it came this way, wanton, unwarned in fraud and bad faith, virtually under a flag of truce. We can not know how long this war will last, how wide it will range now what it will cost us in toil and sacrifices and in treasure. We do know that whatever the cost we will pay it and that our reward will be to hand down to our children the free America which our fathers bequeathed to us." American unite; There are no edits in the other paper so far. ▓▓▓▓▓▓▓▓▓▓▓▓▓▓▓▓▓▓▓▓▓▓ said (not to be quoted) "Where the hell was our Navy?"

Nathaniel J. L. Pieper, San Francisco FBI chief said: "As far as Japanese nationals are concerned, we received instructions from the Attorney General to take certain Japanese aliens into custody for the immigration department."

Twenty-eight were arrested up to one A.M. and an attendant in the immigration station said "One or two more are expected." Pieper wouldn't say how many were arrested, how many to be arrested. In Santa Clara County, where Permanente Cement Plant and Henry J. Kaiser's famous magnesium plant is located, Sheriff William Emig said "One Jap arrested, three in question. Pieper said the legal status of the Japs is in doubt, waiting instructions from the Attorney General. The U. S. attorney was unavailable for comment.

Generally speaking, Pieper said: "We are fully mobilized and ready for anything, cooperating with Army and Navy intelligence, and working on prevention sabotage. So far no cases of sabotage are reported."

Police: Chief Charles "Charley" Dullea, bluff, gruff and self-assured, says there has been no trouble at all in Jap town, no outbreaks no violence. In addition to four regular beat patrolment from the Northern Station Dullea dispatched a special detail of 35 uniformed men, 15 plainclothesmen to Jap town this afternoon about 3. Cops are principally keeping traffic rolling, diverting it from Post-California streets, Steiner-Laguna streets (four blocks each way) area where most of San Francisco's 5000-7500 Japanese live. A few civilian

Hammond -- Page Six

curiosity-seekers poking around early in the evening to see what's doing, and were told to keep moving. Japanese stores were open, life going on as usual.

The police department has an entire personnel of 1400 subject to immediate call. No days off. Everyone is working 12 hours on, 12 off. This/tail end is the vacation season so no one is on leave.

Dullea says there are no restrictions on civilian movements.

100 San Francisco cops have been detailed to the FBI.

Dullea acts as though the situation were well in hand, says belligerently that "We're working with federal agencies on this to prevent any trouble, any outbreaks by an irresponsible people."

WIRE RECEIVED FROM (San Francisco) SUEHSDORF -- TO DAVID HULBURD - Dec. 8, 1941

San Francisco was crisp-cool, bright, clear, sunny today like an autumn football day in New York. Felt like any other Sunday, relaxed, calm, quiet in early morning. Kids playing in street, Italians in Suchsdorf's North Beach neighborhood going to 11 A...mass at Saints Peter and Paul Church (where Di Maggio was married) as usual. Atmosphere was clear, bay glinting with silver of sun on water. A few sail boats pushed out from yacht harbor in the Marina. Day quiet in entertainment field. No football. Some football talk of University of San Francisco's 26-13 licking by Mississippi state at Kezar Stadium Saturday and of Oregon's 71-7 blasting by Texas at Austin. Pedestrians and motorists clogged streets moderately no more than usual for Sunday. Later in the day there were perhaps more official olive-drab army cars rolling around than usual. And the idlers in the streets were talking up the situation. As you passed by you could hear people unburdening their individual knowledge of Japan's navy's strength, our own chances etc. A man explains vaguely to a woman something about the fleet's big guns; small boys and high school adolescents talked loudly, assertively, with gestures and explosive laughter on air raids and where they'd be when they came.

Movies showing: United Artists showing Wanger's Sundown; palatial Fox showing Garbo's "Two-faced woman," Paramount, Crosby's "Birth of the Blues." Fox west coast theater string of seven including Fox and Paramount -- announced once between early evening shows that members of companies K and L of the California State Guard should report immediately to the Armory. But other theaters made no announcements; no interruptions. United Artists suggested that service men leave name and seat location if personal calls should come in. Several did, from enlisted men's families who heard intermittant broadcasts from 12th naval district etc. to report to stations.

Radio: following news bulletins, government agencies began calling at all networks to have emergency announcements read. They began shortly after 12 noon. First on air was Alameda Naval air station, following them. Though not in this order, came 12th naval district, ninth corps area, San Francisco fire department, coast artillery units attached to San Francisco harbor defenses. All messages ordered service men to report to their stations or headquarters immediately. Simple message (ordered by Captain W. K. Kilpatrick, twelfth naval district chief of staff, at 12:30 P.M.): "attention all officers and men, twelfth naval district and Alameda naval air station: Report to your stations immediately." Alameda air station phoned networks at seven P.M. to cancel its announcement because all men had reported. Networks estimated they broadcast news flashes or emergency announcements every ten minutes since noon. Most regularly scheduled programs were hash, a few minutes of this, a few of that, an announcement, then another butchered program.

The Philharmonic concert was absolutely riddled.

Net works on 24 hour duty now for an hour after local fire department announcement was broadcast, blatant, bovine, fog-horn department siren blasted intermittently over the city.

People: radio, newsmen, communications services generally pally, full of chatter, eager to talk about the war. Rollicking would seem to be word for radio stations where cheerful bedlam reigned. "Modern design news bureau" cracked KFRC mutual news room early in evening. Radio men asked as many questions as they answered, flapped the jaw generally on the still lean diet of news. Usually lackadaisical police department, on other hand, all business, all efficiency, refusing to answer anything over phone and demanding that reporters present themselves at a hall of justice with credentials if they wanted information. Collared at the hall, the chief and his minions were their old, generally cooperative selves. Details AP reception direct Honolulu story: San Francisco Associated Press located second floor Bastard-Gothic Chronicle Building Fifth and Mission Streets. Clyde Gilbert Bartel (cq), 42, seven years San Francisco AP, now Sunday cable editor, says office had gotten Steve Early flash Washington and he was busy answering civilian calls for information and making

3.

AP business calls to member papers when operator cut in with info overseas operator on wire with Honolulu call. As Bartel remembers it, this at about 11 a.m. he dashed into Suffy Little AP photographers room across hall to take call. Bartel heard voice, cool, but little keyed with excitement saying: "This is Burns, Eugene Burns. We're being bombed." Bartel said: "Yes, I know you're being bombed and so is Manila." Burns said: "Yes? Well, they're over us now and the attack is still going on." He gave his story in about five minutes. "Be sure to call us back, "Bartel said at end. "Yes," said Burns. Bartel roared back to office, batted out his first story by 11:28, Burns called back about noon spoke ten more minutes with additional details. A third call was coming through but before connection was made war-navy department censorship had gone into effect and Burns unheard from. Bartel says Burns calls came in clearly although both were shouting at each other. Occasionally circuit would fade like shortwave radio from Europe. But generally intelligible. No bose could be heard behind Burns voice. Bartel struck that Burns whom Bartel unknows doing routine job in best newspaper tradition. Unhurried. No dramatics, no gags, no stammering, strictly business. Bartel too pressed by time to think of own reaction.

United press was lucky. The office was closed. James Sullivan, bureau manager, had dropped in, however, to do some routine work after attending church in Berkeley and before the afternoon crew came on. The telephone rang: "This is the overseas operator calling. Just a moment while I complete the call." Sullivan jumped for the radio wire, only ticker in operation on dull Sunday morning, there saw the Early flash from Washington, got back to the phone to hear Mrs. Frank Tremaine, wife of up man in Honolulu say: We are being bombed, they are fifty planes over the city." She didn't identify as Japanese. Sullivan then went to work like crazy. Sullivan thinks call came about 10:45."

CORRECTION AND SUBSTITUTION IN WIRE FROM SAN FRANCISCO (Suehsdorf) TO DAVID HULBURD, RECEIVED 12-8-41.

Please disregard paragraph on United Press getting flash (Page 3, last paragraph) and substitute the following:

"James A. Sullivan, Bureau Manager, got the first flash when the telephone broke the dull Sunday routine. Most staffers were out of the office. Operators said: 'This is the overseas operator, hold on while I complete the call.' Then Sullivan heard (about 11:45 A.M. he recalls) flash bell on the teletype, dashed over to the ticker and read the first flash from Steve Early. He went back to the phone and talked to Mrs. Frank Tremaine, wife of UP man in Honolulu. She said, 'We are being bombed. About 50 bombers are coming over.' She couldn't identify bombers as Japanese."

End

Wire from Hammond (San Francisco) to D. Hulburd - December 8, 1941

Color add: I was up in the country when the news broke. It arrived via radio, party line telephone. The first word was from a Hawaiian boy working at Hagel ranch, who walked up announced unhappily: "Well, they just bombed Honolulu, the sons of bitches." From then on news arrives sporadically as various peoples drove up, plus what we learned from the radio. Our first reactions were almost of relief--tremendous pressure building up for weeks finally resulting in an accomplished fact. People in the country were disbelieving at first, then resigned, calmer than in the city, perhaps they feel they are protected by distance from vital military objectives.

The weather was warm, sunny, typical California winter-springtime with the hills turning green after the first rains. All roads, ferry out of town were jammed with Sunday tourists (this before the news broke); roads were equally crowded later.

Returning to the city, the first thing noticeable was the blackout on the Golden Gate bridge, no lights showing even at Toll Plaza, collectors dropping cheery well-trained "Good evening" for brusque "Thanks." The gate bridge ramps were also blacked out, although the presidio through which they pass was still showing lights. One ramp was partially closed off with police guarding it. (Later it evolved the blackout was a mistake-someone thought he heard Japanese planes, and ordered lights switched off. The lights came back on later).

The San Francisco-Oakland Bay Bridgeport remained lighted, but regular state highway patrol units were augmented by armed companies of the California State Guard (volunteer organization inaugurated after the National Guard units were called to active service.) A hundred men were guarding the Oakland side approaches, Toll Plaza, and the bridge span through the tunnel on Yerba Buena Island, site of the naval receiving station and Treasure Island. On the other side of the tunnel, San Francisco units pick-up patrol, guard dirt and fifty street approaches. They were also stationed along Embarcadero guarding state-owned belt railroad, wharves and warehouses. Altogether, about four hundred guardists on the San Francisco side. These men were ordered on duty from state adjutant general's office, Sacramento, officer of DAT at San Francisco Armory (guard headquarters) said exultantly: "We dare anyone to get in (Embarcadero warehouses, etc.). They wouldn't get two feet:" The general impression driving through all parts of town -- war was still not an actuality to San Franciscans. They were talking about bombings, ship sinkings, etc. but it still was distant, unaffecting them personally. The most striking evidence of this was at the city's hospitality house for soldiers, and sailors. It was jampacked with gay, laughing, cheery men and gals. Although we were told there were only about one-third of the usual Sunday night crowd there due to leave cancellations, there were still fully five hundred on hand. The hostess said many men were writing letters, sending wires, but that was the only difference from the usual weekend. She was swamped with telephone calls from men wanting to know what they were supposed to do, friends trying to get track of others, but those at the dance apparently were unaffected by the situation. Apparently, the news was too big to penetrate in such a short time or else they were expecting it for so long that its final coming didn't make such difference one way or other. The bus was due to leave for Tiburon Naval Base at midnight but was put forward to eight. The sailors were irritated at leaving the gals rather than worried or apprehensive.

Jaltown section on the city was blocked off to all traffic for several hours this evening (making it seem a complete isolated settlement) since the police were expecting trouble. However none materialized. The cops said they were sent out with orders to expect anything, patrol in twos until relieved. They are expecting to be put on a 12-hour duty although not ordered so far. The shades in all Japanese homes were drawn, a few shops continued to be open but the majority were closed. There were few Japanese on the streets except for the curious around the Hotel Aki from which the FBI took the manager earlier, and the Fuji Transfer company across the street where the FBI men were going through the files after packing the owner off to the Hall of Justice. A candid expression of the sergeant on duty: "Why in hell couldn't they have waited until after Christmas." One little Jap came streaking out of the hotel in a great stew, said he was out fishing all day, came back to see a girl, and the FBI held him for questioning all afternoon in with others found the hotel. The majority of the Japanese we saw were either sad, bewildered, or else trying to appear unconcerned, slightly belligerent or tyring to appear nonchalant. The only ones outside the Japanese consulate, somewhat outside the borders of the Japanese section, were a cop, and two curious girls. The cop said no crowd had been up there probably because few people knew he lived there. The fire in the afternoon brought considerable attention, however. The cop said the FBI went over the debris ash by ash. One of the gals said she noted with interest three new trunks arriving at the Consulate last Wednesday.

"I thought something was up then".

The waterfront was dead in the evening, except for the usual crowd of tourists at Fishermens Wharf. Chinatown was crowded with the usual Sunday mob, Japanese owned stores (of which there are many) remained bravely open. Only serious Chinatown crowds were around ideographic newsposters in the windows of Chinese newspaper.

Night owl Beaneries were not even bothering to turn on news broadcasts, radios were giving out their usual swing record programs.

Wire from Arnold Aslakson, Minneapolis, to J. McConaughy,   Dec. 8, 1941

News first broke on the radio about 1:30 p.m., WCCO, CBS station. Sandwiched between the Spirit of '41 broadcast from an eastern naval base, and a World Today news roundup, WLOL Mutual broke at 1:35 into "This is Fort Dix." WTCN, NBC broke the "Voice of Experience" at 1:36. KSTP, NBC sandwiched at 1:29 between the MacAlester College musical program and Chicago Round Table on "Canada: A Neighbor at War." There were dozens of calls to the radio stations asking "Is it true; will the boys home on Christmas leaves have to go back?" One asked: "Is it another play? (Apparent reference to Orson Welles); several women who called KSTP choked up. One said she had a boy in Pearl Harbor. Another one had a boy in Honolulu. Number 1 couldn't believe her ears. A man who phoned WTCN exploded: "Why those sons of bitches!" Radio switchboards were not jammed, however, apparently because of fast radio followup of the first flashes. We are unable to check the phone company on traffic yet. But several people, 50 of whom I called at random, told of running to friends' homes or phoning friends the news.

The St. Paul Pioneer-Press extraed at 4 or 4:15, the Minneapolis Morning Tribune at 4:30. The Trib had two extra pages in the first extra, upped it two pages more for each extra up to the fourth.

Curtis Edwards, WTCN announcer: "I didn't think they'd stick their necks out. I didn't think they'd have the guts." A young newspaper man (not I): "Oh, are they a bunch of damn fools." A painter and decorator: "Oh, oh. We're in it. I didn't think it was going to happen -- yet. We got to go at 'em." A retired realtor: who described his views as modified America First, though not an A.F. member: "How in the hell could we get caught napping like that? To think they were able to come over our base at Pearl Harbor is beyond my comprehension when we know how treacherous those Japs are. I'm disgusted." Draft-age men to each other -- several such conversations: "Well, we're in it. Our number's coming." Bakery Stock Clerk: "Well, it won't last long. They asked for it. We tried to be white and they turned on us like rats." Shoe salesman's wife: "Oh. It's happened. But Japan will take a beating." 16-year-old: "Japan must be about out of supplies. But glad I'm not 17 yet."

An investment secretary and his wife: He: "The U.S. will declare war now." She: "Do you think so, really?" He: "I wonder how long they'll be able to hold out. Will the Russians attack Japan now?" A credit man who said he wanted to "go get 'em" after the Panay: "I think we ought to declare war on the whole Axis. But how could they get caught napping at Pearl Harbor?" A bank auditor: "That bunch of double crossers." An Architect: "It's here at last. Might as well get it over with." Two neighbors to whom he passed the news phlegmatically just said thanks. They went to turn on their radios. Numerous others "hadn't thought much about it," "expected something, but not so soon." A majority expected an attack on Thailand or the Indies. Not Hawaii or the Philippines.

You can't help thinking that people are now more aroused, but it is too early to use any superlatives. Three walked on Christmas-lighted Nicollet Avenue, main shopping street, for half an hour. We saw many little knots of people gazing in windows as if nothing extraordinary. There always 20 or so in front of Powers Department store on the corner watching the animated display of the three wise men, shepherds, manger scene of "Peace on Earth." They listened to the music, remarked at the display, walked on.

When the news first broke, there was a chill rain, turning to wet snow by evening. Many were at dinner, others reading Sunday papers. There was no football. Movies."Keep 'em Flying," Abbott & Costello, at the Orpheum: "Suspicion," Grant and Fontaine, in "Shadow of the Thin Man," "Ladies in Retirement" at the others; no major theatres broke the show with the announcement. But the movie business slipped one-third as people stuck to their radios.

The Pioneer Press editorialized: "The Axis powers have brought the second World War to the Western Hemisphere, the Axis Powers that have recklessly launched

Aslakson, Minneapolis, Dec. 8, 1941   P. 3

this terrible war will find this country better prepared than they have imagined. The spirit of the American people under such provocation is equal to all the cruel sacrifices that this bloody business will impose."

The Interventionist Minneapolis Morning Tribune: "We must realize, each and every one of us, that this treacherous attack is not a detached incident which involves merely Japan and the United States. But on the contrary, an integrated detail, a part of the pattern of Hitler's world war plans... The fight, plainly, is not with Japan alone. It is with the entire Axis partnership of gangster nations, with Germany and its scavening satellites wherever they may fling down their challenge to us."

Through G.V. Cannon, president of Minnesota Marine Veterans Club, went a telegram to FDR: "300 World War Marine veterans in Minnesota request the privilege of service in a suitable classification to relieve younger men." Police Chief Edward B. Hansen asked for 100 extra police (Minneapolis force now 100) to guard defense plants and utilities. The Navy doubled guards at all naval equipment plants. The local America First Executive Committee said: "Japanese attacks, must, of course, be resisted." A group of state and local leaders of the Defend America and Fight for Freedom Committees wired the Minnesota delegation: "It is now clear that this is our war," and called for a declaration against Germany.

Maybe you missed this: Immediately after the first announcements of war, one network, I think it was CBS plowed merrily through the "good news" program with John B. Kennedy, telling the good news of how America is healthy, never ad-libbed a line to tone it down. Terribly incongruous.

End

Wire from Aslakson (Minneapolis) to J. McConaughy - December 8, 1941

Add Japanese side lights - Minneapolis: Local telephoned calls estimated up about twenty percent necessitating about thirty additional operators. Long distance calls are up as much as 45 percent.

Wire from Ben Avery, Phoenix, Ariz. to J. McConaughy - Dec. 7, 1941

News of the attack on Pearl Harbor hit Phoenix at 1 p.m. via the Phoenix CBS station KOY interrupting the CBS program "The World Today" at 12:30 p.m. Mountain time. I was the only person in the Arizona Republic newsroom and was immediately swamped with telephone calls. The telephone company reported no trouble. We hit the street with an extra at 4:45. All of our staff were scattered around, some playing golf, some out joy riding and the news editor was in Tucson.

Remarks of some Phoenicians who called to ask if the report was true:

"Well, I'll be damned. What is our army doing -- have you got anything?"

"What's this I hear about Japan declaring war? -- Have you got anything on the game between the Chicago Bears and the Cardinals? Aren't you getting anything besides that war stuff?"

Many of them, when advised about the war just said, "Well, I hope we blast them off of the face of the earth," or "How many of the yellow so and so's have we killed?" There also were a number of calls from relatives of servicemen in the Pacific asking about certain ships. Arizonians definitely were aroused. There are about a thousand Japanese farmers in the Salt River Valley and for weeks Arizonians generally have commented "If those Japs want to start something they'll sure find a fight" and opinion is general.

The news hit Phoenix on one of the quietest Sunday afternoons I've seen. The weather was warm and sunny and most everyone was out riding around, playing golf or just lolling on green lawns, almost no one was downtown, just a few scattered cars and an occasional pedestrian. Many were out in the country. The news ended the siesta hour though for within a short while crowds were gathering around sidewalk radios from Lord knows where. Many were in theatres. There were no football games. Phoenix' two big theatres were well filled. The Fox was showing "Keep 'Em Flying" but did not interrupt the program. The Orpheum interrupted "International Squadron" an RAF picture and absolute silence followed the announcement for about a minute, then the audience buzzed.

Dime theatres reported the same effect after making the announcement. Governor Sidney P. Osborne heard the news at his desk in the Capitol where he was catching up on his correspondence and immediately called H. R. Duffey, in charge of Phoenix FBI office, then summoned the Arizona civilian defense co-ordinating council into an emergency session at 4 p.m. The meeting was held to issue all council members to stand by for orders if needed in the event of an attack on the Pacific coast and general evacuation of coast residents to Arizona. After the meeting, the governor issued a statement asking all Arizonians to keep cool and do nothing until orders were issued and to leave everything to regularly constituted authorities.

Huge dams on Salt river already were under guard and have been for months. No editorials are available but am airmailing a special delivery with a picture of by-standers holding copies of the Republic extra, watching a wandering organgrinder with his monkey perform on a downtown street.

Wire from James Bell, Topeka, Kansas, to David Hulburd, Dec. 7, 1941.

War came to Topeka at 1:30 PM on a quiet, warm, 56 degrees, sunshiny Sunday. Most Topekans had finished big Sunday dinners and were napping on their sofas. First flash over Columbia's WIBW came at the end of the Spirit of '41 program. I got it over NBC Blue network while listening to the Great Plays series. I was in the bath tub. The second bulletin in re the attack on Manila made me sick. My parents, brother and sister are in Manila. My wife turned pale and said, "There it is." My telephone rang a few seconds later. I was called to help issue an extra and write "What it's like over there" story. Daily Capital switchboards were jammed immediately. One man, with distinct rural midwestern accent, asked: "What the Hell's going on out there? Has Uncle Sam declared war yet? Why in Hell hasn't he? How old do you have to be to get in the Army and Navy?" Others wanted to know if it were true. One mother, with a son at Pearl Harbor, choked up when told that Hawaii had been bombed and said, "Maybe they'll kill my boy, but I know he will be avenged." The telephone company says lines have been unusually busy since first flash. Several persons have attempted to put in calls to Honolulu and the Philippines, without success. The Daily Capital's 4-page extra hit the street just before 7 P. M. Kansas City Star had its extra in town an hour and a half later. Thousands of persons were waiting to get copy of CAPITAL. They went like hotcakes. People drove in from the residential districts to get them.

There was no hysteria. Everyone was interested. No one was very excited. My wife's first expression, "There it is", was common phrase. I would say that Topeka is taking the news with grim determination. Most Topekans, I believe, didn't think it would ever happen. When it did, they took it calmly. There are isolated cases of panic. One woman called the Capital frantically saying that a Jap plane had just dove on her house. It turned out it was a private plane flying over the city at high altitude. Capper and Ratner, with radio addresses coming up, had to change their texts in a hurry. Both pledged their wholehearted support of the President. Alf Landon, in a telegram to Roosevelt, said: "There is imperative need for courageous action by the American people. The Japanese attack leaves no choice. Nothing must be permitted to interrupt our victory over a foreign foe. Please command me in any way I can be of service."

Capper said, "Japan's attack means war and we will see it through. I will support our President."

Junior Senator Clyde Reed, ill in Parsons, left immediately for Washington by plane. Capper returning by train. The news came when many Topekans were in the first afternoon show at movie houses. No pictures were broken into to give the flash. The biggest crowds were at Bob Hope's "Nothing But The Truth." I saw them come out. They were laughing and gay. When they heard the news, their faces sobered rapidly, then they went away quietly. One man said, "Guess we'll have to lick the sons of bitches." An indication that Topeka is taking the news calmly is that all theatres reported nearly normal attendance at night shows. The people are not aroused in the usual sense of the word. They are quiet, calm and determined that the U. S. will win.

Three members of the local Navy recruiting office staff have requested sea duty. I've talked to several dozen persons and none express regret that war has come. All feel it is necessary. The feeling is this:

Right or wrong, we are in this thing now and we've got to win. No use singing the Star Spangled Banner or shooting Jap restaurant owners. We're ready to do whatever is asked of us. Poor old Capper is broken hearted. He wandered about the Capital news room with a long face. I believe there were tears in his eyes. He kept saying: "It's too bad, it's too bad." Later in the evening when preparing to leave for Washington he was brighter and more determined. "I will support the President - it's the one thing left to do," he said. The only sporting event in process was State Field Dog Trials, (hunting). The news took the kick out of the dog lovers sport. The afternoon, which started off spirited, ended rather flat. "I guess our hunting will be confined to those God damned slant eyed bastards from now on," said one sportsman. In Topeka, I would say the single most important development of the day was the joining of Capper and Landon behind Roosevelt. Landon's statement was the most sincere he ever made. When I talked with him I got the impression that he would gladly do any job the President required of him. CAPITAL won't have editorial comment before Tuesday morning. Will wire digest of State Journal's editorial Monday P. M.

                                                End

Wire from James Bell, Topeka, Kansas, to David Hulburd - 12-8-41

Editorial comment of Topeka STATE JOURNAL:

"As a people we must travel a long and difficult road before the U. S. again finds itself at peace with all nations. No one knows the terrible toll we may be called upon to pay for our weakness in those years when we depended for security upon the pledged words of other nations, including the one which attacked us without warning Sunday. But, however difficult the course may prove, we must travel it. Whatever the cost in blood and sacrifice, we must move swiftly to pay it. This is our war. We must win it."

This, I believe, is an extremely good summation of Topeka's general attitude. The city is at work today, but jobs are suffering by the lack of interest of employes. Navy and army recruiting offices report tremendous upsurge of enlistment. The sun is shining, it is warm, and two short hours ago, the U. S. declared war.

                       End

Wire from Harold Boyle, Portland, Me. to J. McConaughy - Dec. 7, 1941.

Portland, Me., a big new naval base for the Atlantic fleet, is just recovering from the shock of the Reuben James sinking after that ship left here for Iceland, received news of the Japanese bombings with more excitement than is common to the Yankee temperament. The news first came by radio (Columbia chain). The newspaper office was bombarded with telephone calls asking "Is it true?" "Does Associated Press confirm it?"

A cold but sunny afternoon here with little going on in a city still somewhat under the influence of the old blue laws except for theatres open. Most excited were about a thousand sailors on shore leave from boats just back from convoy duty. Many expressed real concern over the report that the U.S. Oklahoma had been hit. Several in the newspaper office commented that they had mates on the Oklahoma.

The most common statement in middle-class circles, "Now we can be unified; no more strikes; let's get down to business. Entrance into European war next." A small isolationist group here, followers of Congressman James Oliver, who is an outright isolationist, changed its tune. One: "There's no answer to this one. Give them (the Japs) as good as they send."

General reaction here, from bus drivers to a few wealthy: "A typical, underhanded way of acting. Americans are through taking it lying down." Typical Yankee reaction: "They stabbed us in the back."

Very few Japanese in Portland; this city, which is a no. 1 defense site with naval base, two large shipyards and four army posts, interested in reaction of west coast to talk of bombings, blackouts, etc. Portland is the nearest Atlantic port to Europe and expects similar reaction in the case of war with Germany.

My honest opinion is that the news affected many the same way as in 1917. People are serious; no wisecracking or grumbling about meddling. Said one newspaperman: "I feel sure of one thing. Up to today, I wondered whether we were another France; too soft. What I have seen today convinces me that American

Page 2 -- Boyle, Portland, Me.

(At least Maine people) can fight in the old way."

Quote from lead editorial in Portland (Me) Press Herald, largest newspaper (morning) in Maine in Monday issue:

"No better proof of fundamental Japanese treachery, of which the country has been hearing for many decades, could be found than the foulness of conduct that launched attack upon this nation while it was earnestly trying to seek a peaceful settlement of the Far Eastern question. In 50 years of public life, Sec. Hull said he had never known a document so filled with "infamous falsehoods" as that delivered on Sunday to him by the Japanese emissaries in this country. Of that we shall hear more today.

"The issue is between democracy and despotism. It is we democratic powers against world slavery. It is the U.S. against Hitler, his satellites and stooges. If the congress has the guts which an American congress ought to have, it will refuse from this day to blink at duty. It will recognize verities. It will declare war upon every enemy of peace and decency. We must not only furnish the tools; we ourselves must help finish the job."

Wire from John Durant, Boston, Mass. to David Hulburd - Dec. 8, 1941

In Boston, five days of unseasonable warmth and fog lifted and a sharp, cold wind needled down from the North across clear skies in which the fiery sun was preparing for the final plunge into the West. Boston was pervaded by Sabbath calm with folks, after a hearty noon meal, slouched in their chairs beside the radio, in movies, Sunday driving in the country, or visiting neighbors. There were few people on the streets. All was quiet. Then electrification came at 2:29 as local radio stations announced, "Unidentified planes, presumably Japanese, have just bombed Oahu."

As newspapers, the BOSTON GLOBE, POST, heard the radio report, immediately confirmed by news ticker, editors ordered bulletins and slapped them on bulletin boards fronting Washington Street by 2:45. Pandemonium reigned at BOSTON RECORD where the 4:30 P.M. edition was being made up. The RECORD put a special war edition on the street at 3:18. Small knots of people with coat collars turned up stopped in front of the newspaper row of bulletins, passed on. It was too cold for more than - "why those bastards of Japs."

The four biggest Boston movie houses did not break the program to announce the Jap invasion.

One of overtones of thought I am beginning to pick up is----From now on, England has got to come second and the United States first in regard to production of our planes, tanks, etc.

Editorials in Boston Papers:

HERALD: "America's period of "blood, toil, tears and sweat" is at hand;" POST: "This attack in one instant has destroyed the disunity which has been disturbing America. The causes of this war can be left to the historians to evaluate. The twilight of peace is over;" GLOBE: "United as never before, we will meet this challenge"; RECORD: "We are all Americans now, united, strong, invincible."

Page 2, - John Durant - Boston.

As people clung to their radios, announcements came piling in -- Report for duty at once; Navy recruiting stations will be open at 8 A.M.; all manufacturers of defense materials are to take immediate precautions against sabotage; Metropolitan police ordered to 24-hour duty to protect Boston's water reservoirs; John McCormick (?) Majority House Leader, receives a telephone call from Roosevelt, and his wife at Dorchester home hastily packs his bag for his return to Washington; extra guards rushed to Charlestown Navy Yard; Ex-Governor Curley wrapped up the Japanese decoration presented to him by the Japanese Embassy in 1917 and mailed it to the Japanese; at all power plants were detailed guards; Civilian Defense workers were requested to stand by for instant action; at Newton, hundreds of people were in the midst of anti-air raid practice when the news came and they simply kept on with their rehearsal with grimmer sense of reality; Mayor Tobin spoke, Governor Saltonstall called out the National Guard. One sad note is that Boston still has no air raid warning siren.

Immediate public reaction in the following order was: unbelieving astonishment that the Japs would have the nerve to attack Oahu, wrath at the treachery of the Japs, spontaneous recognition that we are united in the common goal to lick the Japs.

The most important developments were the speed with which the people were notified for events and mobilized for emergency via radio, and the unquestionable and immediate reaction of "at last we are united."

For quotes of the man on the street, I like best the fellow who said to me, "That settles it, we're united now." A waitress - "There's been too much talk and not enough action. Let's get going." A schoolteacher - "Let them have it, they asked for it." A Sailor - "It's me or them - and I'll make damn sure it's not me." A shopkeeper - "This is one war the U.S. will approve of." Everywhere you went it was the same, united at last, go out and get those Japs.

End

Wire from John Durant, Boston - to J. McConaughy - Dec. 8, 1941

Telephone calls in New England were up 25% after the announcement of the Jap invasion Sunday, and recruiting stations here report today a big rush. Before the Navy and Marine recruiting station in the Federal Building opened at 8 a.m. there were 41 men, ages 17 to 43, waiting outside the door to join up, and the offices have been swamped ever since. The Army reports that the number of recruits is "10 times normal." A grandfather, father/and a son, all of the same family, came to the Navy recruiting station here, and there is an excellent chance that all three will eventually be accepted for Coast Guard and Navy service.

Wire from Clayton Fritchey, Cleveland, to J. McConaughy - Dec. 8, 1941

There is a good angle here on the impact of the Jap attack and how all conflicting opinion on the Far East instantly crumbled before the reality of actual war. Yesterday and today 80 delegates to the Institute of Pacific Relations met in Cleveland to thrash out oriental problems and find the best course for the U.S. to pursue. Many of the nation's greatest authorities on the Far East are in confab, along with congressmen, prominent industrialists and such journalistic experts as Hugh Byas and James R. Young, both Tokyo correspondents.

News of the attack broke at the start of Sunday afternoon round table. There was dead silence for two minutes. In those 120 seconds, 80 different opinions were resolved. It was unanimously agreed, as one delegate put it, that "Japan has handed America its long-needed unity on a silver platter." The Institute met here under the auspices of Cleveland's Foreign Affairs Council, directed by Brooks Emeny. Everything was done in a very swank way. Delegates and guests gathered at the Cleveland Country Club Saturday, had lunch, cocktails, dinner, spent the night at the club, then started over again Sunday morning. No speeches were allowed; all back & forth discussion. Among those present: H. F. Angus, Department of External Affairs, Ottawa; Dr. M.S. Bates, Nanking College, China; Robert F. Black, president of White Motors Co.; Kurt Bloch, research director, Institute of Pacific Relations; Congresswoman Frances Bolton, Edward C. Carter, secretary-general of the Institute; Gordon K. Chalmers, president of Kenyon College; Sir Shanmukkhan Chetty, Indian Purchasing Mission; New York; Congressman Robert B. Chipperfield, Frederick V. Field, chairman of the Editorial Board, Amerasia, New York; Congressman Bartel J. Johkman, Congressman Karl Mundt, Count Sarlo Sforza, former Italian Foreign Minister; N.A.C. Slotemaker de Bruine, director of the Netherlands Information Bureau, New York; Congressman John Vorhys; delegates also included half a dozen bank presidents, economists, heads of rubber companies,

Fritchey, Cleveland, Dec. 8, 1941

editors, prominent lawyers, etc. Almost a complete cross-section of people. I never saw a greater mixture of men and women and never heard greater mixture of opinion -- until the radio flashed out the stunning news. If one blast from the radio can unify a group of arguing professional experts it ought to be able to unify everybody else. Most of the Congressmen mentioned above are regarded as isolationists, but not one dissented from quick consensus that America's course had been set.

It is understood that everything said at these conferences is off record, but after a radio bulletin had come in, the Chairman of the meeting finally broke the silence by turning to one isolationist Congressman and asking what answer America would give to the Japanese attack. The reply was: "Our answer is probably being given by the American fleet right now." Applause.

An interesting fact is that not one expert present had foreseen such a drastic offensive. Up to the moment the news broke, the overwhelming opinion was that Japan had no wish to fight U.S., that the peaceful solution of all Pacific problems was possible, and the Japs were too intelligent to commit "national suicide" by going to war.

The only speaker to come close to the mark was James R. Young, who said the action of the Japs had nothing to do with "Government" or "Intelligence" or anything else. Japan, he insisted, was being run by a gang of gangsters in the Army and Navy who were responsible to no one. These "gangsters" he maintained, would do anything to perpetuate themselves in power, no matter what the certain consequences to Japan. Young brought a portent to the meeting. Four days ago he suddenly received through the mails, a file the Japanese had kept on him since his arrest in Tokyo. There was no note of explanation; just the file. Sent from the New York Japanese Consul. There was an air about the incident of someone cleaning out papers before moving. Young also told Congressmen present that in Washington there was available to them Japanese war plans which had been seized three or four years ago. These plans, he said, called for the identical operations which the Japs followed today. If what Young says is true, then the Germans didn't plot the strategy of this attack.

Hugh Byas pointed out that the Japs had struck the same kind of surprise blow at Port Arthur against Russia, and recalled the story of how the Jap ambassador went to the Russian Court Ball while an attack was being carried out without knowledge of the Russians. Byas said he had thought in the present situation the Japs would try to keep the U.S. divided by pursuing the war in such a way as to put us in the position of helping British imperialism.

In an effort to explain the seemingly insane attack, one Institute official said the State Department had received a story to the following effect: the Japan war lords knew they could not win in China, but could not afford to admit and withdraw. A defeat by the U.S. and Britain combined would cause no loss of face. Therefore, the best solution was a short war with the Allies and quick surrender.

General excitement here was slow getting underway. The first flash came over radio station WGAR at 2:30, just as the World Today program began on Columbia system. Station managers here tell me that listeners didn't seem quite to grasp the news at first. Phone calls were nothing like the Orson Welles war. When World War II broke out, it had been preceded by an hour-by-hour radio build-up for several days. This one, of course, broke out of the blue.

More from Cleveland later.

End

Wire from Clayton Fritchey, Cleveland, O. to James McConaughy - Dec. 8, 1941

PLAIN DEALER says: "Once more this nation is called upon to protect its own destiny and that of free people everywhere. There will be no faltering, and a gain, by the Grace of God, no doubt as to the outcome."

CLEVELAND PRESS: "The Japanese found us slow to wrath. They will find us mighty in wrath. They found us unwilling to strike the first blow. They will yet find us striking the last blow...America salutes the President, who fought so nobly for Pacific peace, and who now leads us in the just cause of self defense. America salutes the armed forces, who have never lost a war."

CLEVELAND NEWS: "This war will not end when Japan is defeated, but when the Axis is smashed, whether that takes one year or ten."

Mayor Frank J. Lausche has wired Roosevelt that all of Cleveland is marching at his side.

An American Legion broadcast appeal this morning asked all home and building owners to display the American flag every day from now on.

Radio bulletins cleared the streets of auto traffic last night. This was the lightest traffic casualty list for Sunday night in many weeks.

The only current labor trouble in this area was immediately settled. Four striking units at Great Ravenna Shell Loading Plants called off pickets this morning. The plant is back in full production. The Cleveland Civilian Defense Council met at 11 A.M. Anti-sabotage forces at all industrial and utility plants were immediately increased and priorities established on civilian use of police forces.

Says Arthur P. Gustafson, attorney for Cleveland chapter of the America First Committee: "I'm terribly shocked. I'm hoping we are so situated we can put an early end to this war. It looks like the only way to end it is to demolish Japan. I trust our Naval and Air forces are sufficient."

End

Wire from Gray (Portland) to J. McConaughy - December 7, 1941

Portland was warm Sunday, sky bright above with a haze fringing the city. It was good golfing weather. At Mount Hood, skiers had fresh snow. Church-going Portlanders were listening to sermons when the White House flash came at 11:30 am PST Newspaper readers were sunk in the funnies or scanning the headline, "F.R. makes Final Plea." Home radios were tuned to "Chicago Roundtable" (NBC red), "The World Today" (CBS), "Swingtime Strings" (Mutual) when network newscaster cut in. Listeners sat up shocked, turned up radios, telephoned neighbors.

By evening, the telephone company had increased their switchboard crew nearly 50%, long distance lines were jammed, calls to Chicago were delayed two hours; to San Francisco two hours; to Tacoma--Fort Lewis--one hour; all Seattle circuits were in constant use. At 7:55 pm PST, the Pacific Telephone & Telegraph Company bought radio spots to ask that citizens use long distance only for most urgent business. Extra guards were placed around telephone buildings.

The "Oregon Journal" had the first of five extras with UP bulletins on the street at 2:15. The Oregonian (whose AP Sunday wire ordinarily opens at one o'clock, today opened at 12:30) was out with the first complete paper at 3:30. At 7:30 pm I asked a one-legged newsboy, standing on a downtown intersection on crutches peddling extras, what people were saying, "As a matter of fact," he replied, "I've just been too damned busy to talk to them about it."

To most Portlanders, the news was incredible. None had expected the Japs to get close as Hawaii, which is closer than New York to Portland. When one lad rushed out of his house to tell a congregation leaving Church, some said: "You're fooling." Once convinced, most Portlanders were calmly furious, determined. They said, "Well, they asked for it--now we'll give it to them." "They ought to take every Jap and throw him into jail, American or not." "Let's find Lindbergh and ask him about it." "I'd rather play with a rattlesnake than a Jap anytime." High school boys said, "Well, we'll have to fight now." A Soldier on leave drawled to his buddy, "We'd

Gray -- Page Two

better polish up our shootin' irons." One soldier on Sunday afternoon walked about the Portland business district carrying a portable radio going full force. When telephone lines got crossed, a strange man's voice broke into two housewives' conversation to talk war with them. Finally, they all just listened to his radio blasting news into the telephone. Sugar buying picked up in open grocery stores. Newsreel Theatre inserted a Navy short "The Battle" in the program.

The great unhappy question Sunday afternoon was "Where were our Navy patrols? How could the Japs get that close to Hawaii?" Newspaper executives, extra reporters moved into newspaper offices, glumly hovered about the copy desk to read incoming bulletins. Headline writers dropped the polite form "Japanese", made it "Japs". Oregonian newsmen cheered when the wire editor read an unconfirmed bulletin Jap carrier was sunk. Men called Lindbergh, Wheeler sobs, but inevitably returned to the Navy question. One said "The Navy was caught with their pants at half mast," another, "What makes me sore is that this was the last great nation that had a chance to surprise the Axis, and here they pull the same thing on us Germany pulled on the rest," another, "We oughta be bombing Tokyo.

When a reporter telephoned the news to Portland's acting Japanese Consul Y. Oka, he snapped, "It is just a wild rumor. I have had no word at all. I have just heard what is on the radio; I don't believe so. I don't believe so at all. I think it is just rumor. I think it is just wild rumors, very wild rumor". Shortly he was burning papers in the Consulate stove. Smoke filtered into the eighth floor corridors of the Board of Trade Building. Police threw a guard around that office and the Consul's home. Oka told newsmen between 1000 and 1500 Japanese have been trying to leave the Portland area. American-born members of the Japanese American Citizens League, admittedly facing hard times, told newspapers they hope the fairness of the caucasian Americans would ease their lot as citizens.

At Oregon shipbuilding Corporation's vast plant beside Willamette River,

Mrs. Henry Kaiser christened the SS Thomas Jefferson at 3 pm Sunday while shipyard workers cheered it down skids. Launching guest, Oregon Governor Charles A. Sprague, hurried from there to Oregonian office, sat down at the City Editor's typewriter to peck out wire to Roosevelt .. "1..We must not rest until menace of Japanese aggression in the Pacific is definitely ended..."

Governor Sprague Sunday night proclaimed a state of emergency for the State of Oreg Oregon, precise meaning to be clarified Monday.

Sunday night's wildest rumor here was that San Francisco was being bombed. The region's military and civilian defense forces sprang into action quickly. Bonneville Power Administration doubled guard around the dam, power plant, scatter substations. Portland's city Water Bureau ordered out Bureau employees to guard pipe lines, reservoirs; city bridges were placed under armed guard. At Vancouver, Wash. ALCOA operated its new reduction plant Sunday night with yard lights blacked out. All ships in Columbia River ports Sunday were frozen in port area by navy order.

Editorial quotes: Oregon Journal--"Attack on Hawaii and Philippines, Sunday, was cold, calculating-- and insane. It was planned, suicidal betrayal of peace conversations. To President Roosevelt's personal peace appeal to Emporor Hirohito, it returned a brutal insult of murderous violence.."Now we know the worst, now we can have at an unpleasant task and have done with it as rapidly as we may".

Oregonian--"...Japan, as an empire, is about to go down beneath the waves of the Pacific. America will destroy her--and America suddenly united, whose great strength is as strength of ten through righteous sense of unspeakable outrage... her material dreams will be angled and quite wreckage at bottom of the area. America pledges it. America believes that in that undertaking it carries banners of God."

Wire from Gray (Portland, Oregon) - 12/8/41 3:30 p. m.

Blackouts ordered for tonight at Columbia River's mouth and Gray's Harbor (Aberdeen Hoquiam). May cover entire North Pacific Coast area, including Seattle and Portland

COPY of telegram from Michael Griffin, Louisville, Ky. to McConaughy, Dec. 7, 1941

WINN, NBC, broadcast news 1:30 during program "Great Plays." WGRC, Mutual, at 1:33, during Serenade for Sunday; WAVE, 1:43 during Chicago Round Table, WHAS, Columbia, 1:42 during old fashioned revival hour. Following its beat WINN swamped with phone calls. All stations had to hire extra operators. Bell Telephone Company here reports big pickup of local calls following first flash, but emphasis on long-distance calls after news Japan had declared war. Manager thinks parents calling sons at camps. Courier-Journal extra out 4:30, first since Hitler invaded Poland. Paper had to call printers who were attending union meeting. Papers sold biggest on record, as fast as presses could print at start, according to Jasper Rison, circulation manager. Press roll on first extra 43,000, all sold in Louisville. Total sale of two extras preceding first night edition nearly 70,000 in Louisville alone -- unprecedented here.

First reaction here stunned surprise. Noon newscasts carried no hint, newspaper stories Sunday here indicated Japs backing down, afraid of U.S. A taxi driver thought about announcement a second or two, then said: "Is this going to hurt this country?" Two Fort Knox officers dining in a hotel turned to each other, asked: "What is it, a gag?" When one of them realized report on level he groaned: " Nuts, there goes my trip to Sugar Bowl." Mr. and Mrs. Harry Preston informed by a reporter while they were window shopping on Louisville's 4th Street, principal thoroughfare. Small, blonde, extremely youthful Mrs. Preston bit her lip; husband, tall, slim, also youthful, stiffened. Neither spoke for an instant. "This is a big surprise." he said. "But we have resigned ourselves. Our boy Robert (23) is with the Atlantic Fleet or was last we heard."

Fort Knox soldiers strolling the streets with girls were surprised, but apparently pleased. "I didn't think the Japs had the nerve," said Sergeant R. McCallum. "But we're ready for 'em." Most civilians took it with their mouths

Page 2-- from Griffin, Louisville - Dec. 7

open, had nothing to say at first. This was followed by strong irritation that Japs could have attacked Pearl Harbor and got away with it. Everybody showed exasperation. "What was Navy doing?" "How could an airplane carrier get that close?" were typical angry questions from every type of citizen.

Louisville citizens just getting ready to enjoy what they call "a pretty day" when news broke. Sun was shining, air crisp and cool. Most people at Sunday dinner or getting ready for automobile rides. Downtown streets populated mostly by soldiers and their girls. Sunday traffic, heavy here since Defense effort started year ago, at its quietest, movies doing brisk business, no standout films, none interrupted to give news fearing it might cause commotion, according to managers.

Obviously took a matter of an hour or two for news to soak in, but this warlike community plenty mad now.

For months defense plants here have been strongly guarded, so no extra details put on following announcement, but at Knox extra guards thrown around all utilities. "We're already guarded to the hilt, so guess we'll just go on making powder," said Lieut. Col. R.E. Hardy, Army Engineer in charge of Indiana and Hoosier Ordnance Works (DuPont Powder Plant, Bag Plant at Charlestown, Ind.)

"Somebody is crazy in Japan," said Maj. Gen. Jacob L. Devers, Chief of Armored Force at his Fort Knox office. "I don't see how they can hope to accomplish anything by this attack. As for us here, this thing will of course speed up our whole program of preparation. It ought to bring an end to all these foolish strikes for one thing. I don't plan to do anything about calling men back to the Fort immediately, but if this thing is as serious at it appears to be, we may have to cancel holiday leaves. It may also bring a halt to discharges of men over 28-year limit and, conceivably, we might begin calling back some of those already discharged and placed on reserve. That, of course, is up to the War Department."

Page 3-- from Griffin, Louisville -Dec. 7

Civilian Defense Committee here called meeting for Monday night with Mayor.

Veterans outfits began offering services if needed.

Herbert Agar, away since last spring, dictated lead editorial to Courier via telephone from New York: "War has chosen us. There is no more excuse for doubting that barbarism has come back into our world.... And we must face the terrible truth that the end will not be found in Japan, or on the wide wastes of the Pacific. The end will be found in Berlin.... America will now unite to beat Japan. America must now unite to finish the job by beating Germany, the source of all our woe."

Wire from Robert Hagy, Pittsburgh, to D. Hulburd - Dec. 7, 1941

PITTSBURGH AND THE WAR

The strangest development here involved America First assembled in Soldier's Hall in Oakland Civic Center, three miles from downtown Pittsburgh. Senator Gerald P. Nye, tall, dark, handsome North Dakotan, spoke to 2500 ranked and filers (capacity) from hall-wide platform above which Lincoln's Gettysburg address is spread in huge dark letters against a dirty buff background. I was assigned to cover it for the Post Gazette, and just a few minutes before leaving the office flashes and bulletins came over the AP wire on the Hawaii and Manila attacks.

I arrived at the hall just at 3 p.m., the time the meeting was scheduled to start and found Nye in a two-by-four room backstage ready to go on with the local officials of the Firsters. I shoved the pasted-up news at him. Irene Castle McLaughlin, still trim wife of the dancer killed in the World War I, another speaker and Pittsburgh chairman John B. Gordon, clustered around the Senator to read. It was the first they had heard of the war and Nye's first reaction was: "It sounds terribly fishy to me. Can't we have some details? Is it sabotage or is it pen attack? I'm amazed that the President should announce an attack without giving details." Cool as a cucumber, he went on to compare the announcement with the first news of the Greer incident, which he termed very misleading.

I asked him what effect the Jap war should have on America First, whether it would disband. He replied that "If Congress were to declare war, I'm sure that every America Firster would be cooperative and support his government in the winning of that war in every possible way...but I should not expect them to disband even if Congress declared war." Nye and the others then paraded on to the platform as if nothing had happened. Although the news had come over the radio, apparently nobody in the audience knew anything and the meeting went on just like any other America First meeting with emphasis on denouncing Roosevelt as a warmonger. Mrs. McLaughlin expressed concern for America's wives and mothers, her voice catching as she referred to Vernon Castle's not coming back, dabbed a tear from her eye as she sat down.

The next speaker was ruddy, ruralish Charlie Sipes, Pennsylvania State Senator, locally famed as a historian. Routine America First stuff until, in the midst of an attack on Roosevelt for trying "to make everything Russian appealing to the U. S.", he cried: "In fact, the chief war-monger in the U. S., to my way of thinking, is the president of the U. S.", while the hall, decked in red-white-and blue balcony bunting and "Defend America First" signs was still full of roaring approval, a white-haired, heavy set man stood up from aisle seat well to the rear. The man, although nobody knew him and he was in mufti, was Col. Enrique Urrutia, Jr., Chief of the Second Military area (Pittsburgh District of Third Corps area) of the organized reserve. "Can this meeting be called after what has happened in the last few hours?" Co. Urrutia, infantryman, 31 yrs. in the army, burst out, livid with incredulity and indignation. "Do you know that Japan has attacked Manila, that Japan has attacked Hawaii?"

Apparently the crowd took him for a plain crackpot heckler. They booed, yelled "Throw him out" and "War monger"; several men near Urrutia coverged on him. According to Lieut. George Pischke, in command of detail of 10 policemen assigned to keep down disturbances which usually mark America First meetings here, the committee's blue-badged ushers "tried to man-handle" the colonel. Cops were in quick, though and Lieut. Pischke escorted Urrutia out of the hall (through a blizzard of "war-monger" shrieks and reaching women's hands) at the latter's own request. "I came to listen", he told me in the lobby, purple with rage. "I thought this was a patriot's meeting, but this is a traitors' meeting." Inside, Sipe, a cool hand, tried to restore calm, said soothingly "Don't be too hard on this poor bombastic man. He's only a mouthpiece for FDR. Then Sipe went on with his speech.

A couple of other people addressed the crowd. Finally came Nye. Still no word from leaders about the war. Nye started at about 4:45 p.m. for nearly three quarters of an hour he went through his isolationist routine. "Who's war is this?", he demanded at one point (referring to war in Europe). "Roosevelt's" chorused the rank and filers. "My friends," said Nye callously, "are betting 20 to 1 that if we don't stop in our tracks now, we'll be in before Great Britain gets in." Howls of laughter. A few minutes after this, I was called to the telephone. The city desk had a bulletin on Japan's declaration of war and asked me to get it to Nye. On a piece of copy paper I printed in pencil: "The Japanese imperial govt. at Tokio today at 4 p.m. announced a state of war with the U. S. and Great Britain." I walked out on the platform and put it on the rostrum before Nye. He glanced at it, read it, never batted an eye, went on with his speech...

"It is Nazism to do any thinking here in America," and so on. Nye started to speak around 4:45. I gave him the note at about 5:30 for 15 minutes more, he continued his routine, "I woke up one morning to find that we had 50 ships less -- that President had given them away despite laws forbidding it." "Treason" yelled some. "Impeach him" yelled others. Finally, at 5:45 more than two and a half hours after the meeting started, Nye paused and said: "I have before me the worst news that I have encountered in the last 20 years. I don't know exactly how to report it to you but I will report it to you just as a newspaperman gave it to me." Slowly he read the note. An excited murmur swept through the packed hall. Nye continued: "I can't somehow believe this. I can't come to any conclusions until I know what this is all about. I want time to find out what's behind it. Previously I heard about bombings in Hawaii. Somehow, I couldn't quite believe that but in the light of this later news, I'm sure there's been many funny things before. I remember the morning of the attack on the destroyer Greer. The President went on the radio and said the attack on the Greer was without provocation

but I tell you the Greer shot first. That was the incident the president said was unprovoked and that's cheating."

With that, he disposed of the new war, but more or less upset and flushed in the face, he didn't do much more than flounder through five or six more minutes of stuff about America's prime duty being to preserve democracy lest "victor and vanquished alike fall" and communism "grow in the ruins". Loud applause. "Keep your chins up", said Senator Nye and sat down. Benediction, a couple of announcements and the meeting was over. Plowing through his fanatical followers, I gave Nye a third piece of intelligence -- that Roosevelt had called a 9 p.m. meeting of the cabinet and congressional leaders. I knew he was scheduled to talk tonight at the First Baptist Church (pastor of which is pacifist) and I asked him if he intended to fly to Washington. Flustered, grim-lipped rosy faced, sweating, he muttered, "I must, I must try...", and strode quickly out of the hall talking to somebody about plane reservations..Whether he couldn't get a plane or what, he nevertheless ended up keeping the church appointment, announcing he would take the train to Washington later tonight. At church, before 600 people, he was grim, bitter, defeated. "I had hoped for long that at least the involvement of my country in this terrible foreign slaughter would be left more largely to our own determination."

Then he reviewed events leading up to the war, accusing Roosevelt of "doing his utmost to promote trouble with Japan". Inferring that we were already at war with Germany, he declared: "I am not one to say my country is prepared to fight a war on one front, let alone two." Then several people laughed at a reference (out of habit?) to "bloody Joe Stalin". Nye said coldly: "I am not making a humorous speech." But on the Jap attack he said: "here is a challenge. There isn't much America can do but move forward with American lives. American blood

and American wealth to the protection of our people and possessions in the Pacific."

Leaving the church, another Post-Gazette reporter caught him, asked what course he would prescribe for the nation finally he gave in completely. The fight gone out of him except for enough to make one more crack at Roosevelt. "We have been maneuvered into this by the president," he said, "but the only thing now is to declare war and to jump into it with everything we have and bring it to a victorious conclusion."

Page 6 -- Add to Hagy, Pittsburgh

The weather is fine, sunny and clear and brisk (in the thirties).

Many people were downtown with children looking at the Christmas window displays at Kaufmann's, Gimbels, Horne's and other department stores.

Everything is calm. There is no evidence of street excitement in the afternoon. You wouldn't know war had broken. "Calm prevades the city on the war's outbreak," was the Post-Gazette's two-column Page 1 reaction story headline.

When the Post-Gazette, the only morning newspaper came out, extras sold fast even though most people had the news by radio. The Post-Gazette came out at 6 p.m., an hour and a half before the usual bulldog time. The Press run, on an extra 110,000 instead of the regular bulldog run of slightly more than 50,000. The normal circulation of all editions is 225,000 to 230,000. Now expecting a total run tonight of a half million.

The Post-Gazette editorial comment: "...wanton attack ... there is no doubt that the U.S. armed forces will give a good account of themselves. There must be redoubled effort at home to see that they have the weapons and equipment which they need. Certainly this challenge must galvanize the entire nation to immediate and effective action. Since Japan has elected to fight, it is perhaps as well that she chose to attack the U.S. directly. Nothing could have united the American people so immediately and completely."

Sunday night crowds were as big as usual in the busy city. Hotel lobbies were quiet. Newsmen reported seeing a railroader grab an extra at Pennsylvania station, take one swift look at the banners and say quietly to no one in particular, "Goodbye Tokio". "Well, that settles it," was common comment. Most people appeared to be stunned briefly, then stoical rather than aroused, determined but not excited. A middle aged newsy at the corner of Penn Ave. and Tenth St. said, "We'll know how to fight this war -- I was in the last one."

Page 7 -- Hagy Pittsburgh

The nearest thing to excitement outside the newspaper offices and radio stations was apparent in the city's dinky little Chinatown, just one block in size. The usually stolid Chinese padded up and down Third and Second Aves. shaking hands with each other. Slapping backs, smiling happily while the youngsters hopped about them in the sunshine.

Swiftly moving into action to protect this "stock room of a far flung arsenal" against they hardly knew what, top city officials held a tense, serious half-hour meeting starting at 7:30 p.m. around Mayor Cornelius Decatur Scully's big oval conference table on the fifth floor of the City County building (correct proper name). Department heads gave the mayor, head of Pittsburgh's civilian defense council, brief, terse reports on what they were prepared to do, what they might need in money and men for fire-fighting, anti-sabotage work, etc., what steps they had already taken for emergencies. Half an hour -- that was all. "We mustn't waste any more time on discussing tonight," said the mayor finally. "There are grave problems we must meet as best we can and money will be no consideration in this emergency."

Police Supt. Harvey Scott later held a special meeting of his inspectors, told reporters he already had 150 men on extra detail guarding bridges, plants, reservoirs, main highway junctions. Both Scott and fire chief Nick Phelan said they would ask city council Monday for extra appropriations to augment man power and equipment.

Army and Navy recruiting officers prepared for a brisk business Monday mornings. Out for dinner tonight, I walked behind five apparently carefree young men who acted as if they were starting out for an evening of fun. "Well, you guys," I heard one of them say as they passed a newsstand, "What'll I do -- enlist tomorrow?" He seemed very happy about the whole business. "Why not?" said one, and then they changed the subject.

A cab driver, after reading the Nye story in the Post-Gazette told me: "That guy committed treason out there this afternoon. If I'd known what was going on out there,

I would have had a hundred drivers out there and we would really have strung that guy up." Man next to me (grabbing coffee in the greasy spoon) a laborer, said between gulps of spaghetti, "Now maybe Wheeler and Lindbergh and these other guys will shut their traps."

Wire from Hagy (Pittsburgh) - rec. 12/8/41 11:38 a. m.

Add Pittsburgh reaction:

Downtown theaters jammed Sunday afternoon and night, but unable to find any case where the show was interrupted for a war flash. The Biggest crowds were at Loew's Penn, playing Crosby in "Birth of the Blues" and at Fulton, playing Abbott and Costello in "Keep 'Em isxfx Flying."

The city's P. M. papers had extras out Monday at 7 a. m. -- Press and Sun Telegraph.

Word was spreading today of bizarre ads in lost and found column of Sunday press classified section (paper out Saturday night). Between two ads about last rat terriers appeared the following:

"Tokyo -- 8:05 p.m. -- news in English JLG4, 15D10 MEG., 19.8 M; JZJ, 11.80 MEG., 25.4M."

Farther down the column there was another: "Okyo -- 12:25 A.M.AA Children's Hour. JZJ, 11.80 MEG., 25.4 M; JZJ, 15.16 MEG., 19.7M."

The press was mum on where the ads came from. GBI flooded with calls from ad spotters. Local FBI boss told me he saw no significance in the ads but admitted he had never seen others like them in Pittsburgh papers and that they certainly appeared in a strange place. He said he had turned the matter over to the Federal Communications Commission.

At 10 a.m. today, Pittsburgh police radio broadcast an alarm to pick up men in a car with Michigan license plates, and query the occupants on taking pictures of the Westinghouse Electric and Manufacturing Company plant at East Pittsburgh, booming with defense orders. A few minutes later, police radio, WPDU, announced that military police at West Point wanted three Japanese in a brown sedan, adding: "These may be the same men wanted in connection with the taking of pictures at Westinghouse." Panic, probably.

Add Pittsburgh reaction (Hagy Pittsburgh) - Page 2

Army and Navy recruiting stations jammed as expected this morning. Men lined up in heavy but brief flurry of snow waiting to get in.

People here now definitely aroused as, after first shock and stunned calm, they gradually realize the enormity of what's happened.

(End)

Wire from Grover C. Hall Jr., Montgomery, Ala. - to James McConaughy -

Dec. 8, 1941

When Jean Harlow died the Telephone Exchange here literally burned up; fuse after fuse was replaced. The war flash did not jam wires nearly so much, but the calls mounted approximately a third. The flurry continued until nightfall.

Saturday night I attended a dance at the Officers' Club, Maxwell Field, headquarters of Southeast Air Training Center. Flying officers at my table agreed that the Japs were only bluffing, returned to their puerile pontifications about the dullness of British cadets in training; paucity of trainer planes. There was no sense of the immediacy of conflict at all.

Sunday I had dinner at a lawyer's birthday celebration. The phone rings. "Mr. Pickens says Pearl Harbor and Manila have just been bombed by the Japs." Everybody looked at their plates, while he turned on the radio. "I don't see why in Hell they don't let the older men do the fighting," said 47-year-old lawyer. This was a typical scene.

The war flash caught Montgomery at dinner. The weather was crystal-clear, nippy. Christmas decorations were up on Dexter Avenue, along which Jeff Davis rode to the Capitol on Goat Hill. There was a lot of talk about the Blue-Gray game in January.

A self-conscious flying cadet who wants to fly a bomber lay down on the floor to listen to radio flashes.

At a suburban tavern dozens of young people sat in booths at dusk drinking beer and whisky. I listened to the radio, but even more to personalized chatter. I saw one girl looking furtively at her draftee-fiance.

That night I watched a stenographer and a first grade schoolteacher. They indulged their escorts in close attention to radio bulletins, but they didn't care so much about the details.

A drugstore waitress: "This is it." The State's purchasing agent: "something, isn't it?" Our lady Sunday editor: "Fight like hell."

Essentially, Montgomery was deeply shocked. They had thought and never doubted that the Japs were bluffing. They were deeply resentful over the treachery. Vengeance bent, confident of victory, dazzled by cataclysm, but with little second thought yet of cost. They think it's a damn good thing. There is a sense of relief, like the passing of a painful kidney stone. Hop to it, get it over with.

From the Montgomery Advertiser: "Here was a different America, an America that had been surprised, but one in which surprise quickly gave way to determination. Whatever initial advantage Japan may have gained by choosing Sunday morning for an unannounced and unprovoked attack upon the U.S. bases, has been more than offset by the effect upon the people of this country.

P.S. "Sergeant York" is playing here to capacity.

Wire from Henry Hough, Denver, to D. Hulburd - Dec. 7, 1941.

Jap war query questions:

1/ The radio broke the war news one hour and one half before the first Denver Post extra hit the streets. The Third Post and second Rocky Mountain News extras are now out. Many residential areas where the extras haven't reached still don't know about the war except for persons who listen to the radios. Calls to several persons showed they hadn't happened to listen to the radio today and hadn't heard about the "dumb Japs".

2/ I was waxing the floor when the radio gave the first unconfirmed report about the Japanese attacking Hawaii. It gave me a cold chill. Everybody is interested but very few are excited except soldiers. One waitress in a popular downtown bar said, "These soldiers have just gone wild. They are getting drunk all over the place." Sunday night crowds downtown are thin always with soldiers in evidence everywhere. No particular excitement is evident and no crowds congregating as they do around Times Square in N.Y.

At eight tonight the city editor of the News instructed a reporter to query America First leaders to see what they have to say, papers and Associated Press report no newsworthy incidents in the area around Denver except for precautions to prevent possible sabotage at defense plants and mines. Mutual Broadcasting Co. outlet station KFEL in Denver received a phone call from an irate listener who wanted to know why the "Lutheran Hour" was cancelled. When told that some schedules had been upset by the war news, he snorted, "Do you think the war news is more important than the gospel?"

Telephone operators at newspapers and radio stations report not many calls which surprises the hello girls. Veterans of Foreign Wars and their ladies in formal dress holding a big banquet in the ballroom of the Albany Hotel to hear the national commander of the VFW on a talk broadcast by Mutual had made no provision for the war bulletins to be read during the evening. When I asked them about it, they said they don't think it necessary. Movies didn't interrupt programs today with war flashes, left patrons to hear about the war after they left the theatres. A big line of people waited to buy tickets tonight at the Denham theatre where Major Bowes Amateur Hour is playing. In homes, family gatherings are huddled about radios listening to war reports and exchanging opinions.

3/ Denver today was sunny and warm with most people out riding in their cars as usual on pleasant Sunday afternoons. No games were scheduled today. The Junior Civic Symphony concert at Municipal Auditorium had the usual small turnout at 11¢ per ticket.

4/ No editorial comment available yet.

5/ No important incident of development except for steps taken by police and defense forces to safeguard defense spots from possible sabotage.

To sum up, everybody is keenly interested but very few are excited, some are mad. Nobody is afraid.

End.

Wire from Clem Hurd, St. Louis, Mo. to D. Hulburd - Dec. 7, 1941

St. Louis, Mo. Dec. 7 news of war came by radio, no paper published until about 6 o'clock when Globe Democrat got on street with eight page paper. Post Dispatch and Star Times each has its own radio station which supplied frequent bulletins. Globe Democrat second extra contains disconcerting one column headline Manila Quit; Army placed on alert reading of item indicates no retreat merely typographical error quit for quiet. At Radio Station KSD of Post Dispatch a local program of Champion Buglers of Jefferson Barracks and Fort Wood had just finished program at 1:30 with Sgt. C.K. Bob Young, champion of Jefferson Barracks blowing to the colors. Few minutes after program ended news came in by AP -- an interruption was made in University of Chicago Round Table program just started. One Army major present for preceding program remarked "Darn, I just had a chance to go to Hawaii and turned it down." At KMOX, Columbia network, break was made by chain program "World Today" at 1:40. Many people called radio stations and newspaper offices for verification but switchboards of Bell Co. were not swamped. However, there was unusually heavy traffic through St. Louis on long distance calls to points west of here. Calls to Denver and San Antonio were delayed up to one hour. Extra girls were called to St. Louis exchanges, all of which are dial operated, in anticipation of rush which did not develop until 6 P.M. Telephone traffic chiefs went to their offices on hearing news on radio. Fifteen extra girls were called in to handle long distance calls, mostly to West Coast; from points east of here all calls to West Coast must pass through St. Louis or Chicago.

A few quotes: "What were those 350 soldiers doing in barracks -- were they playing poker or do they sleep until noon." "I bet those Germans told them to do it." "Roosevelt finally got it, now he will have to send that one bomber that the British didn't get over to take care of the Japs." Roland G. Usher, author of famed Pan Germanish and head of Dept. of History, Washington University, told Globe

Page 2-- wire from Clem Hurd, Dec. 7

Democrat first reports indicated to him the German Air Force took part in the attack over Pearl Harbor. It had long been his belief, he said, that Germany has been trying to bring the United States into war against Japan. At reception attended chiefly by members of moderately fashionable Pilgrim Congregational Church some of the following were heard: "They ought to blow the Japanese Navy out of the water." "They can't start bombing Tokio any too soon because look what the Japanese have been doing to China for months -- but we're a people of higher ideals and should not do that unless they force us to. We don't want to remember that we began the war that way."

People of city in general took news quietly -- few people on streets downtown. Day was cold, about 40 degrees, and sunny -- no professional football game. Big movies as follows: Fox Theatre showing "Keep 'Em Flying," Ambassador "Little Foxes," Missouri "One Foot in Heaven," St. Louis "Appointment for Love," Loew's, which postponed "Two Faced Woman" because of Archbishop Glennon's objections was showing "Design for Scandal." No announcement made at Loew's but large radio in lobby drew crowd of about two hundred -- little comment except for expressions of incredulity at first. At other theatres mentioned a regular news broadcast is given every three hours, Pearl Harbor news contained in broadcast at 1:38. News received in silence, but at Fox later announcement of Senator Wheeler's statement "Going to lick hell out of them" was applauded. Jefferson Barracks Air Corps replacement training center, bordering city, asked theatre managers to notify any soldiers from that post to return immediately, but no general announcement to that effect was made. Many soldiers visiting city packed up and left immediately for camps on hearing of attacks.

Quote from Globe Democrat editorial: "It is a stunning and ghastly act to undertake a major war. Only with the deepest reluctance and realistic foreboding does this country take up arms -- yet we will do so with the stanchest confidence,

Page 3-- wire from Clem Hurd, Dec. 7

grim and courageous acceptance of duty and an impregnable will for victory. God grant this be a quick and decisive war. Whatever its length or the sacrifices it entails, America is ready.

Wire from Keen (San Diego) - 12/7/41 - 12:26 a.m.

The news came to San Diego between 11:30 a.m. and 12 noon Pacific Standard Time via radio on a beautiful, sunshiny day as San Diegoans either cruising about idly in their autos, mowing lawns, trimming hedges, loafing around the house, or reading Sunday papers.

San Diego has two direct network outlets, NBC (KFSD), and Mutual (KGB). On KFSD, a play was in progress; on KGB, George Fisher, the "Hollywood Whispers" reporter, was reeling out film gossip when the first bulletins broke.

Immediately thereafter, at intervals of fifteen minutes or less, came radio announcements ordering all men of the 11th Naval District back to their posts at once. Leaves from Camp Callan and Ft. Rosecrans were canceled.

People at first seemed stunned by the news of Honolulu and Manila bombings. "Sounds unbelievable -- like another Martian broadcast," was the sentiment of some. Gradually the realization came that this was the real thing. And when the call for servicemen to return to their posts was issued, the full impact struck and spread. A large number of people knew of the event, passing word along to others personally or by telephone before the first San Diego extra hit the streets 2:15 P.M. (PST)

In the morning, the usual huge Sunday pleasure-seeking mob of service-men were swinging through downtown San Diego, frequenting bars, and other entertainment spots. For at least one hour after the radio calls started asking men to return to posts, number of uniforms didn't seem to diminish. Then suddenly they began disappearing, and by early afternoon, comparatively few service men were seen along San Diego's various pleasure rows.

The major afternoon activity/ was the pro-football game, Los Angeles Bombers v. San Diego Bull Dogs, traditional rivals and big crowd attracter. However, with servicemen eliminated and everyone else glued to radios, the crowd usually 10,000 for

1.

such a game, was held down to 3,5000. Too early for spectacular interruption of movies.

Some reacted in forced humorous manner. "Wanny buy a house cheap?" asked residents of near the waterfront, where San Diego's defense industries and navy and military bases are located, and where bombings, if any are likely to occur.

Slowly mounting anger was most typical, however. It wasn't manifested in any violent outbursts, but was best exhibited by the scene at the San Diego waterfront during the entire afternoon.

As Navy men rushed back to shore stations and ships, civilians sped to the waterfront to watch the activities. A transport was loading up at a dock; sailors were boarding shoreboats; a great throng was standing silently, glumly, without a smile, observing. That crowd, looking west across San Diego harbor, and out beyond Point Loma to the Pacific where her enemy was raining destruction and taking lives, possibly of their own sons and brothers, was the most grim, silent crowd I've ever seen. From it rose an atmosphere of determination and unity.

Sailors' wives, some with children, were there to bid husbands farewell, possibly for the last time. There were no hysterical scenes; almost all the women were sad but dry-eyed.

The average comment of the servicemen, aircraft workers and other civilians on the streets was: "It's the best thing that ever happened. Now we'll get in there and lick them to a pulp."

The major development after the news broke was the mobilization of service men. Following on the heels of that, San Diegoans by hundreds offered volunteer services to local defense council for duty as auxiliary police, air raid wardens, medical corpsmen, nurses' aides, etc. Everybody wanted to do something to help.

Not a Jap was seen on the streets here throughout the day. Harold Nathan, FBI head here, said his crew was completely mobilized and waiting for word from

Washington. A roundup of Japanese nationals due momentarily. The exact number of Japs here is considered secret by FBI, but at the local Buddhist Temple, the Japanese Church, they estimated there were 450 Japanese families in San Diego County, approximately 2,000 people. Parents mostly aliens, and children born here. The occupation of most is farming. There are very few Japanese fishermen in San Diego, where the Portuguese and Italians have the fishing fleet monopoly.

No Jap stores have been closed yet, and no anti-Japanese outbreaks have been reported by the police. The Japs seem to be keeping under cover, and in interviews professing loyalty to the United States.

Outward signs of war -- police clearing all streets adjacent to the Consolidated Aircraft Corporation's giant plant, and other defense industries of parked autos to permit the fullest access of emergency vehicles; guards with fixed bayonets at the Naval Training Station; comparative scarcity of service men in night clubs, beer halls and shows; people clustered about radios on streets downtown. No greater restriction in people's movements than usual -- it has been very strict in the last year in the vicinity of the Naval bases. For the first time, Camp Callan, selectee coast artillery training center, forbade visitors to enter except on official business.

No editorial comment yet available. Will file more early in the morning on this and more on San Diego public reaction.

(END)

Wire from Harold Keen, Edit. Dept. San Diego TRIBUNE-SUN to David Hulburd - 12-8

Editorial comment from San Diego UNION Monday morning:

"Japan yesterday signed her death warrant as a world power when she treacherously attacked Honolulu and other American and British outposts in the Pacific . . . By this action, which equalled in cruelty and treachery anything ever perpetrated by Adolf Hitler or any other criminal in history, Japan removed herself from the pale of toleration. This spark in the Pacific, which was ignited by a fawning puppet of Hitler and probably at his instigation, sets a new blaze which may prove to be the backfire that will save the decent peoples of the world from the full effects of the catastrophe that has been raging in Europe for more than two years . . . By this act, she started a string of events that quickly will send her reeling back into the medieval age from which she was rescued by this country just a century ago.

"Despite all the criticisms that might have been directed against the Roosevelt Administration for its handling of certain phases of the international situation, there has been room for none and there has been precious little voiced over its direction of affairs in the Far East." (This is significant because the San Diego UNION is strongly Republican and violently anti-Administration).

"Japan was appeased time after time . . . For four years we kept our markets open, supplying her with materials which enabled her to wage war against China . . . Now, she appears in her true colors, wrapped in the bloody flag of an international outlaw."

Another editorial urged avoidance of hysteria.

More "man in the street" comments: "It's about time we got out there and cleaned 'em up,"--Wally Kazikowski, 18, Marine. "We've been ready for it, and now we don't have to wait any more," - Clyde B. Casebeer, 20, Marine. "The Japs are digging their own grave; we're ready to put 'em in it," - Brad Thompson, 18, aircraft worker. "We should have killed off those damned Japs a long time ago," - Eugene Smith, 22, salesman. "I'm glad it's come to a showdown and now we can teach those Japs a thing or two," - F. Bringas, 24, aircraft worker.

End.

Wire from Robert Kintzley, New Orleans States, December 7, 1941 - to David Hulburd

The flash came to Orleans families as they gathered about the dinner table or in the living room waiting for the bell. The temperature was 50 degrees, thin-blooded natives were mostly indoors, too early for most for movies. There was a feeble, pallid sun. The flash broke into local, peaked juvenile singing for Red Goose shoes on WWL, (1:44 P.M.), in Great Plays program on WDSU, dance recordings on WNOE. The first and only extra was the TIMES-PICAYUNE at 3:25 P.M. with double 8-column, 215 point banner. The PICAYUNE staff was the only Sunday crew here. Switchboard, paper and radio were temporarily congested. Most calls were on casualty identifications since there were many from here in the war zone.

People in grog shops drank beer; shows ran no flash; the general spirit was the awful realization rather than flag-waving. Civic leaders didn't find ready tongue. Association of Commerce President Robert L. Simpson said, "This is a horrible situation, but we've got to see it through." Others were of similar tenor, not blasting the Japs. The Orpheum Theatre interrupted "The Men in her Life" at 9 P.M. to announce from the stage that all service men were ordered to report to posts. About 25 arose, marched out grimly -- no demonstration. Saenger Theatre with "Sergeant York" and Loew's with "H.M. Pulham, Esq." noted nothing unusual.

The best indication that the people were aroused was the good business (no figures) Navy and Marine Recruiting Stations did when they opened after the flash. Twenty seconds after Colonel Frank Halford, in charge of Marines at Southern recruiting division, opened office in came Lyman Crovetto, 29, dice dealer: "I'm rarin' to go," and when told his married status with a son, 10, might rule him out, his face fell: "I just have to get in." He left after physical to see if his beautician-wife would sign affidavit releasing him from support. When Federal Building elevator operator told drunk prospective recruit Navy recruiting station was closed, he said, "Ah'll wait," and went to sleep on chilly steps.

Best quote from Gung-Hsing Wang, Chinese Consul-General here was: "...This will be the last time Japan has a chance to hit below the belly." He added jubilantly: "As far as Japan is concerned, their goose is overheated." He was called from bath tub to the telephone after an attache had told a reporter: "He's busy in the bath tub. What's the trouble?" From British Consul-General John David Rodgers: "It's been a terrible day, hasn't it?"

The best news action was around the iron-fenced Japan Consulate on aristocratic St. Charles Avenue. The crowd hit 2,000/ mark around 5 PM with 6 cops and 3 motorcycle patrols. Burning of Consular papers in two wire trash burners worried next door resident because of flying embers. Attaches chased unburned wind-tossed fragments about while crowd hissed. The Fire Department doused the fire, cops grabbed the wet pile over a foot high, and took it to the precinct station. Around 11 P.M./to the handful of cops and newsmen left, Consul Kenzo Ito sent out eight cans of Schlitz and thermos of tea. One cop nabbed the beer to take home; the tea, eight cups and saucers were taken back with regrets.

PICAYUNE editorial excerpts: "The militarist gangsters at Tokyo will find they have worsened their own bad case before the bar of world opinion and weakened their military position by the foul and ineffectual blow ... Yesterday's sinister developments have aroused Americans as no previous occurrence of this war has done...The American people do not shrink from the conflict thus forced upon them."

Most important development probably was the determination to all-out smother Japan. Typical cock-sureness: "We can lick 'em hands down. They got it comin'." They mean it, but they were solemnly undemonstrative.

Louisiana State University students massed in Baton Rouge, marched to see President Major General Campbell B. Hodges, who came out in lounging robe and told them it was their duty to study hard. He envisioned a long war and said students would probably get their chance.

End.

Wire from Jack Meddoff, Buffalo, N.Y.
            to James McConaughy -- December 8, 1941

Nearby Fort Niagara troops today quietly took over the job of guarding the great defense industries of Buffalo and the Niagara frontier, supplementing police, deputy sheriffs and private guards. Workers on day shifts reaching plants of Buffalo Arms Corporation, Bell and Curtiss-Wright Airplane plants and other defense factories, found uniformed soldiers grimly on guard fully armed. The first electrifying reports of Japanese attacks broke into the calm of a bright, pleasant December afternoon, but hours passed before the sensational news reached the majority of the people, and its grave import was impressed on the public mind.

The first report here was flashed on four radio stations almost simultaneously at 2:29 p.m. and people at home or in cars who had radios turned on were stunned by the sudden news. "This is Camp Dix," and "Spirit of '41," both ironically enough were military-type programs, were interrupted as the flash broadcast on stations WGR and WKBW. Thousands in downtown and neighborhood movies knew nothing about it until they came out, and some didn't even know for hours afterward because the first extra did not hit the streets until nearly 9 p.m. Sunday, just a few minutes before the regular first-edition time of Buffalo's only morning paper, the Courier-Express. The only p.m. paper, the News, did not go extra. Buffalo and environs took it calmly, the usual Sunday afternoon and evening routine being followed and no excitement visible anywhere. A banner crowd at the American Hockey League game Sunday night, the 10,000 spectators cheering and shouting at players as if no war had descended.

Radio stations WBEN, WKBW and WGR, carrying NBC and CBS and NBS war bulletins, were on the air all night long and will remain on a 24-hour basis during the emergency. Reaction of man in the street was evidenced when I asked a number of them, picked at random.

A few quotes follow: "We should get at Japan and get at 'em quick andthen go over and get Hitler". -- William H. Moesel, 16 Floss St., Department Store salesman.

page 2-- Jack Meddoff, Buffalo -- Dec.8,1941

"I blame Hitler; he made Italy stab her friends in the back and now he has made Japan do it. We ought to declare war on Germany too" -- Leon Sikorski, 360 Doat Street, tailor.

"Italy and Germany told Japan to do it; we ought to get all three of 'em and get 'em good." -- Joseph Brucato, 71 Johnson St., Buffalo Athletic Club waiter.

Franklin A. Dearing, 34 Horton Place, shorthand reporter in the District Attorney's office -- "We ought to kick hell out of the Japs and then kick hell out of the rest of the gang."

John W. Caudell, 95 Livingston St., retired merchant; "I hope we knock hell out of them but don't say hell, it won't look good."

Richard Potkowski, 17 years old of 58 Harmon Street, just discharged from the 27th Division at Fort McClellan after 14 months, said: "I'm ready to go right back in now and help show the Japs where they fit."

Meanwhile soldiers and sailors, home on furloughs, crowded railroad terminals hastening back to posts. But there was no outward excitement, everybody was calm about the whole thing.

Buffalo News in a lead editorial today says in part: "America must and will strike back at Japan with all her force and determination. Whatever be the cost in blood and treasure it shall be paid.... From now on our war effort must be total. No half-measures will suffice."

Courier-Express also made a war lead editorial saying in part: "...The war is on. It is not a war of America's seeking. In no American mind can there be any doubt about the ultimate outcome of this war.... Japanese Empire has signed its own death warrant as a world power. But in signing their country's death warrant the Japanese war lords have given a temporary reprieve to their model and mentor, Adolf Hitler."

page 3-- Jack Meddoff, Buffalo -- Dec. 8, 1941

When the first radio flashes broke Sunday afternoon, more than 2,000 Girl Scouts were singing a Christmas program in Kleinhans Music Hall and offering a silent prayer for a Happy Christmas all around the world, all unaware of Jap attacks.

Newspaper switchboards, normally quiet Sunday afternoons were deluged with calls from anxious parents and relatives of men in the Pacific Fleet.

Buffalo men in their forties began volunteering to Navy within an hour after the first flash was heard. Chief Yeoman Gerald P. Milan said he got more than 25 calls at the Navy recruiting station Sunday night from men wanting to fight the Japanese. He said some told him they were way past 35 but felt physically fit and if accepted "would join up in a minute."

......

Wire from Jack Meddoff, Buffalo, N. Y., to McConaughy - 12-8-41

Most interested person scanning the last war news and listening avidly to the radio is Frederick W. McMillin, Jr., of 176 Sanders Road, Buffalo, a salesman for the Federal Portland Cement Company, whose brother is known as the Navy's "dictator" of the Pacific Island of Guam -- Capt. George Johnstone McMillin, 52, who makes his home in Youngstown, Ohio. Said McMillin: "My brother is known as 'King' by the 23,000 natives of Guam - the Island - and, this is little known - is actually the property of the U.S. Navy and not of the Government. My brother was sworn in as Governor-Commandant of the Island April 19, 1940, for a two-year term."

McMillin's last letter from his brother came two weeks ago. McMillin said his brother has pointed out in letters that Guam has no natural harbors and only one landing field and there is a visible Japanese Island only forty miles away. Said McMillin: "In his last letter my brother told me of evacuating the island of all women and children six weeks ago. This left him without his family consisting of his wife and two children, Adelaide, 16, and George Jr, 14. They are in Long Beach, California, having arrived in this country the day before Thanksgiving day. Another daughter, Ruth, 21, is with her husband, Lieutenant William Mack, in China, at present. Capt. McMillin is an Annapolis graduate, 1911; took part in Vera Cruz disturbances and then was on the U.S.S. Delaware in the World War and served aboard the battleship Sacramento on convoy duty off Gibralter; was later assigned to Mare Island Navy Yard off California. On Guam Island he lived in a Palace built by the Spanish in 1600's in the capital city of Agana, population of 12,500, a modern little city. The palace is as large as a city block and its attached gardens also are a block in area. Seven miles away is the seaport town of Piti which is in command of a Marine Corps battalion headed by a Colonel. They supply the police force. There are only 53 Japs on the island but they have lived there a long time."

End

Wire from Edward Morrow, Omaha, Neb. to J. McConaughy - Dec. 8, 1941

Omahans who generally follow the midwestern custom of dining Sunday shortly after 1 o'clock, were mostly finishing dinner when the radio programs (one was Sammy Kaye's orchestra) were interrupted to bring news of the bombing of Hawaii. Half empty theatres interrupted pictures to flash the news on the screen and some customers got up and left. The show at the biggest house, the Paramount, was Sergeant York. Movie business thereafter was very light.

Telephone calls, both local and long distance, shot up as friends and relatives called each other with the news. Omaha office of the Northwestern Bell called 12 extra operators, mostly for long lines work. The World-Herald did not have an extra until 4:45. The World Herald sold 19,200 extras containing fairly complete account of what had happened. This was the entire run and newsboys were unavailable to handle more. Many of those who bought said they were going to keep the first extra, which had an 8-column "War" across the top, as souvenirs.

There isn't the faintest doubt that people here are aroused as indicated by quotes of World Herald reporters picked up on the streets.

Best came from one of three soldiers who stopped to read a radio bulletin. The one soldier whistled, said, "Boy, take your last look at Omaha for a long time. Which way's the war?"

The afternoon in Omaha, after a sunny morning, was windy and cloudy and bleak. Soon after word came here, FBI men plucked K. Hayashi, member of the San Francisco Japanese Consul staff, from a United Airlines plane here. He wanted to proceed by train but was told to stay here. He refused to go to a hotel and remained overnight in the airport waiting room.

The World Herald was swamped with calls from relatives of soldiers, sailors and civilians in the Orient and had to call three extra phone operators. Nebraska has always been a great feeder for the navy and probably has more men per capita in the navy than most.

The World Herald, which started out being Isolationist but has been wavering considerably in the last months, though it hasn't relented in hating Roosevelt, called for all aid to the President. The editorial said in part: "Japan's unannounced attack, treacherous and murderous, upon American outposts in the Pacific, has shattered the veil of illusion and wishful thinking that all too long has befogged the American mind and hindered vigorous and effective action by the government and the people of the U.S.

"We face the naked fact. No longer can it be glossed over. We are at war -- at war in the Pacific as in the Atlantic. And the measure of our unreadiness is startlingly evidenced by the fact that Japanese aircraft carriers, submarines and bombers, even parachute troops, were able to cross thousands of miles of the Pacific Ocean and reach Oahu undetected until they began shooting.

"No use now to quarrel over that dismaying and humiliating disclosure.

"From this day forward, citizens may expect the utmost vigilance and efficiency to the fullest possible extent on the part of the government and our military arms.

"Around our President, Franklin D. Roosevelt, our Commander in Chief, all citizens from today and to the end will be rallied, giving all that they have to his support and encouragement. May the God of hosts bestow upon him wisdom and strength and grace of his tremendous task."

End

Wire from Bob Munroe, Miami, Florida to David Hulburd - December 8, 1941

The Outstanding reaction here was first disbelief, then a rush to newspapers, radio stations to confirm, swamping switchboards already congested due to lack of trunk lines, apparently continuously tied up with government and other emergency traffic. It is estimated that more than ninety percent of callers expressing opinions said U. S. should have entered war sooner. Exceedingly vague geographical sense apparent. One man inquired seriously of radio station WIOD, "Will President Wilson speak tonight and if so, what time?"

Three Miami-Miami Beach broadcasting stations broke news at 2:23, 2:29 and 2:32 respectively. WKAT had blue network NBC show, "Great Plays." WIOD had NBC Red "University of Chicago Round Table." WQAM had "Spirit of '41."

All interrupted then and frequently throughout the day and night giving local and wire news. WQAM show involved interviewing torpedo boat crews and sound effect of boats roaring off into the distance. Termination program just fading when war bulletin flashed.

University of Miami, Coral Gables, officially ordered closed for the day, Monday, but neither of two Deans in charge during the absence of President B. F. Ashe from city would say anything except, "No special reason," and no plausible reason apparent to outside observer. University has large number of cadet fliers in training, both American and British. Guards placed around campus.

Miami Daily News, owned by former Ohio Governor James M. Box, presidential nominee in 1920 with Roosevelt as running mate, was on the street with extra edition at 5:13 PM, claiming 12-minute beat over Miami Herald, morning paper opposition. The News will say editorially Monday, "Not even the bitterest critic of the Administration can charge that the U. S. asked for this war with

Japan. President Roosevelt and Secretary Hull have treated Japan with unexampled patience, not only throughout the last eight years, but even through the very last days and hours, when the final treachery was being compounded. In return they received the sly, sneaking stab in the back, a trick that Hitler and Mussolini hardly needed to teach the Oriental.

"Now that the war has come, there is only one weapon in the armory of American traditions: It is steel, applied with the fully flexed muscles of the vast productive organism which nerves our armed forces. We will fight with vigor and conviction, but not with over-confidence. We are faced with a brave and reckless foe, who for many years now has been piling up a store of secret armaments. Let us beware the complacency which lost the day for France and almost lost it for England.

"We will fight with perfect unity on the home front -- that is, with perfect unity of all our people who are first and foremost Americans -- for Japan's wanton attack has at last ended the unreal debate over whether we are or are not at war. The nation must now close ranks to see the struggle that has been thrust upon us through to a victorious finish."

Miami Herald said editorially, "The U. S. will fight this war in the only way it knows how to fight - fearlessly, as one, and with every resource at its command. Every humane and human interest in the moral code of our people propels us on -- to victory."

No Miami movies were interrupted for war news bulletins and no evening attendance fall off was noted. Think the people on the whole relatively calm and philosophic following first excited reactions. There were no big sports events in progress at the time. People were mostly motoring, fishing, golfing, etc., outdoors in warm December sunshine, and few interrupted their pursuits except momentarily. A member of a foursome playing bridge at the Miami Biltmore Country Club in the locker room as first news was given on the radio inquired loudly, "Where in Hell is the nine of spades?" The most frequent comment heard was, "I'm glad we're in it. The sooner we get it over with the better." Also, there was some criticism by competent military fliers re the Navy Patrol failing to spot the Japanese aircraft carriers. Radio telephone-equipped sport fishing fleet off Palm Beach, notoriously garrulous among themselves, received the war news afloat and became unnaturally quiet for the balance of the day. Coconut Grove coastguard, air base and other local military units redoubled the 24-hour guards and personnel and individually expressed eagerness to fight and unanimous optimism as to the ultimate result.

END

Wire from Clarke Newlon, Dallas to James McConaughy - Dec. 8, 1941

Twenty-five hundred people sat in the Majestic Theatre at 1:57 Sunday afternoon. They had just watched the finish of probably one of the most dramatic war pictures of the year -- Sergeant York. On the film flashed the title. Then there was a break in the sound and over the speakers came the announcement that Japan had attacked Pearl Harbor, Manila, Japan had declared a state of war with the United States. There was a pause, of a pin-point silence, a prolonged "Awwwww" and then thunderous applause.

This, however, was not Dallas' first news of the opening of hostilities. At 1:10 p.m. radio station KRLD broke into its Columbia program "The World of Today" (a news program) to give Dallas and KRLD's listeners the news. From then on its phones were swamped and the station devoted more than half the remainder of the day to news breaks and resumes. Usually open until 2 a.m., KRLD stayed on all night. NBC's WFAA broke the news at about the same moment and within the next three hours the station's telephone operator estimated that 400 weeping women telephoned all asking the same question: "Do you have the casualty list yet? When will it be broadcast?" All said they had sons or brothers or sweethearts in Pearl Harbor or Manila. The men called too. They wanted to know: "Is Roosevelt broadcasting tonight? Are we in the war for certain now?" Both men and women inquired if this meant the end of all furloughs. WFAA broke into a local sustaining program with its first war news break. The title "You Might Be Right." The station stayed on throughout the night, as did Mutual's WRR.

The Dallas Journal issued three extras, at 3:50, 5:09 and 8:07 and delivered a free paper to every regular subscriber. Estimated sale: 46,000. The Dallas News issued its first extra at 5:50 and sold 20,000 within fifty minutes. Switchboards of both the News and the Journal were swamped with the same hysterical relatives of soldiers and sailors at the scene of the Japanese bombing.

Wire from Clarke Newlon, Dallas, Dec. 8, 1941 p. 2

Clyde Stewart, manager of the Dallas Telephone Company, a division of Southwestern Bell, said that his office used a larger force Sunday afternoon than had been on any "normal occasion" and the long distance calls after seven were long delayed due to the rush of business. One boy called Dallas from Camp Hulen near Houston with the information that he had waited an hour to get his call through and had called as had hundreds of others in camp because his company had been told they might be called out on thirty minute notice.

Dallas got the news as it sat, mostly, at the traditional southern Sunday dinner and took its war news with fried chicken and hot biscuits. It was a raw and cloudy day out with the temperature around fifty, unpleasantly cool for Texas autumn. There were a few people on the streets, but up and down every business and residential street the noise of radios drowned out normal Sunday traffic sounds. The concensus of a score of quotes: "I'm glad the suspense is over. Now we can get busy and get something done."

Typical: Lewis Fisher, 25, dismissed from active duty Nov. 7th because of dependency: "I'm ready to go back now that there's something to do and someone to fight.

Mrs. H. F. Dudley, housewife, husband barely over draft age: "I'm upset, but think it's better now than later. I'm ready for my husband to fight."

Charles W. Hopkins, employee of U. S. Steel Corporation: "We'll stomp their front teeth in. Japs are the same caliber as Hitler."

Earl R. McGraw, roofing contractor: "Suicide for Japan."

Roy Carter, credit man, "Not fully prepared but we can take care of it."

Mrs. Jim Stewart, housewife: "We'll whip hell out of 'em."

Most important result so far seen: Every man in or out of draft age told his friend: "Better grab a gun, Bud," and laughed, but every man and every woman seemed to have been aroused from the numbed lethargy that constantly-hammered and recurring

Wire from Newlon (Dallas) to D. Hulburd - December 8, 1941

headlines of Russia-Germany-England war have brought about. There was more of the feverishness of September 1939. The war was real, and very close once again.

Editorial excerpts: The Dallas Journal, "We submerge all differences in the common determination that we shall support the government of the United States with every resource and every effort of every citizen in this country."
The Dallas News: "The war we face is different from any war we have ever known. Our peril is far greater than before. We will win/ with the full strength of America in the effort. That we will not win if we do not exert that full strength is a contingency so much to be feared that we dare not risk it." The Times Herald: "The harder we hit, the sooner shall we prove to the despots that we have the power to crush them and the sooner shall we have peace and security".

Wire from Harry Schwandner, Milwaukee, to James McConaughy - December 8, 1941

Milwaukee received its first war news in a Bulletin read over WTMJ, <u>Milwaukee Journal</u> radio station at 1:58 p.m. Sunday. Popular University of Chicago Round Table of the Air was interrupted to give the flash. It came as a profound shock to Milwaukee, strongly isolationist, happy hunting ground of America First Committee. Wisconsin football fans were listening to the broadcast of the Chicago Bears-Cardinals game (of interest because Wisconsin is the home/of Green Bay Packers) when the announcer interrupted the game to give the first flash of war. The news was startling to Milwaukeeans. Thousands telephoned to the <u>Milwaukee Journal</u> for verification. Switchboard was jammed with calls for hours. Reporters had to wait for 15 minutes to get through the telephone jam. Radio men from WTMJ swamped out operators. Most callers asked "Is war declared? Is it true what the radio just said?" Word spread rapidly through the city, recovering from midday dinners.

The telephone company reported that a huge flood of calls. The city was excited. Isolationists swung over with interventionists in a "let's go" attitude.

Lansing Hoyt, chairman of the strong Wisconsin charter, America First Committee, told a <u>journalist</u> reporter at his home that the United States would "bomb to the ground" Japanese cities. He said: "We have been for defense all along. Now we are for offense. It looks like war against the Axis." Hoyt is Milwaukee Republican chairman and a brother-in-law of John Cudahy. Hoyt has been a leader in arranging Isolationist mass meetings in Milwaukee, at which Wheeler et al spoke. Edmund B. Shea, prominent Milwaukee attorney and president of the Milwaukee chapter, Committee to Defend America, said that all Americans should united in the common cause of defending the nation. Shea had announced earlier Sunday a series of meetings to whip up sentiment in Milwaukee against isolationism, with Senators Pepper, Murray, Ball, Lee Bridges as speakers. Gov. Heil sent this telegram to President Roosevelt:

"The news of Japanese aggression is a distinct shock to citizens of Wisconsin. I pledge you the full and unified support of our people. May the Lord give you help and strength in this hour of grave peril."

The desk clerk at Milwaukee's largest hotel, Schroeder Hotel, said that the guests couldn't believe their ears at the news. "It was like a dash of ice water," said the clerk. Walter Stern, a retired president of a flour mill, said: "I'm shocked beyond words. Well, we're ready. It is full steam ahead now." Harry M. Silber, an attorney said: "I'm so surprised that I hardly know what to say. But I'm sure we'll take good care of them." The Rev. J. R. Linsen Mayer, pastor of the Roosevelt Drive Presbyterian Church, in a middle class district, gravely told the latest war news to a silent audience of 100 gathered for a hymn sing. Then he prayed for defeat of "the forces of Japanese aggressions," emphasizing that the record showed that the United States had been attacked without warning. The general Milwaukee scene:

It was a quiet Sunday afternoon, with no big events to attract crowds. The city's main street, Wisconsin Ave., was jammed with parents and their children looking at Christmas store window displays. A raw wind whooped in from the south at 25 m.p.h., lashing Lake Michigan into whitecaps and foam. Lead clouds hung over the city, blotting out the sun. A favorite Sunday pastime of Milwaukeeans is to drive slowly along Lincoln Memorial Drive along Lake Shore through the city's beautiful parks. Thousands were doing that Sunday when their cars' radios gave them the first war flashes. Many startled listeners parked along the drive to listen to the bulletins. As word spread along Wisconsin Ave., crowds gathered in knots to exchange news. Downtown bars suddenly were jammed with pedestrians who wanted to get close to a radio. They talked earnestly and grimly. Milwaukeeans who have long felt that the United States shoud stay out of Europe's war were

Schwandner, Milwaukee - Dec. 8, 1941

fighting mad that the Japs had attacked the U.S., killed U.S. soldiers. They felt that here at last was something to get mad about, fight for.

The Milwaukee Journal and Milwaukee Sentinel extras were off the presses about 5 p.m., hit the streets about the same time. Extras sold heavily. The Journal reported sales of 66,000. Downtown crowds grabbed extras fast as newsboys offered them. Cries of newsboys, "Japs declare War on U.S.," rose above the Christmas chimes that tinkled on Wisconsin Avenue from loudspeakers on street corners. In the crowds were young soldiers and sailors on leave with their girl friends. Service men looked grim. Their girls were whitefaced, some tearful. Young men and women generally seemed grimmer about the news than the older folks.

I am rewiring, Monday, the first editorial comment.

Wire from Harvey Schwandner, Milwaukee - to David Hulburd - Dec. 8, 1941

First editorial comment, Milwaukee Journal: "We are all in it today... Guns have spoken; the only answer is guns.... For those who go where bombs fall and torpedoes cleave the waves, the task appointed is plain. For those who stay, the task also is clear, -- to back up with all we have the men we send to assert the creed of freedom, the obligation we owe ourselves and owe Island peoples whose government we have undertaken, whom we are pledged to defend. Americans stand together today in determination. We pray that the struggle may not be long continued, the cost in life and human values too great. But short or long, we are all in it -- to aid our Government with material things, with counsel, with the unfailing assurance of support, whatever the price to be paid."

Wire from Sullivan (Seattle) to D. Hulburd- December 7, 1941

Police detail in the oriental section in Seattle was doubled to guard against disorders. Police and the FBI guarded the home of Yuki Sato, Jap consul, and officers refused admission to a group of neighborhood children calling to give a Christmas present to one of the Consul's children. But Gordon Lewis, 8, son of a navy lieutenant-commander, talked his way in, handed schoolmate, Syuki Sato, 8 a toy automobile and a dimestore dive bomber. The Consul's children leaned out of the windows, talking to neighborhood children.. Said the Consul to the press: "I am very sorry, no statement." Jap stores and restaurants stayed open but the Jap quarter was almost devoid of Japs. They stayed in their homes.

There are about 6,000 alien Japs in and around Seattle. Long distance telephone communications, when war news broke, were tremendous in the Seattle area, and the telephone company had to send out for all its extra operators.

A few hours after the news broke, soldiers began leaving Seattle by bus and truck for Fort Lewis, Fort Lawton and other posts, sounding good humored but fatalistic good-byes.

The most immediate visible result of the war is prompt patrols -- police, soldier, sailor, deputy sheriffs, state police, company guards and others of defense regions, bridges guarded, Seattle 28 mile pipeline guard txtff tripled, extra guard around water purification plant up in Cascades, light power, gas and other utilities guarded.

Remarkably fast, Rear Admiral C. S. Freeman at Bremerton, Commander 13th Naval District: Gen. Kenyon A. Joyce, Commanding IX Corps at Fort Lewis; Capt. Ralph Wood, Commanding Sand Point Naval Air Station, Governor Arthur B. Langlie, City officials, Civilian Defense leaders, all got in communication with each other and agreed on what was to be done--px protect all strategic points, calm citizens, be on alert.

The war news first came to Seattle via radio, NBC and CBS stations, between

11 a.m. and noon. On CBS, it broke into the program of the New York Philharmonic Orchestra. The Post-Intelligencer had an extra on the street 3 hours later, the Times was on the street in about 4 hours after the news was received. The Times staff, not due until Monday, all came down to work.

Telephone calls also served to spread the news. Hundreds of persons called friends. In one 15 minute period, the Times got 700 phone calls asking what papers siren was screaming for. The Times said "War declared", most frequent comment was, "Is that all?" Comment:

"Well, this spoils our day at home, my husband is being called down to the office"-- housewife.

"My husband will be working longer hours from now on, and do we need the overtime"-- wife of a defense worker.

"It's awful, what will we do? What are you going to do? We'll be bombed within a week" -- war-conscious but rather neurotic woman business executive.

"I'm going back home to my folks in Wisconsin" -- young Zoman nurse.

"And I'd have to pick a day like this to go see "The Man who Came to Dinner." --young girl who had a Sunday afternoon date.

"Japan asked for it, and Japan will get it--in the neck" -- James Y. Sakomoto, Seattle-born publisher of Japanese-American newspaper.

At seventh avenue and Olive street, two soldiers and their girls stepped off the curb smiling, while newsboys nearby shouted and waved black headlines, in Aurora Avenue. A sailor with a bag containing roller skates, marched briskly into the neighborhood roller skating rink.

This first and immediate reaction is sobering now. As twilight falls, people are calling each other on telephones, talking its over more quietly. More intelligent questions are coming to the newspaper offices. The flippancy is nearly gone. State, city and country agencies are functioning nicely, shutting off alarm

Sullivan -- Page Three

and hysteria, but grimly getting ready for the worst.

Busy here, but will file more.

When the news came to Seattle the city was basking in sunlight, day was cold. People were going to church, starting out on Sunday drives, eating late breakfasts, listening to radios, reading Sunday newspapers. At the Orpheum Theatre, a line stood waiting to get in to see "Maltese Falcon" and "Target for Tonight" and other theatres were getting early Sunday crowds. Over various districts of the city, an Army or Navy plane would circle and people looked up with lovely interest.

A 12-year old freckled-faced fat boy, making change for a package of cigarettes in a neighborhood drug store, asked the customer: "What do you think of the Japs? Say, we've got to give it to them."

In homes, neighbors drifted in to talk over news; telephones kept ringing with friends on the line.

Those out driving heard the news by car radios, or noticed state patrol cars assembling around Lake Washington floating bridge, Boeing Field, Point Wells oil storage area, Fort Lewis, Sand Point Naval Air Station and other strategic points.

Four fishermen on Tolt River county north of here heard the news by car radio. They dropped all fishing for the day and got back to the city by noon to be with families.

Wire from M.S. Sullivan, Seattle, Wash. to J. McConaughy - Dec. 7, 1941

Sidelight; Marine Corps recruiting station opened at 6 tonight (Sunday) "by demand", had 78 enlistments by 9 o'clock, 3 more in office enlisting when recruiting officer called the newspaper. Navy and Marine recruiters are starting enlisting tomorrow from 6 a.m. until 11 p.m. daily.

This is late, and reactions calming down. Lots of people on the street looking at Christmas windows, buying newspapers. A line now a block long for "Maltese Falcon" and stage play "Man Who Came To Dinner" packed. No theatre interruptions, but news bulletins flash on. Service men left when the bulletin said to go to stations.

John Boettiger in the editorial called "War Comes To the U.S.": "We must now really go all out for the war effort. Now that the die has been cast, the thought of defense is secondary. It is not altogether impossible that a Jap aircraft carrier could slip through close enough to our coast to conduct a foray upon our airplane and shipbuilding plants. In this war it will be labor that has the greatest opportunity. Strikes of any kind should be wholly outlawed."

Most general reaction here was astonishment and "How do they (Japs) think they can get away with it?"

Exact position of ships out of Seattle unknown, but Alaska Steamship Co. has three vessels enroute north and several ships of America Mail Line may be in combat zone.

Would say single most important development is rush to guard strategic points on Puget Sound. Would say people aroused to belief Japan should be crushed at once.

Wire from M. S. Sullivan, Seattle, Washington, to David Hulburd - Dec. 8, 1941

TIME'S editorial -- "War has come. The bickering (of our country) has been stilled as quickly and completely as the clicking of a light. Here are the days when we of America are a united people behind our Commander-in-Chief, our President, and behind those to whom he delegates his authority. Some of us have sat smugly back in a feeling of security -- but (Japan's attack) is probably the very jolt America needed to snap it out of its lethargy."

End.

Wire from Toms (Indianapolis) to D. Hulburd - December 8, 1941

The news reached here near one-thirty central standard via radio flashes over all stations many catching bulletins interrupting broadcast of Chicago Bears-Cardinals pro football game jamming all switchboards but there are no extras at the moment. The Indianapolis Star Bulldog reached the streets shortly after 9 last night. The Indianapolis News issued an extra at 7:30 this morning, three hours ahead of its usual time. Most people expressed themselves in moderation and noted immediate retreat from customary language of isolationists in this inland belt. The first word of conflict brought remarks like:

"No fooling, we're in it."

"Let's recess politics".

The matter was taken seriously here and there was a tendency toward panic by persons living near big naval powder deport and new ordinance plant under construction. Many took advantage of the sunshiny afternoon to motor after lunch yesterday so downtown streets were sparse and movie attendance extremely light. "Suspicion", "Sundown" and "Birth of the Blues" were showing but there were no interruptions.

If any supplemental fact of note was apparent it was the hegira of motorists to country roads. The Indianapolis Star carried a page one editorial "Japan has attacked. With no warning war is thrust upon us. Is America united? Is Indiana united? There is but one answer. Yes. Hoosier boys are at the Pacific battle front, on the sea and in the air. You can show you are backing them up as they fight your battles. Let old glory give the answer. The Star suggests that the flag be flown today from all public buildings & from factories and other private industries, from the stores and schools and from homes. It will thrill every heart against the trying days ahead. It will put courage and faith in victory in all of us. Not only today, but every day. Keep the flag flying."

Will follow News editorial.

Wire from William L. Toms, Indianapolis News, Ind. to David Hulburd -

Dec. 8, 1941

Indianapolis News of Charles Warren Fairbanks' family in Page One editorial says in part:

"The American people will not live in slavery. Better death in defense of liberty than life under the totalitarian heel. That is today's challenge to every American.

"The time has come to lay aside partisan, sectional and other differences. There is only one division - Americans and the enemies of Americans. And there is only one choice in this country - to be Americans all the way. It is not American to delay a necessary act of Congress, to put any private business above the public business, to lay down a tool in any defense industry. It is American to strip for the fight and drive through to a quick and complete victory.

"To the discharge of this obligation the American people address themselves, under President Roosevelt, as one man fighting for all that he holds worth while in this world.

"Hitler is attacking, indeed, but through the Japanese, as he has so long tried to do.

We must fight with everything we have. It will not be easy. But the greater our concentration and the greater our sacrifice, the sooner the victory."

End.

Wire from Wm. Vaughan, Kansas City, Mo. to J. McConaughy - Dec. 7, 1941

It was cloudy this morning when Kansas Citians went to church, but by the time they started home for the traditional Sunday dinner of the middlewest the sun had come out. It was another perfect, unseasonably warm day in a string of similar ones. The temperature was to rise to 55 degrees by 4 o'clock. Before then the news had come that Japan was at war with the U.S.

The first word came through radios and was missed by many families who were at dinner when the flash was read. A copy reader on the telegraph desk of the Kansas City Star, down for an early trick, caught the flash from the Associated Press and sprinted up a flight of stairs to the studios of station WDAF. At 1:33 p.m. the news of the first White House announcement went on the air, interrupting the Chicago Round Table. At 1:39 Station KMBC broke in on the religious Round Table, a panel of Kansas City pastors sponsored weekly by the council of churches. Other stations hit at about the same time, but WDAF claimed the first break, beating the regular network flashes by about ten minutes.

Kansas City's two newspapers, the Star and the Journal, held back extras until they could make a creditable showing on the streets. By 7 o'clock both were out -- the Star with four pages, the Journal with eight. By 8 o'clock, the Star had jumped to 16 pages for a second extra edition. (The Star's extras were of its morning paper, the Times).

The Journal carried in the 3-column front page space in which Harry Newman had written an editorial every day since he took over the paper a month ago, Newman's by-lined comment, which began:

"The little yellow man is really yellow.

"Almost 100 years ago this Sunday afternoon an admiral of the U. S. Navy -- reached into the dark drawer of Medievalism and pulled the intellectually and physically dwarfed Nipponese out into the light of civilization and education.

Page 2 -- Vaughan, Kansas City

"The cycle seems to have come about again and that same navy -- seems duty bound to put them back into the drawer and into the dark."

Charles V. Stansell, Associated Editor of the Star hurried to the office to write for the second extra edition:

"There can be but one reply to the deliberate dastardly and unprovoked Japanese attack upon the U. S.

"A war fought with the clear knowledge that our government made every effort to achieve a peaceful and honorable settlement of the outstanding problems on the Pacific and that it was unprovoked aggression of which history can offer any record rewarded by one of the most flagrant examples of unprovoked aggression of which history can offer any record.

"There must be no illusions. This is not a war that can be fought with one hand behind our back. It is not going to be a cheap or a painless war. It will be a war with /a seasoned and desperate antagonist, an antagonist, moreover from whom every form of treachery must be expected as a matter of course.

"But whether our losses are small or great, whether the struggle requires months or years, we must make sure of one thing -- that although Japan has struck the first blow, we shall strike the last and the result of that last blow shall be the complete destruction of the Japanese empire. To the end that our children and our children's children may live in a free and decent world."

Although it listened to its radio, quickly bought out extras and flooded newspapers with telephone calls, however, Kansas City took the news more or less in its stride. There were cars on streets, many of them with horns tooting. They arrived downtown and on the country club plaza where colored lights outlined the Spanish type buildings in the spectacular annual Christmas display.

At Loew's Midland Theatre, the manager, John McManus, seized an opportunity in a B picture called "Niagara Falls" when the sound track contained no dialogue and announced to his audience that Japan had declared war he was the only first run theatre manager to do so. The Midland, where "Sundown" was the A picture and the N Newman with "Skylark" reported good houses tonight, perhaps better than average. The Uptown "Swamp Water" and the Orpheum "Look Who's Laughing" decided people were staying home to listen to their radios.

Most conversation about the war, on the streets at least, was good-humored, almost gay with a sense of relief, of "Well, here it is at last." Newsboys yelled, "Gotta whip those Japs" and their customer grinned back at them. Calls to the newspapers indicated, however, that in many a Kansas City home, the bombing of Hawaii held more of sorrow than of adventure. Mothers of sailors on the Oklahoma who had been looking forward to Christmas visits from their soldier sons, called for more information, many of them in tears. Service men themselves wanted to know about the concellation of furloughs, about any orders for reporting to ships or camps.

At the USO club soldiers danced to a juke box, played ping pong and gathered around copies of newspaper extras. They spoke bravely of what "we'll do to those blankety blank Japs" but their interest did not seem particularly deep.

In the afternoon, 1,000 Catholics gathered for the dedication of a De La Salle Academy gymnasium, heard the grim news from their bishop, the very Rev. Edwin Vincent O'Hara. Other Kansas Citians heard further bulletins at a sparsely attended night hockey game between Kansas City and Omaha.

The Southwestern Bell Telephone Co. had no accurate check on call volume, but thought it had risen although not enough to tie up switchboards.

The job co-ordinating all of Kansas City's defense activities will be directed by Rear Admiral Hayne Ellis, retired.

Appointment of Admiral Ellis was announced early tonight by L. P. Cookingham,

Page 4 -- Vaughan, Kansas City

city manager, who with Mayor John B. Cage, conferred with Ellis.

Admiral Ellis will serve as director of Civilian Defense at a salary of $1 a year. The appointment of a director was authorized last week by the city council, which created a municipal defense department. Under the ordinance the mayor will appoint an executive advisory committee of 25 members, which will appoint a large advisory committee including city, state and county officials and representatives of organizations participating in (probably word missing here)... There are expected to be more than 100 members.

Cook, labor and business leaders were unanimous in statements calling for crushing of the Axis.

All utilities and big plants, including North American Aviation, Inc. Bomber plant being built in Kansas City, Kansas, and Remington small arms ammunition plant at Lake City Mo. added guards, took all precautions against sabotage. Police and deputies ordered to stand by.

Wire from Charlton Whitehead, Norfolk, Va. to J. McConaughy - Dec. 8, 1941

After midday-dinner stupor of the majority of Norfolkians, they were kept home by the coldest day of winter, broken at 2:26 p.m. by a brief bulletin over local NBC outlet WTAR, stating that Pearl Harbor had been attacked. Incredulous listeners swamped newspapers and radio, but 10 minutes later NBC news-room confirmed the report. Indignation mixed with fear was most noticeable. On the street corners, where loungers gather to watch the Sunday parade, and in homes, the reaction was "I don't believe it," or "For God's sake why do we always let foreigners get the jump on us," Also heard was the belief that Roosevelt had engineered this so we would be at war, which he wants. Everyone, including Congressman Winder R. Harris, asked, "How could such a raiding force approach without a Navy patrol or at least warning of impending raid."

The first bulletin interrupted Sammy Kaye. The other radio station, WGH, a Mutual outlet, not until 4:20.

Within less than two hours, Chief Police John Woods had rounded up and jailed 14 Japs in Norfolk, all known.

Movies report no bulletins issued, moviegoers not knowing of the war until they got out. However, after 6:30, the Navy's request that men on the delta and the Little report immediately to their ships was announced in all theatres. No falling off of attendance was reported, although the day was poor due to cold. No football or other big crowds were out today.

Brigadier General Rollin H. Tilton, commanding the Harbor Defense of Chesapeake Bay bulletined through WTAR that all officers and men were called to return to their posts. However, late tonight the radio reported that the Third Corps Area Army was rescinding this order. Meanwhile, calls were continuing for all Army men to return. There was much discussion, does this mean Christmas leaves will be cancelled.

Although Commandant of the Fifth Naval District Rear Admiral

Manley H. Simons issued an announcement that guards were doubled, he has not called men back. Two ships, the Little and the Delta, however, are recalling their crews. It was rumored they will be sent to the Pacific. There is much wonderment will some of the Atlantic Fleet now here be sent too.

Telephone lines are jammed with calls. Long distance and local calls are very slow, Army and Navy officials burning up the wires, and everyone calling everyone else to tell the latest rumor and news.

The first and only extra was put on the street about 7 o'clock, four pages, published by the Virginian Pilot morning sheet. All carrier boys were recalled from morning and evening papers. The extra was a sell-out within an hour, never reached the suburbs.

The local recruiting office announced that it would remain open all night. Only one man has enlisted so far. He wanted to beat the Japs with his own two hands.

There was much consternation when the night train arrived from New York as no passengers knew of the war until their arrival here.

As a typical Navy town, Norfolk is ready for whatever happens and the concensus is that our Navy can whip the pants off the Japs in a hurry if given a chance. No one seems sorry to see war come, except that they hate to see youngsters killed.

End.

Wire from Charlton L. Whitehead, Norfolk, Va. to Time - Dec. 8, 1941

Editorial comment in VIRGINIAN PILOT morning paper: "Proclaim Fact America entered war with clean hands."

"The Mikado's military Junto has united the whole American people" in one criminal weekend by "a shocking act of violence."

"As never before they (Americans) will be united in the nation's defense, for they have a common enemy, the nation concerning whose policy of conquest in the Far East they never differed, and concerning whose unprovoked and treacherous attack they can have only one opinion."

Editorial continues calling attention to isolationists' miscalculations as to where the threat to America lay. The evening paper, LEDGER-DISPATCH, editorials were in a very similar tone.

Today Army and Navy recruiting offices here were swamped with applicants, more than 60 men applying in Army and nearly 100 applying in Navy during morning. Feeling at fever pitch among civilians, but the Navy is cagey because it is shocked by the ease with which Japan invaded our strongholds. Remarks such as, "I want to beat the yellow Japs with my own bare hands" heard everywhere. All the people are united in the hope that the Japs will be wiped from the map. As an important naval center, Norfolk air raid precautions are most thorough. Navy families here are wildly worried about friends in Honolulu. The Naval Base, newspapers, radios are swamped with calls about casualties. The first edition of the afternoon paper today sold out in an hour, with men and women rushing out of offices to hold up carriers on the street. Extra guards were placed Sunday night all around all Navy and Army Posts, and Utilities in the city. 21 Japs in this area, all known here, are in jail held by Federal authorities.

End.

December 7, 1941

To: David Hulburd

From: Wilmott Ragsdale   Wire from WASHINGTON

1:00 Japan envoys asked appointment with Hull. It was scheduled for 1:45 p.m. 2:05 p.m. envoys arrived at the state department, twenty minutes late. They sat alone in the gloomy, diplomatic reception room under the portrait of Elihu Root. They were stared at from across the room by the cold bronze busts of Washington and Lafayette until:

2:20 p.m. they were led into Hull's office through the office of the Secretary's office force instead of directly through Hull's office door as usual. To a score of photographers and reporters, they nodded "yes" when asked whether they had asked to see Hull. At this time Hull must have known about the attack. The Japanese may not have known the exact time or at all.

2:26 p.m. the radio flash gave Roosevelt's statement that Pearl Harbor had been attacked. The Japs had handed Hull the reply to his "document" or principles presented last November 26. Hull "carefully read the statement ... turned to the Japanese ambassador and with the greatest indignation said: "...never seen a document more crowded with infamous falsehoods and distortions etc."

2:40 p.m. (about) two Japanese masks walked out of Hull's office, got their hats, and pushed through forty reporters to the elevator.

"Is this your last conference?" No reply.

"Have you any statement? Will there be a statement from the Embassy? No reply.

"Did you reply to Mr. Hull's document?" "Yes."

2:50 p.m. a telephone conversation with ▮▮▮▮▮▮▮▮▮▮▮▮▮▮▮ who said: NOT FOR ATTRIBUTION "Of course I can't tell the strategy but we will follow you

1.

immediately. We hope Russia will let us use Vladivostok, but we don't know. We will ask immediately. Of course we can't get there with ships, but we could fly in."

3:10 p.m. DOS Chief of Information Michael McDermott came from Hull's office to the Press room and read the Secretary's statement on his meeting with the Japs. Forty British and American correspondents crowded around to get Mac's husky words. One Japanese correspondent for the Tokyo paper Asahi, Paul Abe, an American citizen and former student of Oregon State College wrote the statement down carefully presumably for dispatch to his paper. Chief Domei correspondent Cata was at the Embassy. He is a Jap citizen and will be held with another Jap reporter for exchange for the American newspaper men in Japan and occupied China. Abe and the other American correspondent for a Jap paper, Clark Kawakami are expected to stick in United States. Clark was married two months ago to a Japanese movie actress and had planned to send her back to Tokyo on the next boat. Another correspondent for the Tokyo Asahi, Nokamura, received the news first from a UP reporter. His face contorted, his hand went up to his shoulder, he said: "serious."

A reporter telephoned the Jap embassy and asked whether it would seek police protection. The spokesman replied: "No, we have great faith in the fairness of the American people."

3:38 p.m. ███████████████ called to see Sumner Welles. He said Welles may have been surprised by the character of the attack, "but you know Mr. Welles, he certainly didn't look it." ███████████ said NOT FOR ATTRIBUTION "We will attack Japan with you. The Indies have been notified of the attack and are ready."

Upstairs in the Far East Division, the Foreign Service officers were gathered in the halls talking about the attack. There was criticism of the Navy. "Where were the patrols? How could they have let an aircraft carrier get so near the Islands. The carrier must have got within two hundred miles. Are they playboys or sailors?"

5:14 p.m. reporters were called into Howard Bucknell's office (assistant chief of information DOS). Before he read a statement, the crowd heard the radio flash from Tokyo that the Japs had declared a state of war. Bucknell's statement was that all official Japs and official Japanese establishments in U. S. territories would be accorded full protection."

The questions whether the U. S. can use Vladivostok -- the only near base to Japan -- is hot hot under the surface. Hull and Roosevelt may see Litvinoff tomorrow. Vladivostok is 600 miles, Manila 1,600 miles. Previous guesses of ▇▇▇ ▇▇▇▇▇▇▇▇▇▇▇▇▇▇ NOT FOR ATTRIBUTION have been that Russia would not let Vladivostok be used because of fighting one war in Europe. But ▇▇▇▇ NOT FOR ATTRIBUTION, said the Russians would let Vladivostok be used "if they think it is in their interest."

The Chinese in Washington were hilariously happy at having for fighting allies both Britain and U. S. People in corner drug stores were not excited by the news. Said one guard at the State Department: "We have been talking about this since I was a boy. I'm glad it's decided now."

The war with Japan means immediate "dislocation of vital supplies of tin, rubber, etc. from Malaysia, Dutch Indies, and India", according to ▇▇▇▇ ▇▇▇▇▇▇▇▇▇▇▇▇▇ NOT FOR ATTRIBUTION. He also said the Department has one report, not released, that the Japs have made a landing on the Thailand coast and that a Japanese submarine has been sighted 800 miles off the U. S. West Coast. Off the record this Jap landing on the Thai peninsula will be to cut the railroad from Singapore to Bangkok.

Subs and raiders will immediately begin attacking supply ships bringing vital materials from the foregoing three areas to the U. S. "It is our first worry. It all comes back like a nightmare to me now. How we plead on our bare knees four years ago, that the U. S. buy and stockpile these materials so the Navy could be free when this happened. We have been getting it fast these last three or four months, but before that we didn't get enough. The first thing Japan will do will be to dislocate these roots. Of course they can't cut off our supplies, but they can divert much of our Navy and cut some of them."

Thailand forces: From a military intelligence report, a State Department official told me these are the military forces of Thailand: 80,000 regulars and 300,000 reserves. The Thai minister told me several days ago, "Of course we have all our mechanized equipment on the French Indo-China border." The fellow giving me the Thai forces remarked, "Mechanized equipment means they have got spears."

There are 40,000 Japs in Peru. NOT FOR ATTRIBUTION ▓▓▓▓▓▓▓▓▓▓ fears they may attempt to blow up the Cerro de Pasco mine which is American owned and a big producer of copper and lead essential to U. S. defense.

Japan has been importing half the rice necessary for her city population from Formosa, and French Indo-China. The Navy may cut this.

DOS has no new figures on Japan's oil supplies. Last July the army military intelligence said Japan had enough oil for about a year of all-out war. Since the freezing order Japan has got not a drop of gasoline from the U. S., Netherlands Indies; has got small quantities from Sakhalin, the island they own half of with the Russians, directly north of Japan.

The Japs forced the American oil companies in Japan to acquire a six months advance supply back in 1934.

Kurusu, who was then director of the Foreign Office Economic Bureau was the Chief Negotiator with the American Embassy and oil companies in forcing the companies to store this oil.

(MORE COMING FROM ED LOCKETT)

December 7, 1941

To: David Hulburd

From: Ed Lockett

Wire from WASHINGTON

Tall, bald Eric Friedheim, INS roving newsman in Washington, was having a drink in the Press Club at 8:40 Saturday night. Just as he was finishing the Scotch and soda, someone came up to the bar beside him. He turned, recognized an acquaintance, small, brown-skinned, black-haired Masuo Kato, jovial little Washington correspondent of Japan's Domei News Agency. "Hi, Kato," said Eric, "did you hear about the President's message to the Emperor of Japan?"

"Good God, no," said Kato, "I just cabled the office: all quiet here tonight; no news."

If Kato is telling the truth, he was as unaware of Japan's plans to invade Hawaii and the Philippines on Sunday at Dawn as apparently was the U. S. Navy, the U. S. government at home, and, conceivably Japan's own Ambassador Nomura and Special Envoy Kurusu. This pair, and tall, courtly Secretary of State Cordell Hull, were conferring on the "critical situation" obtaining in U.S.-Japanese relations "within an hour" of the time Nippon turned her war dogs loose on U. S. territory. Washington was recovering from Saturday night peacefully enough on Sunday when the news came. In the AP news room, on the third floor of the Washington Star Building, Bill Peacock, running the Sunday desk, was busily laying out the report for the wires. In the UP news room, black-haired, swarthy Arthur de Greve, veteran night wire top reporter was at his desk going over the big batch of handouts, culling the useless material from that which would go into the night report. Tall, lanky Arthur Hachten, INS oldster, was in the INS newsroom preparing for the work that would come a little later when the night wire opened at 3 p.m. Big, heavy Harold "Duke" Slater, running the Sunday day wire was reading

1.

the paper, his work nearly done. At approximately 2:20 the telephone rang in all these offices, and all three men picked them up. From the other end of the wire came these words: "This is Steve Early. I am calling from home. I have a statement here which the President has asked me to read." Then Early read to the three services the President's statement (pick up text from ticker) which told the U. S. that Hawaii was being bombed. He closed up the brief conversation with the observation that he was going directly to the White House, and "I will tell you more later."

Before Early could get out of his house, however, he had to make another telephone call to the Press associations - this time again on a three-way hookup, to advise at 2:36 that there had also been an attack on Manila.

Tall, lean Eddie Bomar, the AP's military analyst, was in the office at the time of the calls; he and John Lear and an AP feature writer, set out for the White House, were the first to get there, and were in the press room five or ten minutes before other newsmen turned up, learned from the police guards that Mr. Early had arrived, but wasn't quite ready to see them for a few moments. Meanwhile, the offices started mobilizing their staff. Stocky, black-haired, taciturn Douglas Cornell, AP White House man, was painting a door in his basement when his wife called him to the telephone, and the office told him to get the hell over to the White house pronto. He got.

Heavy, jovial, fat newsman Mike Flynn of the Wall Street Journal, was getting ready/to go to an oyster roast when his wife called him, just after his office called him. His oyster-roast host telephoned, asked him why he was late getting there. Mike said: "Sorry, but I'll see you after the war," and lit out for the White House.

Merriman Smith, small, black-moustached UP White House man, was shaving when his wife told him she had heard a radio announcement about the attack, and as he picked up the telephone to call the office, he found the office was calling him. He set out for the White House too.

Eric Friedheim was at the Redskins-Eagles football game as was his boss, bald William K. Hutchinson, INS Bureau Chief in Washington. "Hutch" knew where Eric was sitting, and after the boys in the press box got the news, passed it around, "Hutch" sought out Eric, sent him Whitehouseward. Half a dozen other reporters were in Griffith Stadium watching the ball game and didn't get into the busy scene of operations until afterwards. Hardly half a dozen reporters had got to the press room when the blue-coated policeman stuck his head in, announced: "Mr. Early will see you." The reporters filed into Steve's office found the red-faced secretary hunched behind his desk, looking very serious, unruffled. On his right sat his secretary, pretty, blonde, blue-sweatered Ruth Jane Rumelt, her notebook ready. "I have just a little additional information to give you, besides that I have already flashed to your offices," Steve began. "So far as is known now, the attacks on Hawaii and Manila were made wholly without warning - when both nations were at peace - and were delivered within an hour or so of the time the Japanese ambassador and special envoy Mr. Kurusu had gone to the State Department and handed to the Secretary of State the Japanese reply to the secretary's memorandum of November 26.

"As soon as information of the attack on Manila and Hawaii was received the War and Navy departments flashed it immediately to the President at the White House, thereupon and immediately the President directed the Army and Navy to execute all previously prepared orders looking to the defense of the U. S.

"The President is now with the Secretary of War and the Secretary of the Navy and steps are being taken to advise congressional leaders."

As reporters raced back to the press room, half a dozen late arrivals tagged at their heels, demanding a fill-in, and soon the press room was filling up.

At 3:23 p.m. Early's girl Friday popped her blonde head into the room, interrupted topspeed preparation of bulletins based on the opening press conference, reading from the shorthand in her notebook:

"So far as present information goes, and so far as we know at the moment, the attacks are still in progress. We don't know in other words that the Japanese have bombed and left. So far as we know both attacks are still in progress."

She had hardly gone before she was back again with another bulletin which she read from shorthand notes:

"The President has just received a dispatch from the War Department reporting the torpedoeing of an army transport, thirteen hundred miles west of San Francisco. Fortunately, the transport was carrying a cargo of lumber rather than personnel."

Back the reporters raced to their phones and by this time NBC had received permission from Steve Early to set up its microphone right in the press room. This had never been done before, but Steve said certainly and the electricians moved in and started setting up things.

At 4:09 p.m. and 50 seconds, Baukage of NBC was on the air, cut directly into the national network from the White House press room for the first time in history. Too late, CBS saw the NBC preparations under way, got permission from Early, and started setting up. CBS was more than two hours getting on the air direct from the White House.

Sharply at 3:35 p.m. Steve Early deserted his own office, walked into the press room himself, said he had an announcement: "The army has just received word and reported to the President signals of distress sent out by an American vessel believed to be an army cargo ship, seven hundred miles West of San Francisco." This concluded, he turned to go, then halted a moment to say: "So you can see that the Japanese submarines are well out in the Pacific."

This news threw the press room into another dither of flashes, and reporters were battling for the two booth telephones in the White House press room that are for public use. All of the press associations, many big newspapers, have direct telephones into the press room. Copy paper was getting scarce by a little after

4 p.m.; the news hawks used it up taking notes, and a few were writing. Mostly the news went out from the White House by telephone, however, and was rehandled in the newspaper offices.

At 3:57 Miss Rumelt brought word that Steve again wanted to see reporters, and they crowded into his office. Steve looked very serious. He was looking down at the floor intently as the newsmen crowded around his desk. He carefully waited for them all to get inside, had attendants close the door when the men were in, said:

"I have just called you in to bring you up to date on developments. The President now is with the Secretary of War and the Secretary of the Navy, and the Chief of staff, General Marshall. The President has just decided to call a cabinet meeting for eight-thirty this evening, and at nine o'clock to have the congressional leaders join with them in a joint meeting.

(Pick up conferees from ticker please)

Here a reporter inquired if the President intended to call in the leaders of both parties in Congress. Steve said yes and added: "I call your attention to the fact that is the same group he has been meeting with in the past. I say that, so you can give this an international meaning. He has not yet called in the chairmen of the military committees of Congress. You can also say that the President is assembling all the facts as rapidly as possible, and that, in all probability, he will as quickly as possible make a full report to the Congress. That's all I have, gentlemen."

At 5:58 came another call from Steve Early's office to the press room, and by this time the press room was packed with reporters, radiobroadcasters, and both CBS and NBC had set up microphones in the White House press room itself. With Baukage maning one; several CBS staffers handling the Columbia mike.

The press packed Early's office to the walls, and this time photographers, both stills and movies, were permitted to go in, and cameras ground as kleig lights turned the office into daylight, sent sweat streaming down the faces of tired newsmen.

"I call you in," Steve said, "to tell you that both the War and Navy, since the first report (of action in Manila) have been endeavoring to get in touch with commanding officers in Manila, and have been unable to do so. I suppose they are busy. Therefore, the President is now disposed to believe, and to hope, that the first report was an erroneous one.

"However, the President has just talked by telephone to Gov. Poindexter in Honolulu, and he confirms the report of heavy damages and loss of life there, including the city. He said that a second wave of planes was just then coming over."

Only a few minutes later, at 6:07 exactly, Early left his own office, came to the busy press room where reporters were still handling the bulletins from the latest press conference, and announced:

"The Navy has just reported a squadron of unidentified planes over Guam."

By this time, the photographers were taking pictures of the hot, busy, noisy and crowded press room itself. Some reporters had sent out for sandwiches and coffee. It looked like a long vigil.

At 6:24, blue-sweatered Miss Rumelt came back into the press room again, waved reporters to silence and attention, announced:

"The Navy just advised the President of dispatches that Guam has been attacked."

Again, at 6:54, Ruth Jane was back in the press room, and for the first time, her announcement after the press room snapped to attention was something of an anti-climax. She had come, merely, to say that the President had added white-haired Hiram Johnson to the list of congressional leaders invited to the White House tonight. She explained that Johnson was invited in his capacity as ranking minority member of the Senate Foreign Relations Committee.

By 7 p.m. the press room was a mess of torn papers, cigarette stubs littered the floor, the atmosphere was stuffy, hot, and reporters were growing very tired.

Glamorous Lee Carson of the INS was sitting at a typewriter, hammering out a night lead, her long bob, unusual dark coloring, and pretty gray suit much the most attractive spot in the room. Big, fat, Fulton Lewis got on deck about 6:45 in relieving his pretty secretary, Jean (koming); the Nelson Rockefeller office had its bald, blue-suited Robert McGill sitting in on the goings-on; Western Union had a flock of delivery boys popping in and out.

The White House boys got bits of developments in other departments by grapevine during the afternoon, and a small portable radio in the corner was running all afternoon. The folks in the White House press room learned, for instance, that speaker Sam Rayburn was out riding in his automobile when the news of the attack broke, that his frantic office was unable to get him and notify him until he returned to his home late in the afternoon.

Vice-president Wallace was in New York City, heard the news presumably over the radio, quickly got in touch with the White House by telephone.

The President was in his study most of the afternoon, close to the telephone, constantly in touch with the Army and Navy by telephone, an anxious listener who finally, dissatisfied with the reports he could get indirectly, put in a telephone call direct to Governor Poindexter in Honolulu.

Silently, during the afternoon, the secret mechanism always ready to swing into action for overall defense of the United States swung into action. Big, red-faced, tall, rugged Col. Ed Starling, White House Secret Service detail chief was quickly telephoned at his home after the news of the attack came; quickly came to the White House, started the process of calling in every one of the men assigned to the White House. The White House guard noticeably thickened; White House and capital police were stationed at every one of the entrances to the rolling White House grounds.

By 4 p.m., fully 500 persons had collected on Executive Avenue just outside the west side entrance to the Executive offices, attracted by the photographers' activities and the news they had heard over the radio. For a while they gathered around the southeast entrance to the State Department Building, across the street, but finally the activity around the executive offices drew them away and to the White House entrance.

Shortly before 7 p.m., Solicitor-General Charles Fahy slipped into the White House, probably through one of the living quarter entrances, was only discovered by reporters when he left at 7:09. He said he had been closeted with the President for only a few minutes, was very reluctant to talk at all. Finally, as reporters crowded around him when he was leaving, he thought a few moments, intently, announced in his whisperlike voice: "My visit had to do with the aliens--the Japanese--living in the United States."

It was just after this that the White House, fast coming all alert to the critical situation, clamped down a ban against any photographs in the White House grounds when George Dorsey (Identification later) one of the newsreel men, went into Steve's office, asked him what about pictures of the cabinet entering tonight, and the congressional leaders to come later.

"No, sir, no sir," Steve cracked. "We're not going to have the White House lit up tonight. Absolutely no pictures of the cabinet."

This was emphasized about ten minutes later when a Secret Serviceman called on the picture boys to halt as they started taking pictures of Fahy.

"No more pictures on the White House grounds," said Mike, and that was that.

Shortly after this Steven Early told a half dozen pressmen, for their own information and not for publication, that henceforth reporters could expect reports on developments following and concerning land-based operations, but that nothing could be expected from the Navy for obvious reasons.

"Every ship afloat has killed the radio, of course," he said. "We cannot expect to learn anything about sea engagements. About all you fellows can do now is clean up the story of land operations."

At 7:44 tall, graying Bill Hassett, Steve's assistant, came out into the lobby of the executive offices, gathered newsmen about him, and announced:

"The War Department has supplied the White House with a preliminary-- it is only preliminary--report on casualties. This report places the military dead at 104, and the military wounded at more than 300, on the island of Oahu alone. This is only a preliminary report, remember, and it gives no information whatever on civilian dead and wounded."

By 8:20 the press room was a complete wreck, with new telephone wires littering the place, tripping reporters up occasionally as they dashed about; all the radio networks had installed mikes by a little after 8, and each of the broadcasting announcers had little staffs of secretaries, researchers and reporters clustered about him.

Funniest diversion of the tense, wearing afternoon and evening was when slight, extremely comical Fred Paslay, crack reporter for the New York News, thought his telephone was installed. It looked very formidable and official, wearing a sort of skirt of wires around its base, and Fred picked it up to call the office. But no office did he get. Instead, as he put the receiver to his ear, the lilting, breezy tunes of a dance band came to his ears. Nothing else could he get, for half an hour. He tried innumerable times; each time he got an orchestra. Finally, one of the two dumb looking telephone company workers tangling up the wires in the room did some giggling, got the phone working right.

The Cabinet got to the White House right on time, for once-- although Secretary of the Navy Knox just got in under the wire at 8:30, the appointed time.

The first member of the Cabinet to arrive was big Jesse Jones, Secretary of Commerce, at exactly 8:20. Vigilant police carefully checked his big limousine through the Pennsylvania Avenue gate and into the grounds of the White House. In the order named, then came Wallace, Perkins, Ickes, Wickard, Morgenthau, Stimson --

tall and white-haired Hull, with two bodyguards; Biddle, and finally Knox. They entered the living quarters of the White House. (9:45 p.m. received)

To: David Hulburd
From: Felix Belair

Dec. 7, 1941
10:31 P.M.

Wire from WASHINGTON

Scene at Jap Embassy

Early in the afternoon the crowd began gathering across the street from the Japanese Embassy on Mass. Avenue. Occasionally, slant-eyed house boys could be seen them peering out from behind drawn curtains. Police orders were enough to keep back the constantly growing crowd that kept on the look out for the story book smoke that always comes from the chimneys of foreign embassies of nations about to sever their diplomatic relations with their resident countries. The Japs had used more modern methods. Just before three o'clock in the afternoon a couple of lackies were seen by local reporters to carry out half a dozen square five gallon tins the stuffed with papers over which they poured an unidentified liquid. There were a few whiffs of yellow smoke and, presumably, the papers were gone. Reporters were unable to go within fifty feet of the scene.

Around seven o'clock, Major Ed Kelly, Superintendent of Metropolitan Police, approached the Embassy gates but was refused admittance. He went around to the side door to the kitchen, emerged a few minutes later to say he had come to inquire how many policemen the Embassy required. (As if he didn't know) If he received any reply from the kitchen door, Kelly kept it to himself. Then he got into his car, blew the siren and moved down Mass. Ave.

To: David Hulburd
From Wilmott Ragsdale

Dec. 7, 1941
11:17 P. M.

Wire from WASHINGTON

A Japanese correspondent said upon leaving for his Embassy:

"Am I happy that Otto Tolischus and other American correspondent are in Tokyo."

To: David Hulburd
From: Wilmott Ragsdale

Dec. 7, 1941
10:32 P. M.

Wire from WASHINGTON

War caught approximately 200 United States Marines at post in North China. They are stationed in Peking, Tientsin and Ching Wang Tao.

Roughly, there are 5,000 Americans in Occupied China and 500 in Japan proper. Since last May, the number of Americans in Japan proper has dropped from 5,295 to 500. There have been several warnings from this Government that they should evacuate. The figure for Occupied China is about the same as it was last May.

--- ---

To: David Hulburd
From: Jerry Greene

Dec. 7, 1941
9:50 P. M. -
10:25 P. M.

Wire from WASHINGTON

Washington Color:

Washington tonight is a city stunned, not afraid, not excited, but like a boxer who, after three rounds of sparring catches a fast hook to the jaw, rocks back, rolls with the punch. Tonight Washington is rolling back from the clout but in the rolling, sets itself grimly, solidly for the counterpunch.

Thin, sharp remnants of the afternoon's cold wind dither across bleak LaFayette Square directly in front of the White House tree limbs stick up bare and stark above the scant light of the posted lamps. Benches are deserted for the first night in weeks; two draftees hurry past the bronze of Andy Jackson in LaFayette Square the snap in their steps, the square of their shoulders a sudden contrast to the demeanor of the draftee who slouched across the mall in early afternoon. Across the Square from the White House, the massive veterans' Administration Building remains one of the few in Washington without lights burning late into the night.

Pennsylvania Avenue is a mess for blocks on either side of the White House, traffic jammed, moving slowly with waits for from three to five light changes before cars can move a block. There is a silent deliberation in the movement of the cars. The driver, passengers in each turn their heads, stare with unmoving lips at the White House from the time they come within range until they are beyond.

Hundreds of pedestrians in a steady flow ease past the tall, iron picket fence separating the White House grounds from the Avenue. They are in groups of three to five. They move along quietly, talking if at all in whispers, subdued murmurs. Silence on the Avenue, despite the mob of cars, the mass of people, is apparent, deep enough to gnaw at the nerves.

Everybody, motorists, passengers, pedestrians alike, is watching the White House ~~silently~~ quietly, without noise, waiting, hoping somehow to see a visible sign of retaliation. Not even in mingling with the groups can one pick up enough audible conversation to catch the tenor of conversation.

Significantly, two fur-draped "chippies", passing up business opportunities, grasp the iron pickets, stare wide-eyed at the softly lighted white expanse of the executive mansion, mumble to themselves until the cops tell them to move along with the rest of the crowd. Even then the gaze of the girls turn backward toward the president's home, not toward business.

From outward appearances, there is little unusual going on in the White House. Across the leaf-littered lawn shine the soft beams of the great lamp hanging in the portico in front. A chandelier blazes from a thousand facets inside the main door. One cop walks his beat in measured steps directly underneath. Upstairs, deep inside are other burning lights clearly evident through uncurtained windows. A line of cars reaching almost from the brilliantly illuminated executive offices to the Pennsylvania Avenue Gate is first indication that business progresses. Further evidence is quickly apparent in the appearance of West Executive Avenue. Cars pack every parking space.

A stocky motorcycle cop, without his overcoat and sneezing frequently, blocks the entrance, permits only those cars which are on official business. Along the iron picket fence, an occasional cop keeps the crowd moving. But across West Executive Avenue, in front of the State Department, a mass of neck-stretchers fumbles around unmolested and unseeing.

East Executive Avenue is bare, deserted, despite the lone light burning over the East Portico of the White House.

One cop and three smutty red lanterns block traffic off East Executive Avenue at the Pennsylvania entrance. The traffic block extends over the entire White

House area. On 15th Street, at the west side, lanterns, cops, barricades have closed the entire elipse to traffic.

There are few cops, comparatively, around the White House itself. Patrolman Edward H. Ring of the 3rd Precinct, pacing back and forth before the Main Entrance Gate, on duty since 5 P.M., cold and nursing a pair of hurtful feet, had this explanation:

"They sent a bunch of us up here this afternoon but we had to break it up. You know how people are. This is the worst mess at the White House I have ever seen. I mean in the way of traffic. But let two cops get together and four people come up to see what's going on. Let 10 cops gather around and a hundred people come around. So that's why there are only a few of us here. Excuse me. You'll have to move along, there (to the crowds). Sorry, people, but move one way or the other.

"I hear the Army is coming up here tonight or tomorrow. Now don't quote me. That's just a rumor. But I guess they need it.

"I had a fine one while ago." A young draftee come along with his girl and asked me what all the fuss was about. I said, "Brother, you better take your girl home and get some sleep. You are in a war." He says, "You're nuts. What war?" So I told him and his girl turned pale and he give her the eye and they went off in a hurry. I guess it was the old last-chance game."

Strangely, there were few lights on in the State Department Building, but those few, on the East Side facing the White House, were staggered in the form of a rough "V", running from roof to basement.

At Treasury, as at State, there are more milling crowds, moving around slowly, aimlessly. Yellowish lights flicker out from scattered offices in the nation's counting house without pattern.

Down on Constitution, past the dark, empty elipse, there is a renewal of the same quiet, questioning, endless stream of automobiles all eyes turned toward the squat, trim Navy and Munitions Buildings. And there, Washington is seeing war close at home for the first time in a generation.

There aren't many lights on in either building, peculiarly. Navy flickers out at intervals like the orange spots on a new checkerboard. But there are more of the usual uniformed guards inside the brightly lighted entrance.

The cold steel of war shimmers icily along the front of the War Department Building. Troops in tin hats, with full equipment, packs, rifles, ammunition, fixed bayonets, stand stiffly before the entrances. The bayonets are like swift licks of flame in the moving, switching glow of a thousand automobile headlights. Faces under the tin hats are hard, lined, unsmiling. Before the main door of the Munitions Building one nonchalant husky eyes the mob, a submachine gun slung over right shoulder, close at hand.

There are more of these troops at the new War Department Building a few blocks to the north, where the engineers are hurrying in and out with more signs of hot activity than was seen at any other one spot.

But most significant of all was this: Of all the government Buildings seen in a quick survey of downtown Washington, in only one were all lights flaring, were all offices obviously occupied, with all help moving at top speed. That was the narrow, tall office building just to the north of the Munitions Building---the headquarters of Selective Service.

••••

TO: DAVID HULBURD

FROM: FRANK MCNAUGHTON   W 12 - 4:30 Dec. 8, 1941

WHITE HOUSE CONFERENCE LAST NIGHT

"As you already know, Japan has attacked the U.S."

With these words, President Roosevelt, sitting in his big armchair behind his desk in the second-floor red room study at 8:45 last night, opened his conference with Congressional leaders -- the conference that led to Congress' all-time speed record for a declaration of war at 1:32 P.M. today, exactly 48 minutes less than 24 hours after the Japanese attack.

Congressmen were not caught by surprise. One leader, John W. McCormack of Mass., was unable to get back to Washington for the conference. Senate Majority Leader Alben W. Barkley flew in from Kentucky. Most of the others were in Washington.

They arrived at the White House singly and in pairs, were received by the usher and sent to the second floor. They were advised that the President would receive them in a few minutes. A cabinet session, grim and deadly, was still going on in the Red Room. Outside this room, the men who speak for all parties in Congress held an indignation meeting. Long, belligerent Senator Tom Connaly of Texas, Chairman of the Foreign Relations Committee, smoking a cigar violently, said the Japs had asked for it and they would get it. The talk turned to the thousand and one rumors that had swept Washington -- parachute troops landing in Hawaii, battleships sunk, Wake and Midway Islands captured.

A buzzer sounded, there was a scraping of feet and chairs inside the Red Room, and a girl announced that the Congressmen should enter. They filed up to the front of the room. The Cabinet discreetly moved to the back of the room, took other chairs and remained throughout the session.

The President was deadly serious; there were lines deeper than usual in his face; there was no smile, the switch to turn that on was dead. The President held a sheaf of papers, Navy reports, and his desk was piled with them.

Page 2 - To David Hulburd from Frank McNaughton - 4:30 Dec. 8.

He passed out cigars, Cuban Habanas dressed in the label of the Comision Nacional De Propaganda Defensa.

Then Mr. Roosevelt began reading the Navy reports to the Senators and House members. His tone was grave. He emphasized that the information he had received was spotty, and far from complete. Pointedly, Mr. Roosevelt reminded the Congressmen that while these attacks were under progress, the Japanese diplomats, Nomura and Kurusu were at the White House playing a game of diplomatic duplicity upon aged, sincere, peace-loving but now terribly enraged old Cordell Hull.

The President reviewed the major reports, said that they were still coming in at a very rapid rate and that no general overall picture could be formulated in detail. He said, however, that the Japanese had undoubtedly launched a craftily-planned "attack in force" upon every possession and strip of territory the U.S. had.

More coming

12/8/41

To: David Hulburd

From: Felix Belair Jr.
Washington, D.C.

Subject: Roosevelt Goes to Congress

Grim determination was written on every line of his face as Franklin Roosevelt was wheeled out of the south door of the Executive Mansion and helped into his waiting limousine to begin what was to be his last journey to the Capitol until his State of the Union Address in January. His appearance had been awaited by a swarm of tense Secret Service men in plain clothes, who stood about in little groups on the south lawn. Ten highly polished black limousines bearing the seal of the President had been rolled into place. Up ahead and reaching nearly to the west gate the motorcycles of escorting police idled awaiting the signal from big Ed Starling to get rolling. More Secret Service men than had been assembled to protect the President even on the occasion of his three Inaugurals put their automatic riot guns into place, cocked and primed for any emergency. They wore no topcoats, these protectors of the President. Topcoats slow down the draw from the hip of the 38 service revolvers all carried.

Some said the President looked as mad as a wet hen. More probably he had been, but that was last night. Now he had a job to do. He was unsmiling as he sat back in the well-padded rear seat, adjusting his big dark Naval cape. His son, Captain Jimmy of the Marines, sat beside him, trying to express the seriousness that the occasion required. Slowly the Presidential motorcade circled the south lawn, spattering gravel from the driveway about the neatly trimmed grass. Past the east gate a fair-sized crowd cheered from either side of the street south of the Treasury Building. But here was no campaign parade and there were no campaign cheers. The President, however, was not too impressed with the solemnity of the occasion to fail to respond to the crowd. The smile and the wave of the hand was there, although the hand waving was a little less vigorous and the smile was not from ear to ear. The President's response each time was entirely in keeping with his silk hat and formal attire. It was a solemn obligation he was about to ask Congress to shoulder and it had best be done soberly. The President's mood was sobriety from start to finish. Probably never before during his life had the President been so completely protected. Although he rode in a closed car, a Secret Service man perched preciously on either running board. On either side his car was flanked by an open Secret Service car with three men on each of their running boards and four more inside cuddling up with their sawed-off riot guns. Another Secret Service car followed that of the President and ahead of him went "Big Bertha" or "the Queen Mary," a Rolling arsenal if ever there was one. If ever a President rode in a mechanized division it was Roosevelt today.

The Capitol grounds was alive with cops, Marines and plainclothesmen brought in from Baltimore, Richmond and Philadelphia. It would have been worth any man's life to try to break the lines. Reporters going to work as usual entered the House and Senate wing of the Capitol, found themselves confronted by Marines with fixed bayonets. A reporter tried to get into the House press gallery without showing his white card and was knocked back ten feet by the skinniest Secret Serviceman he ever saw. Another was absentmindedly entering the gallery with a rolled-up newspaper. It was snatched out of his hand so fast he scarcely noticed it. Washington cops and plainclothesmen discovered places around the Capitol grounds today they never knew existed. They were posted on both sides and behind the Capitol building, through the galleries and on the floor of the House. It was the same at the White House. They were on the roof of the Executive Office and patrolled the roof of both wings of the mansion itself.

In other words, the protection was more than ample and the day passed without incident.

#3
Washington

All over the White House establishment there was eloquent proof of the nation's peril. Reporters, radio commentators with their sound men, photographers and newsreel cameramen were falling over themselves. Appreciated only by the handful of reporters regularly assigned to cover the place in war and peace was the fact that a goodly number of the young men in the lobby and press room had no connection with the press or any other medium of public opinion. They were members of the White House Secret Service detail. An NBC technician discovered mumbling something over a microphone in his office downtown, almost had the same device shoved down his throat because of Steve Early's notice earlier that there would be no more broadcasting from the press room. Telephone linemen worked feverishly throughout the day installing phones for special newspaper bureaus to whom the idea had never occurred before.

But through all the bustle it was apparent that after hectic yesterday, the White House establishment was beginning to settle down. /To The White House establishment nothing could be worse than yesterday. Steve Early talked less excitedly to reporters at his morning press conference, weighed the few questions that followed his opening statement before answering. ████████
████████

Extra couches and overstuffed chairs were strewn about the lobby. Secretaries, stenographers and messengers moved a little more swiftly from office to office. Gone were the jitters of yesterday. Now war had become a reality, there was nothing to do but see it through. And this appreciation of the finality of the thing reached down to the last typist. All day long newsmen popped in and out of the Executive Office between visits to other departments and press conferences. At any moment a big story might break and it would be wise to be on hand for a first-hand version if possible.

(more coming later)

12/8/41

(by phone) 5:50 p.m.

To: David Hulburd

From: Felix Belair Jr.

Subject: Roosevelt Goes to Congress CONTINUED

The White House had become the funnel through which all news of Far Eastern operation must flow. At the Navy and War Departments old drinking companions of newsmen were saying: I'm still your friend but you'll have to get it from the White House or not at all. At the White House genial, ███████ Bill Hassett said it would take a few days for us to shake down and then there would be some thought of policy about communiques. He did not say who would issue them but if Steve Early has his way he will not be the mouthpiece for the War Ministry.

All Washington was in the middle of a shakedown cruise and the White House was the focal point. Today the White House showed signs of settling down. Not far behind would come the rest of the capital. Once war came Washington started looking facts in the face. In a week or so Washington would begin to make sense.

Franklin Roosevelt has passed from reformer to emergency President to War President. From now on he would see none but of those officials engaged in the conduct of the war abroad and home.

Wire from Jerry Greene, Washington, D.C. -- to David Hulburd, December 8, 1941 -
4:30 p.m.

Washington color:

Tight knots of people pressed smotheringly around half a dozen portable radio sets scattered through the crowd lining the sidewalks of the Capitol plaza. Minutes before, the Presidential caravan had swished up the drive, depositing the Roosevelt and Cabinet officers at the south entrance to the Capitol itself. Metallic voices from the radio speakers describing the scene inside the House Chamber were the only sound to rise above the heads of the tense, still spectators.

There was nothing to be seen except the hard, grey walls of the Capitol, bright and solid in the clear, pale noonday sun, except the dozens of policemen stalking about at every corner, in the street, along the sidewalk. Yet the face of every individual, the faces of all those huddled over the radios, were turned directly toward the towering pillars of the Capitol. There was a church-like hush, a sullen, angry silence. It would be ten minutes before President Roosevelt mounted the dais to ask recognition of the war by Congress. But those in the crowd outside who did speak, spoke in whispers.

What was the silence of shock last night, today was the cold, determined hatred of an outraged people. There was something of the tension of a lynching mob, a mob where there are no masks, where each individual is happy to be identified with the purpose of the assembly. A youngster barely above high school age, her bare legs tinged with purple from chill, above the anklet socks, clung tautly to the arm of her escort, a slight young lad in uniform of a Navy enlisted man, a youth whose jaw muscles rippled as he stared ahead stiffly through horn-rimmed glasses. "Gee," the girl whispered audibly, "Ain't there a way a woman can get into this thing?"

Fifty people were close enough to hear the remark but not a head turned in curiosity, not a smile cracked. The sailor did not answer. The girl chewed her lower lip.

Greene, Washington, Dec. 8, 1941 - ~~drinks~~ 4:30 p.m.

There had been cheers when the President passed by; there were cheers when he left. There were more cheers after the message than before. But before the hurried glimpse of Roosevelt and afterward, there was quiet, quiet as if those who were watching realized that there was scant time for vocal demonstration.

All over downtown Washington those same knots of people ~~drinks~~ ganged around parked automobiles which had radios, listening in the same unsmiling, intent seriousness. There were no wisecracks, there were few exchanges of remarks of any kind.

Washington was at work when the President went up to Capitol Hill, and, beyond a mob around the Treasury Department building, there were comparatively few lining Constitution Avenue to watch the procession.

Down Along the West End of Constitution Ave., more of the machine gun army guards, more of the stiff, tin-hatted troops with fixed bayonets stood at every door of the munitions building. Not yet were there more than the usual blue-uniformed cops at the Navy building.

But over under the shadow of the Lincoln Memorial, a tough, efficient squad lounged at easy alertness back of a drab, snub-nosed machine gun, set up to command the approach to the Memorial Bridge. Troops with fixed bayonets paced their beats at the bridge entrance. There was a duplication of this scene at the 14th Street bridgehead, except here those men not attending the gun warmed their hands before a small fire back at one side.

Without hysteria, without fuss, but with a solid, harsh determination, Washington went to war.

TO: David Hulburd (via telephone Dec. 8, 1941
　　　　　　　　　　　　　　　　　　　　　4:50 p.m.   - em)
From: Crosby Maynard

　　　Add Washington scene during the President's speech.

　　　25 officers, top men in the Navy's Bureau of Aeronautics, gathered a few moments before 12:30 p.m./today in the large corner office of their chief, Rear-Admiral Jack Towers. Towers was not present, was said to be with the Secretary at the Capitol.

　　　Gray and white-haired four-stripers were very much in evidence; there were a few commanders, a very few of lesser rank. All were in uniform, all were serious, most were very calm, silent. The greetings exchanged were formal. Salutes, ranks were strictly observed.

　　　They listened to the President in absolute silence. Cigarettes burned out. New ones were not lighted.

　　　As the President finished, there followed the first bars of the Star Spangled Banner.

　　　An unidentified officer said one word:

　　　"Gentlemen!"

　　　25 officers came to their feet at rigid attention.

　　　As the last words died away there was a very short pause.

　　　"Gentlemen, we have work to do".

　　　The officers filed out.

　　　　　　　　　　　　　- - - - -

December 8, 1941
7:40 p.m.

To: David Hulburd

From: Wilmott Ragsdale

ROOSEVELT:

FDR is standing up well under the pressure. He had only five hours sleep last night, looked fresh but grim today when he made his address to Congress.

During the afternoon he demonstrated once again his ability to snatch relaxation from heavy hours. After talking with Litvinof, he relaxed on his office sofa and slept soundly for an hour.

TO: DAVID HULBURD   5:05 P - 12-8

FROM: FRANK MCNAUGHTON   Wire from WASHINGTON

CHAMBER COLOR

The air was snappy, crisp. The atmosphere one of high-voltage tension ready to spark and bridge the gap to war at the slightest touch of the switch when Congress -- knowing war, thinking war, talking war, ready for war -- started streaming into the Capitol today.

There was not a man who did not know that before nightfall, the awful strength of America would be thrown into a struggle six thousand miles away that coiled and plunged its sting into even thick-hided isolationists, forced them to get their heads up and see what the world was about.

"Hell, it's the only thing to do. Shoot the God damned living Hell out of them," exploded isolationist Dewey Short of Missouri, Republican rable-rouser and bitter opponent of the President. There was only one cry -- war. There was only one question -- would it only be Japan, or Germany and Italy with her? No one knew. Everyone speculated that by laying off Germany and Italy, forcing them to take the initiative as Japan had taken it, the collective mind of America's millions could be solidified on anti-Axis war as it has become united, overnight, on a war with Japan.

Early this morning, a heavy guard of Marines was posted around the Capitol, more than 200 Secret Service men spread through the Capitol, searched even the Speaker's office. Fully 400 policemen were lined up at the south side of the Capitol, reviewed, and then stationed in and around the building.

The Speaker's office was a madhouse. Egg-bald little Sam was seen. Army men, Navy men, telephoning frantically for late news, pulling legislative wires, conferring with Majority Leader McCormack, Minority Leader Joe Martin,

Page 2 - To: David Hulburd
From: Frank McNaughton 5:05 P - 12 - 8

Foreign Affairs Leader Sol Bloom, greasing the skids for the war resolution. A similar scene was going on in the Senate Foreign Relations Committee room over at the other end of the Capitol where Barkley, Tom Connally, Vice-President Henry Agard Wallace were meshing the gears for a quick take-off to war.

Down on the first floor, on the House side of the Capitol, the staff of aged house chief doorkeeper Joe Sinnott were going crazy. Tickets for the galleries were being dispensed there - one for each Congressman. The Senators tickets had been sent to Barkley's office.

(more coming)

Second Take - Chamber Color - From McNaughton 12-8

Dozens of Congressmen wanted one-two-three tickets: They get one. A messenger from the office of Admiral Harold R. Stark, Chief of Naval Operations, waited for an hour in the line outside Sinnott's door. It became a jam, a crush, as the hour neared for the President's address. The House was to meet at 12 Noon, but it was 12:5 before bald, raspy-voiced little Speaker Sam Rayburn whanged his heavy gavel - he keeps two handy, a light and a heavy - called the House to order, then ordered "all unauthorized" persons who had cadged seats at the rear of the chamber, to clear out. There was a bustling, scraping of chairs, and dozens of gate crashers moved back behind the iron and bronze railing in the chamber. Most members of Congress, heeding Rayburn's orders telephoned night-long last night, were in their seats by noon.

Tall, toothy majority leader John W. McCormack, a Massachusetts Irishman to the core, his iron-grey hair flying wildly, his black suit flecked with cigar ashes, hot-footed it to the rostrum, whispered in Rayburn's ear. Little Sam, in a freshly-pressed blue business suit, nodded vigorously, his pince-nez glasses bobbing on his nose.

McCormack scrammed back to the two desks on the Democratic side, in the middle of the chamber, took a seat behind the House microphone, pushed slightly at the broadcasting mikes placed in front of him. Minority Leader Joseph W. Martin of Mass. - hitherto voting isolationist with the majority of his Party - rushed about conferring with the Republicans, patting them on the shoulders, pulled out his written speech, gave it a glance, shoved it back into his pocket.

Doorkeeper Sinnott announced a message from the Senate. It was the passage of House Concurrent Resolution 61, agreeing to a joint session. Three minutes after the House met, the Senate was filing into the chamber. Vice President Wallace helped along octogenarian, fiery old Carter Glass of Virginia; the Republican and Democratic leaders, McNary and Barkley walked arm in arm; aged, infirm Republican

Second Take - Chamber Color - From McNaughton 12-8

Dozens of Congressmen wanted one-two-three tickets: They get one. A messenger from the office of Admiral Harold R. Stark, Chief of Naval Operations, waited for an hour in the line outside Sinnott's door. It became a jam, a crush, as the hour neared for the President's address. The House was to meet at 12 Noon, but it was 12:5 before bald, raspy-voiced little Speaker Sam Rayburn whanged his heavy gavel - he keeps two handy, a light and a heavy - called the House to order, then ordered "all unauthorized" persons who had cadged seats at the rear of the chamber, to clear out. There was a bustling, scraping of chairs, and dozens of gate crashers moved back behind the iron and bronze railing in the chamber. Most members of Congress, heeding Rayburn's orders telephoned night-long last night, were in their seats by noon.

Tall, toothy majority leader John W. McCormack, a Massachusetts Irishman to the core, his iron-grey hair flying wildly, his black suit flecked with cigar ashes, hot-footed it to the rostrum, whispered in Rayburn's ear. Little Sam, in a freshly-pressed blue business suit, nodded vigorously, his pince-nez glasses bobbing on his nose.

McCormack scrammed back to the two desks on the Democratic side, in the middle of the chamber, took a seat behind the House microphone, pushed slightly at the broadcasting mikes placed in front of him. Minority Leader Joseph W. Martin of Mass. - hitherto voting isolationist with the majority of his Party - rushed about conferring with the Republicans, patting them on the shoulders, pulled out his written speech, gave it a glance, shoved it back into his pocket.

Doorkeeper Sinnott announced a message from the Senate. It was the passage of House Concurrent Resolution 61, agreeing to a joint session. Three minutes after the House met, the Senate was filing into the chamber. Vice President Wallace helped along octogenarian, fiery old Carter Glass of Virginia; the Republican and Democratic leaders, McNary and Barkley walked arm in arm; aged, infirm Republican

Page 2 - Second take - Chamber Color - From McNaughton 12-8

isolationist Hiram Johnson of California linked arms with tall, silver-haired Elmer Thomas, Oklahoma Democrat. It was arranged as a demonstration of solidarity, politics out, a Democrat and a Republican in many cases marching along together.

(more coming)

Third Take - Chamber Color - From McNaughton 12-8 5:55P

    Up in the Executive Gallery, Mrs. Eleanor Roosevelt, in black hat, black suit, wearing a silver fox fur, peeked from behind one of the tall, upright girders installed a year ago to keep the house roof from falling in. She had one of the poorest seats in the House.

    Sinnott announced the Supreme Court, and they marched in, Chief Justice Harlan F. Stone's bulldog jaw set in hard lines.

    Old isolationist, British hating Republican representative, George Holden Tinkham of Massachusetts waddled around the wall of the House, his beard freshly combed, wearing a freshly-pressed blue suit in strange contrast to his usually disheveled garb. He hauled up a chair close to the left of the speaker's rostrum, bowed, sat down.

    Secretary Hull led in the Cabinet, and he looked almost like a ghost risen for the occasion. Tall, slightly stooped, he seemed almost exhausted. His face was deeply lined, sad. His white hair was neatly brushed, set off by his blue suit, black tie and white soft-collar shirt.

    One Missouri Congressman, carrying a check for $3,000, vainly tried to buy Defense Stamps at the Capitol post office, finally wound up investing in National Defense Bonds.

    In full uniform, Admiral Stark, General George C. Marshall, Brig. Gen. Henry H. Arnod talked earnestly together on the House floor, finally took seats over at the left of the Chamber, in front of the diplomatic corps from which the Axis diplomats, to a man, were missing. Cadaverous, tall Lord Halifax leaned over, whispered long and fervently to Admiral Stark, checking up on the latest information for Britain, too, was fighting at Hong Kong and Singapore.

    Joe Martin pointed a stubby forefinger at the chest of isolationist Ham Fish, lectured him, and Fish nodded vigorous agreement. A dozen children were on the floor,

Page 2 - Third Take - Chamber Color - From McNaughton 12-8

sitting in their parents' laps. Back at the rear of the Republican side of the Chamber, delegate Sam King from Hawaii talked with round-headed, bald and bitter Harold Knutson, only man now in the House who voted against war in 1917, ▓▓▓▓▓▓▓▓▓▓▓▓▓▓▓▓▓▓▓▓▓▓▓▓▓▓▓▓▓▓▓▓▓▓ -- talked with first one member, then another.

The President got 1-1/2 minute ovation when he hobbled up the ramp to the speaker's dias on the arm of son James who was in his Marine uniform.

For the first time in eight or nine years Republicans generally applauded Franklin D. Roosevelt. Only a few sat on their hands -- Hiram Johnson of California, William Lambertson of Kansas, Ulysses S. Guyer of Kansas.

(More coming)

TO: DAVID HULBURD

FROM: FRANK MCNAUGHTON

12-8 6:05P

Fourth Take - Chamber Color

It was the first time the Republican Party, in bulk, en block ever gave Franklin D. Roosevelt anything but the silent treatment.

The President, in formal morning attire, took a firm grip on the reading clerk's stand, flipped open his black, looseleaf notebook like every schoolchild uses, adjusted his glasses, took a long, steady look at Congress and began to read.

The hum and overtones which had rumbled through the galleries, across the floor for an hour, died out instantly. The Chamber was brilliantly lighted, and as the President read, he gazed almost directly into a battery of floodlights which had been arranged for the photographers. A thousand people were behind the rails, another two thousand in the galleries. The press gallery was jammed to brimming, a hundred reporters tried to peer through the doors.

Speaker Rayburn, introducing the President, made it snappy: "Senators and Representatives, I have the distinguished honor of presenting the President of the United States."

It was Roosevelt at his best; an hour later, the House at its best.

A year ago, Franklin Roosevelt trembled as he adjusted his nose pincers to read his annual message to Congress, a message condemning the Axis. He almost dropped his glasses that day. Today, that tremor was gone. His hand was firm, its muscles bulging as he gripped the desk, as he thumbed the five pages of big print. His face was grim; a wisp of iron-grey hair hung slantwise along his forehead. But the main thing -- the hand was firm, the voice steely, brittle with determination.

When he said America would remember "this onslaught," Republicans and Democrats broke into applause. In a front row seat, Chief Justice Stone, whose legal precepts have struck hard for freedom, nodded his approval. Again, when Mr. Roosevelt said "righteous might" will win through, the Congress, the Supreme Court, the Diplomatic

Page 2 - Fourth take - Chamber Color - From McNaughton

Corps leaped to their feet, gave a full minute of wild applause ... "We will gain the inevitable triumph -- so help us God." Again Congress applauded. The Roosevelt jaw was thrust out, there was no show of weakness, no lack of confidence. It was an almost brutal display of the will to win. Then -- up with his right hand, a determined smile, a wave to Congress and to the galleries. Again wildness.

It had taken exactly 10 minutes -- undoubtedly, according to Congressmen, the shortest war message ever delivered to an American Congress.

Speaker Rayburn congratulated the President, accepted a copy of the address; Wallace congratulated him. Rayburn proclaimed the joint session ended.

The phrase is McCormack's - "The President at his best; the House at its best."

(more coming)

TO: DAVID HULBURD

FROM: FRANK MCNAUGHTON   6:18 P 12-8

Fifth Take - Chamber Color

Immediately, McCormack moved to send the President's message to the Foreign Affairs Committee, have it printed, Rayburn declared the motion adopted, then McCormack waved a sheet of white paper, said he had sent the resolution to the Clerk's desk, moved to suspend the House rules and pass it immediately.

Aged, grey-haired, ill House reading clerk, Alney E. Chaffee, read the resolution, House Joint Resolution 254, declaring war on Japan. Rayburn asked if a second were demanded. Joe Martin said a second was requested. Vainly, Jeanette Rankin, at the rear of the Chamber, leaped up to her pipestem legs, protested shrilly, sought to lodge an objection. Rayburn almost brutally ruled that an objection could not be entertained, that no unanimous consent request had been propounded. McCormack used just 20 seconds to defend his motion, said Japan had attacked, moved its adoption. Joe Martin followed, reading his prepared speech that he had written out painstakingly in his hotel room at nearly 3 o'clock this morning. It was a plea for all-out unity, no more strikes, full prosecution of the war. The members leaped up, cheered little Joe, rushed over to congratulate him.

There were yells of "vote, vote, vote," from the democratic side. Rayburn, pounding like a piledriver, shouted, "It won't be long," and pleaded, "Let us maintain order at this time particularly."

Little Sam's voice was almost reverent. Then Ham Fish said his piece, rather read it from a crumpled sheet of onion skin paper, in a high singsong voice and with apparent nervousness. He would, at the proper time, he said, seek an assignment with a combat unit "preferably colored," as he did in the world war.

Again Jeanette Rankin flounced to her feet. "Sit down, sister," yelled short, thin John M. Dingell of Michigan.

Rayburn recognized Chairman Sol Bloom. Bloom hunched over the microphone, like a brown teddy bear in his brown suit, and said one short mouthful: "Speedy action, not words, should be the order of the day." Then little bantam-like Luther Johnson of Texas demanded war, immediately. McCormack slipped over to the Republican side, whispered in Joe Martin's ear, patted Joe affectionately on the arm. Politics was adjourned.

Grey-haired, ex-war nurse Edith Nourse Rogers of Massachusetts said Japan had "stabbed us in the back." The President used the same term against Mussolini in his Charlottesville speech in the summer of 1940. Black-haired, pretty, Mrs. Katharine Byron of Maryland, mother of five sons, widow of a Congressman, said her husband served in the world war, said she was "willing to give my sons if necessary," said she favored war. So did black-haired, formerly oppositionist Joseph E. Casey, Massachusetts Irishman.

(more coming)

TO: DAVID HULBURD

FROM: FRANK MCNAUGHTON   6:42 P 12-8

Sixth Take - Chamber Color

The House was getting restless. Speaker Rayburn called on Republican, white-haired, swarthy-faced, bulky Charles A. Eaton of New Jersey, one of the few Republicans who, years ago, was declaring that aggression was a plot of world conquest, and who, when Japanese were stripping English women in Tientsin, pleaded for a strong American course; told Congress "there are some things a man had better die against than submit to once."

An orator of the Old school, Eaton shunned the microphone, boomed in a loud roar that America had met "the call to unity . . . the call to courage . . . the call to victory." It would be necessary to kill this accursed monster of tyranny and slavery," . . . it would "be a long battle," but America would not stop short of victory.

At 1:04P, Rayburn ordered the roll call. Again Jeanette Rankin tried to interrupt proceedings, and stop the roll call. She was again brutally thrust off by Rayburn. She sat down in a back row seat, drummed her fingers on the arms of the seat, smiled in a bemused manner.

Down the line, without a break, the isolationists voted for war. Even Tinkham, pointing his beart at a rakish angle, bellowed his "aye" vote. Fish of New York, Knutson of Minnesota, Ludlow of Indiana, Mundt of South Dakota, Peterson of Georgia, Rabaut of Michigan, holding his little daughter in his lap, Rankin of Mississippi, Vorys of Indiana and dozens of others who have been the House core of ostricism. The clerk reading the roll call, Irving Swanson, called, "Rankin of Montana."

"No," Jeanette Rankin smiled. "SSSSSSSS." The hisses echoed through the House Chamber, and Rayburn violently pounded the gavel, until the razzing subsided. Swanson proceeded with his roll call.

Jeanette Rankin still smiled. A dozen Republican Congressmen rushed back to the rear of the Chamber, ganged up and sought to change her vote -- Everett M. Dirksen

Page 2 - Sixth Take - Chamber Color From McNaughton 6:42 P 12-8

of Illinois, Francis D. Culkin of New York, Forrest A. Harness of Indiana, Harold Knutson of Minnesota, white-haired Democrat isolationist, James F. O'Connor of Montana, Bulky George H. Bender of Ohio, Karl Stefan of Nebraska, curly-haired James Van Zandt of Pennsylvania, Baldish blocky Karl Mundt of South Dakota, tall George Dondero of Michigan, big-raw-boned Paul W. Shafer of Michigan, and James W. Mott of Oregon.

She smiled, argued, refused. What did she tell them? That it might all be a mistake, it might be propaganda. How did Congress know for sure that Hawaii had been attacked? It might be another Presidential ruse. There was so much propaganda nowadays. Look at the Kearney and some of those other incidents. It might turn out to be nothing more than propaganda. No, she wouldn't change her vote. ▮▮▮▮▮
▮▮
▮▮

(more coming)

TO: DAVID HULBURD

FROM: FRANK MCNAUGHTON 6:58 P - 12-8

Seventh Take - Chamber Color

There was no weeping in the galleries, or on the floor when the house voted. It was a grim resolve to go to war. There was another burst of cheering when, at 1:26 P.M. Sam Rayburn whammed the gavel, announced the vote as 388 Aye, one No. Immediately thereafter, the house indulged in another spree of cheering. The Senate sent in its Senate Joint Resolution 116 - identical to the comma with McCormack's Resolution. Quick as a flash, McCormack was on his feet and asked unanimous consent to "take from the speaker's table" the senate resolution and pass it.

"Without objection, the joint resolution is read a third time and passed," Rayburn yelled. Then the proceedings by which the House had passed its own resolution were "vacated."

At 1:32 P.M., eight minutes short of an hour after the President finished, Congress had voted war against Japan. There were no tears. The tension was not as dramatic as when the House passed the amendments to the Neutrality Act. Why? Because this time, America had been attacked, and Congress' will was not to be doubted. Its will was to declare war, fight like Hell, and as the resolution stated, "All of the resources of the country are hereby pledged by the Congress of the U. S. all in for an all-out war, nothing less.

The Senate scene was somewhat the same. Tom Connally plunged in with his resolution. Short discussion by Connally, by Arthur H. Vandenberg. No disagreement. Then the roll call. Two names stood out above the rest in that roll call. Little squint-eyed Gerald P. Nye, who has been the darling of the American Quislings, intimate of Charles A. Lindbergh. He couldn't muster the guts for a No. He voted Aye.

(more coming)

TO: DAVID HULBURD

FROM: FRANK MCNAUGHTON   7:07 P 12-8

Eighth & Last Take - Chamber Color

Robert M. LaFollette, Jr., voted Aye. Venerable old George W. Norris of Nebraska also voted Aye. There was not a dissent, 82 to nothing, a complete shutout of America First, a route of isolationism beyond even the expectations of the President's advisers. Japan accomplished what the emergency, what the eloquence of the President couldn't budge.

The Senate passed its resolution at the chime of 1 P.M.

Again there were no tears.

It was an almost anti-climax in the House and in the Senate. There was no prayerful silence such as when the roll was called on amending the Neutrality Law, no days of debate, no squabbling, no backbiting. It was just the American Congress, its neck bowed, its back arched, and itself buckled down to the job of giving "blood, sweat and tears" in any volume necessary to defeat the most audacious attack of the aggressors.

End.

To: David Hulburd
From: Crosby Maynard

Dec. 7, 1941
11:05 P.M.

Wire from WASHINGTON

Army Statement on Censorship

"Gentlemen, I need not tell you that the United States is at war. You all know that. I have no additional news for you, now. I have called this conference so that we can have a clear understanding of the position of the U.S. Army in the future, as concerns the news which will be released and which you can print."

The speaker was long, lean, hook-nosed Brigadier General Alexander D. Surles, Chief of the Army's Press Relations Section. The occasion was an emergency meeting the Army and the Press held in the untidy press room of Washington's Munitions Building at 7:30 tonight, scarcely five hours after the announcement of the bombardment of Pearl Harbor.

More than 50 reporters were crowded in the small room a few minutes before General Surles arrived. Many of them were White House correspondents, comparative strangers to the War Department, seeking an additional shred of news. Most were in evil temper, because getting into the Munitions Building had suddenly become very difficult. The mild mannered police who had patroled the building on Saturday afternoon had been replaced with regular Army men, in full equipment, gas masks, fixed bayonets, their rifle loaded with live cartridges. The soldiers had orders to exclude all who did not have full War Department credentials and were doing so very effectively.

Throughout the afternoon the radio had issued frequent bulletins telling all officers on active duty to report for work tomorrow in uniform. Most of those at the Department tonight had put away civilian clothes. General Surles was in mufti, apologized, said he hadn't had time to change.

He came to his point immediately. After emphasizing the gravity of the occasion, he said:

"I know there will be questions you will want to ask. I am here to answer them, so far as I am able. But first, let me say this. Our relations in the past have been very pleasant. Now, we reach a new phase in those relations. All irresponsibility must stop.

"I shall do my best to keep you informed of all events that concern me and would be of interest to you. But the time has now come when any failure to protect any information which comes to your possession can mean the loss of American lives.

"So, it has become necessary for the War Department to invoke the act of April 16, 1918 (50 U.S. Code 34). It is a somewhat detailed act but, as it concerns you immediately, I emphasize these points. You and your papers cannot print any reference in any way to troop movements, disposition, location, designation, components or strength outside of the continental U.S. No references can be printed to the movements of troop transports, even if they are in the waters of the continental United States. That is about all. Are there any questions?"

General Surles was asked almost at once to define irresponsibility, in the sense which he intended it to be taken.

"I mean," said Surles," that in the past, certain information has been printed by certain publications which must have given considerable comfort to potential enemies. Now, all loose observation of our regulations must cease. I don't want, even now, for the word 'censorship' to be used, unless it becomes absolutely necessary. Restrictions are necessary. Restrictions are what we are imposing tonight. They must be observed and I am sure that they will be."

He added that there would be no relaxation of the restrictions until conditions warranted, but that when, and if conditions changed, the regulations might be modified.

"I know there will be questions you will want to ask. I am here to answer them, so far as I am able. But first, let me say this. Our relations in the past have been very pleasant. Now, we reach a new phase in those relations. All irresponsibility must stop.

"I shall do my best to keep you informed of all events that concern me and would be of interest to you. But the time has now come when any failure to protect any information which comes to your possession can mean the loss of American lives.

"So, it has become necessary for the War Department to invoke the act of April 16, 1918 (50 U.S. Code 34). It is a somewhat detailed act but, as it concerns you immediately, I emphasize these points. You and your papers cannot print any reference in any way to troop movements, disposition, location, designation, components or strength outside of the continental U.S. No references can be printed to the movements of troop transports, even if they are in the waters of the continental United States. That is about all. Are there any questions?"

General Surles was asked almost at once to define irresponsibility, in the sense which he intended it to be taken.

"I mean," said Surles," that in the past, certain information has been printed by certain publications which must have given considerable comfort to potential enemies. Now, all loose observation of our regulations must cease. I don't want, even now, for the word 'censorship' to be used, unless it becomes absolutely necessary. Restrictions are necessary. Restrictions are what we are imposing tonight. They must be observed and I am sure that they will be."

He added that there would be no relaxation of the restrictions until conditions warranted, but that when, and if conditions changed, the regulations might be modified.

Surles was not prepared to say tonight what the penalty would be for violation of the April 1918 regulations. The statute provides for fine and imprisonment but the severity of the penalty varies, depending on war footing. Presumably, the more severe penalties will be meted to convicted violators but Surles said that was entirely a matter for the courts and not for him to say.

As Surles was finishing, an aide brought him a note, and he announced that orders had been dispatched to Hawaii and Panama authorizing the immediate arrest, by the Army and the FBI, of suspicious aliens.

Finally, as an afterthought, General Surles said that Secretary of War Stimson, Assistant Secretary McCloy and General Marshall had been at their desks when the news broke and, as he was going out the door, he said in answer to a question that he did not believe Christmas leaves would be cancelled.

December 8, 1941
7:43 P.M.

To: David Hulburd

From: Wilmott Ragsdale

Wire from WASHINGTON

Kurt Sell, DNB correspondent and well-known figure around Washington for more than ten years, arrived at the White House to turn in his building pass. "Do you want my card?" "Yes" was the emphatic reply of the first guard, who grabbed it.

Meanwhile FBI men went to Sell's office and collected all U. S. Government identification cards which would permit him into federal buildings.

There are no longer any Italian correspondents in the U. S. Sell was the last German correspondent in Washington.

(Washington - by phone) 12/8/41

To: David Hulburd
From: Robert Sherrod

    For N.A.

Specific paragraph of 1917 Espionage Act is No. 32. But War Department is invoking much broader powers in announcement expected momentarily, covering legal restriction of all information concerning routes, schedules and troop movement, and of transports within or without the U.S. Under act of 1898 as amended 1918. Casualties will be announced but names of unit will not be. Navy also invoking Espionage Act forbidding publication of news considered "of value to the enemy."

TO: DAVID HULBURD

FROM: WILMOTT RAGSDALE

7:35 P 12-8

There is increasing evidence that nobody in Washington was prepared for the attack Sunday.

When a reporter went to the Navy Department at 4 P.M. Admiral Blandy, Chief of Ordnance, was in line to get in and had difficulty because he had no pass. He got in on a driver's license. He had been to the Redskin Football Game. The Navy was letting odd assortments of people in who did not have passes. In the press room the reporter found half a dozen people with no passes at all.

Meanwhile the War Department was so strict that nobody without a special Sunday pass was allowed entrance. When the guards were stationed around the Department later, they were asked whether their rifles were the new Garands or Springfield. "Neither," they replied, "they're shotguns."

End.

From: Washington (by phone)

12/8/41

To: David Hulburd

From: Jerry Greene

Subject: Economic Defense Board and Your Query

Hector Lazo, son of a former Minister to the U.S. from Guatemala and now executive director of the District Stores, a nationwide cooperative chain, today was picked as head of EDB's new European division, will assume his duties this week. Lazo's headquarters are in XXX Washington. He attracted attention of EDB's executive director Milo Perkins because of both his executive ability and his knowledge of Europe.

His appointment rounds out the geographical expansion and reorganization of EDB.

Colonel Royal XXXXXXX Lord of EDB said approximately 100 men were transferred when Carl Spaeth from the Rockefeller committee to EDB.

EDB today cleared x a way last of its red tape, will begin actual requisitioning of inactive stockpiles tomorrow with tin seizures. Formal clearance is expected from OPM tomorrow for seizure of tinplate now lying in seaboard freight-yards, formerly consigned to Europe.

(Washington - by phone) 12/8/41 - 6:40 p.m.

To: David Hulburd for Business

From: John Crider

Subject: Far East Metals

From ███████████████████████████████ not for attribution to him:

Metals most affected by the war are tungsten, chrome, mica, and graphite. About 25% of our next year's supply of tungsten was to come from China via the Burma Road. The Government has about 7,000 tons of tungsten stocks, of which 5,000 are tightly locked up by Treasury procurement for release only on Army or Navy orders.

We were getting about 30 to 35% of our chrome from the Philippines and New Caledonia. Government stocks hold about 400,000 tons of chrome, which is about a five-months supply. Turkey is one of our other sources of chrome, but we may still be able to get this.

The only source of high-grade mica splittings in the world is India. This type of mica is indispensable in electrical equipment. We use about eight or nine million pounds of this a year, and virtually all is going into defense. The procurement division has some secret stocks of this stuff, and industry also probably has some stocks.

Ceylon is the only producer of a certain grade of graphite. The Government has no stocks of this, but industry probably has some. Other types of graphite come from Madagascar and Mexico.

Since June the U.S. and Britain have taken the entire output of the commodities named above from the sources indicated, with small quantities going to Russia.

If Singapore holds out we will probably continue to get material from southeast Asia, but it is a certainty that most of the shipping from Asia will now be routed around Cape of Good Hope.

Wire from Robert Sherrod to D. Hulburd - Dec. 8, 1941 (Washington)

A Congressional leader who has access to reports from the Pacific (off record: ███████ told a reporter: "This is the blackest day in American military history since 1812." This might tie in with Congressman Dingell's demand for court martial of five army and navy leaders, including Admiral Kimmel and General Hap Arnold. (See press dispatches).

(Washington - by phone)   12/8/41   6:10 p.m.

To: David Hulburd

From: Robert Sherrod

Reliable sources say they know definitely the U.S. had not reached an agreement with Russia by Dec. 1 on what Russia would do if the U.S. and Japan went to war. One source says there is much gnashing of teeth around the State Department because a quid pro quo was not reached at the time we agreed to send Lend-Lease material to Russia. He doubts that an agreement has been reached in the past week.

TO: DAVID HULBURD   Wire from WASHINGTON

FROM: WILMOTT RAGSDALE   7:17 P 12-8

STATEMENT BY EX-AMBASSADOR DAVIES

The following statement on the Russian position in the Far East hostilities was prepared by Joseph Davies, former Ambassador to the Soviet Union, at the request of TIME. It may be quoted directly.

"The question of an attack from Vladivostok or from American Air Bases in Siberia upon Japan's wooden cities, is one for the Military High Commands and the Governments of Britain, the Soviet Union and the U.S. Japan's infamous attack provided unity not only in the U.S. but assured a united front on the world battle lines. Japan has a non-aggression pact with the Soviet Union and Japan is in deadly fear of bombing from the air because of her wooden cities. Japan would undoubtedly desire to try to keep the Soviet Union out of the fight. Hitler's interest might be to have the Soviet Union attacked on two fronts. If the mobilization of Japan's troops in Manchukuo means an attack upon the Red Banner Army on the East, it is certain that she will be gravely menaced by bombattacks from Vladivostok.

"The next few days ought to throw some light upon what the plan is. If Japan, as now seems indicated, wishes to take advantage of the non-aggression pact with the Soviet Union, the Allied Commands will have to determine their policy with long-range consideration as to which would be best; whether to run the risk of a pincer German movement against the Soviet Union or to bomb Japan from the air. There is always the question involved of winning a battle and possibly delaying victory. As long as the Government of the Soviet Union maintains its entity and the Red Army remains intact, Hitler will never feel secure on the land. Britain and the U.S. control the seas and have enormous supplies of man power and industrial production. The Soviet Union has proven its great effectiveness. It may be a long haul but ultimate victory is certain."

End.

(Washington - by phone) 5:50 p.m. 12/8/41

To: David Hulburd
From: John Crider
Economic Action

U.S. business found itself submitting this week to the necessity for tightened Government control. The smoke hardly cleared from Japan's first treacherous attack on Hawaii when long-readied economic machinery started moving in Washington:

Using his customs and asset-freezing mechanism, Secretary Morgenthau loosed some 4,000 Treasury agents to forcibly cover all economic ties between Japan and the U.S. Every Japanese bank or business concern in the U.S. was visited, taken over.

The economic defense board invoked a "total embargo" on shipments of every kind to Japan or its occupied territory.

President Roosevelt, meeting with heads of Government financial agencies, decided to keep the securities, bond and commodity exchanges open unless some chaotic uncontrollable condition developed. However, the commodity exchange administration on Tuesday innovated by freezing futures in soybeans, wheat, butter, eggs and flaxseed at the Monday level.

Invoking the trading with the enemy act, Morgenthau closed the borders to Japanese or their agents, and declared it illegal to transact business with Japanese.

Plans were immediately announced for putting the defense industry of the nation on as nearly a continuous operating basis as may be possible.

The time had arrived for formalizing control in certain areas such as in fuels, transportation and capital issues which, until Monday, had been supervised by loose cooperative arrangements between Government agencies. While something

#2,
Economic Action

along the lines of the capital issues committee of World War I was forecast, Morgenthau said he preferred the informal cooperative method if it continued feasible. Capital issues will be controlled.

Price control automatically got a new set of teeth with the declaration of war. Lawyers disputed the expense of price Tsar Henderson's legal powers in the absence of a precise legislative definition, but no one doubted that from Dec. 8 Henderson would no longer have to rely upon "jawbone control." The necessity for administration's much-chastised price-control bill became academic. In any event, Henderson will need, and probably will employ, greater power than that bill contains.

Morgenthau, as yet unrelenting in his demand for a limitation of corporate profits to 6%, said higher taxes proportionate to the greater war expenditures now needed, would be required; that the public would be more willing to pay in a state of declared war.

The President and Vice President of the New York Federal Reserve Bank stayed at their posts all night Sunday with beds handy in case they got time for a nap.

Morgenthau said the Government did not enter the bond market to support prices when war was declared on Monday. He found the price drop in Government bonds on that day most gratifying.

Fighting a war of great distances, Washington immediately turned its attention to tighten up domestic consumption of fuel needed by the Navy and Air Corps.

LONDON CABLE Unnumbered

From Mary Welsh to David Hulburd -- December 8, 1941

Herewith Britain's reactions, including Commons: Public reactions: excepting newsmen only the fewest Britons heard the news until BBC's nine p.m. news (the week's widest audienced program), when cool, pedagogue-voiced Alvar Liddell led off the news with "President Roosevelt has announced that the Japanese have bombed the Hawaiian base of the United States fleet at Pearl Harbor." In the West End Restaurants, bars, hotel lobbies, the news spread like fire in heather, but in the average, especially lower class, English home the news which was so undramatized by BBC carried little significance. No news was flashed on movie screens as in the United States and no further BBC bulletins until midnight, and the average Britisher went to bed before that, mildly remembering Hawaii was somewhere in the Pacific and wondering what the bombing meant -- little more.

But among politicians, diplomats, United States and British journalists, there was wild excitement with offices frantically trying to reach country week-enders, embassy phones and Western Union head office snowed under. There were no crowds at Whitehall or the American Embassy where Marine Guard strength was doubled. The embassy was a beehive bedlam all night, with everybody rushing to duty, sending out for food and drink, including Champagne, for, like most Americans in London, the Embassy wanted to drink privately and unofficially, not to death and destruction but in relief and to the clarification of the morass of academic issue-dodging.

Winant, who had been week-ending in the country with Churchill, conferred with Churchill until 2 a.m., then had a long conference with Biddle, and was working again by 8 a.m. Today the embassy is still a minor bedlam, but the average Britisher is still calm though sympathetically. This morning seven British friends telephoned me offering sincere and still surprised condolences, such as "Terrible to think it's spread even to you." And "So sorry about your fleet losses." But "Too bad for you, but I'm feeling a slight sadistic pleasure that the war has caught up with our people who rushed over to your country." (There's always been resentment of Britishers who escaped the war to America.)

When questioned on their apathy, bookkeeper, barman, secretaries, elevator men explain: "It's a long way away." And "Won't it stop lend-lease things coming here?" And (cockney) "Thar's a certain amant of excitement abaht it I suppose."

Certainly primary reactions of the British mind, as evidenced by Public, Commons and the press, are firstly the war's effect on lend-lease, secondly worry over Pearl Harbor fleet losses, thirdly that the U.S. won't declare war on Germany. Few, even politicians, seem to grasp the enormous reorientation of war strategy now necessary. They are still thinking of Britain's front line, not perceiving that British and United States are chiefly factories delivering goods to action via whichever route is most sensible. Housewives even mention they are afraid Britain will get no more lend-lease food. Certainly the average Briton doesn't see the declaration's production impetus and therefore is unable to weigh it against naval losses and lend-lease holdups.

There's evidence that sentimentally, illogically Britons in their secret hearts are slightly sorry they no longer stand alone. Old soldier who remembers how he earned a shilling daily in the last war and could buy fried eggs and french fried for ninepence at Passchaendale, and how at the Yankees arrival the same dish shot up to two shillings sixpence. He's worried the Yanks will say they won this war, too.

Herewith Commons: Since Commons customarily doesn't meet on Mondays, many M.P.'s started out at the crack of dawn to reach Commons on time, found no trains, thumbed lifts, arrived breathless. Commons' catering manager Robert Bradley, whose staff is ordinarily off duty, rushed out to markets, started fires himself, then found the staff turning up voluntarily, and lunch buns, sausages, cakes were ready on time. By 2:45 crowds were standing at the members' gate giving their

page 3 -- unnumbered London cable from Mary Welsh, Dec.8,1941

usual little cheers for their favorite ministers, and the central lobby was jammed with MPs and friends, especially Americans hoping to gain last minute entrance to the House. Lady Astor telling a friend "I simply can't believe it" was interrupted by a Russian haltingly asking her to find some MP friend of his, and Astor replied "Certainly will. I don't like your politics, but you're great fighters."

Mobs pushing into the Chamber were suddenly shoved aside making room for Churchill and his wife, Churchill looking tired eyed but amused at the crush, and Clemmie smiling, wearing her most informal hair scarf, sports fur coat, flat heels. (Flash: We've just heard a rebroadcast of Roosevelt's declaration and now comprehend Churchill's amazing gravity and general Common's solemnity, which obviously grows out of the fact that the United States didn't declare war on Germany, which all but the pessimists here were hoping and expecting.)

Commons was nothing like the broadcast of the joint House session in the United States. There was only a mild ripple of cheering a couple of times, once at Churchill's "The Japanese began a landing in northern Malaya ... and they were immediately engaged by our forces which were ready." And "The root of the evil and its branch must be extirpated together." Churchill with typed quarto-page notes on a new (since the bombing) black leather dispatch box, read his speech using black-horn rimmed glasses. He didn't produce any usual dramatics, telling inflections or brilliant pauses, didn't give the final sentence about light any of his usual oratorical mastery.

Although the MPs and the gallery didn't know his now obvious reason for restraint, they followed his lead, responded in minor note, causing the <u>Herald Tribune's</u> Joe Evans when exiting to say: "Don't know why I came ... wasn't hardly worth it."

Undoubtedly Roosevelt's declaration will be a bitter disappointment here. The narrow Commons balconies held an array of Ambassadors, including Polish, Brazilian, Turkish, Chinese, also Canadian High Commissioner Massey, United States Naval Attache Vice-Admiral Robert L. Ghormley and temporary Air Attache (in Lee's absence) Colonel Arthur McChrystal, both for the first time in uniform. The only empty seats on the Commons floor were Conservative back-benches where sit various MPs now with the forces abroad, etc.

Clemmie sat among the diplomats and RAF in the right balcony, Lords and other diplomats in the left balcony (both have only one row of seats), Pamela Churchill was among the press who were noisy, running to the telephone.

Lobby conversations afterwards were amazingly noncommittal, everybody wanting more news and wondering about Germany. Press reaction was general and interpretative rather than exciting, with Mirror's Cassandre saying: "It would not have been commensurate with Nipponese dignity to have kept silence at a batch of awkward questions put to them by paleskinned foreigners .... Mr. Kurusu has blandly denied ... the effect of this soothing syrup has been rather similar to a fireball being tossed into a gunpowder factory. The morality of the New Order, both eastern and western brands, is such that the sound of a dove cooing is a signal to take cover. The olive branch has become a lethal weapon."

Following from Osborne: Winant, looking no more cavern-eyed than usual, had an off the record press conference with U.S. reporters this afternoon. U.S. Marines with sidearms were stationed today at the previously unguarded Embassy, questioning all comers, including Winant himself. Officials here generally are in a position of "You know more than I do if you read the papers", and awaiting specific information from Washington. There was greatest interest this afternoon in the President's speech which was rebroadcast here at six thirty London time. The weather almost forced BBC to cancel the rebroadcast.

page 5 -- Unnumbered London cable from Mary Welsh - Dec.8,1941

You can assume Americans in the Dorchester, Savoy, Cumberland lounges tensely listening.

Hundreds of the 25,000 Americans in theBritish and Canadian forces, especially air, are already beseiging the Embassy and military super-wigs for transfer to U.S. forces. No specific information on Washington policy and no arrangements for such transfers yet. Also none for U.S. civilians here who want to enlist. These arrangements will be made but, of course, depend somewhat on the President's speech. Chicago Tribune's pale, pudgy veteran Larry Rue is taking a merciless kidding for the Trib's recent exploit. Nearly all Americans I've talked to today and tonight had a sudden overwhelming feeling that they belonged at home. Sketchy available news reports leave everybody tense, uncertain, hungry for more American news. Newswise there's also a keen interest but no specific information yet on what, if any, information and censorship facilities the U.S. will establish here and how they will be keyed with the British.

LONDON CABLE No. 3432

From Walter Graebner to David Hulburd, December 8, 1941

Re 949, from Vaidya:

It is too early yet to give a birds-eye view of Colonial reception but significant developments are already occurring in India which now obtains a key position in the war set-up.

Gandhis has requested the recently released Congress present in Moulana, Abdul, Kalam, Azad, to convene at meetings with a working committee and all-India Congress Committee "at an early date" and has made a further friendly gesture by suspending civil disobedience pending the meeting's decision and thereby presumably/having given Britain the opportunity to revise the attitude to India.

Indians in Britain who share the Congress viewpoint opine thusly; It's no good for Britain to continue to portray India as a "difficult" problem, as if it is some jigsaw puzzle for British statesmen to solve as a peacetime hobby. India's tremendous manpower and abundant natural resources must be made use of now by accepting India as a free, friendly partner in the allied setup and thus make the Allied Front overwhelming against the Fascist front. The Indian Nationalists' non-violence principle can go overboard over-night as most Congressmen accepted it as a matter of necessity. Actually, India can start with certain advantages, such as through 20 years of political agitation she is morally mobilized while for military purposes there is a good, drilled force numbering several hundred thousand composed of Congress militia and Moslen League Volunteer Corps. Incidentally, these are the/only two Indian political parties which count, although and though on internal matters they may differ, they are united in the demand for India's independence. The time has long past for Britain and the Indians to quibble over formulas for a constitution, the Indians will be satisfied if given control of all portfolios including defence, finance, foreign relations, etc., though they are willing to take Anglo-American aid for the interim period. In return for such a liberal gesture on the part of the Allies, particularly Britain, India is capable of putting at least 10 million soldiers (this figure is based on Indians' minimum manpower resources) in the field within 2 years while India can be turned into an allied arsenal for defence between the Pacific and the Mediterranean by gearing up her industrial potential with allied technical aid.

Some British publicists claim India's war efforts are progressing but that isn't so; in more than two years Britain's been able to raise only an army of 750,000, viz. the size of the Rumanian Army, while regarding war production, India in spite of her resources is unable to produce tanks, planes, motors or battleships.

In fighting Japan, Anglo-Americans must reckon to face a force of anything up to 10 millions. The American contribution can be chiefly naval and even if America has enough troops for Malaya, they will have to be carried across a wide ocean which is infested with hostile craft. Britain can muster 5 million soldiers of which a large proportion will have to remain in Britain against threat invasion and for possible counter-invasion in Europe.

She has in addition a garrison in Africa and the Middleast and only the remainder can go to Malaya. As regards Australia, her army will always remain in the vicinity of half a million because of her limited population, and in addition nearly half the Anzacs are already engaged in the Middleast.

From where, then, can the Allies secure numerical strength and armaments for defence of the south Pacific or Middleast, which according to reports last week, the Nazis soon intend invading by air, except from India? India was never pro-Fascist and is willing to throw in her lot with anti-Fascist forces provided she ~~has~~ is accepted as a free and equal partner in the allied fold. There is no need to question Indians' fighting qualities, they have proved it in Libya, Abyssinia and Iraq.

LONDON CABLE NO. 3433

From Jeffrey Mark to D. Hulburd - Dec. 8, 1941.

Regarding the Jap war, I feel sure London reaction is much less intense than you'd imagine. Frankly, the man in the street has as yet no conception of the real implications. He has talked about it at lunch today but reverted to other subjects. Similarly, there's no overwhelming preoccupation in this morning's newspapers. For instance, last night in a pub just after the/nine o'clock news, I heard a party saying the Japs had bombed Hawaii. The most serious observation I heard was, "Hitler has been trying to make a Pacific diversion for a long time."

It is important to realize that to Britishers, Hawaii is not a naval base but a South Sea island with a Hollywood ukulele and hula hula trimmings. The feeling now is that Uncle Sam has been caught with his pants down. The first thought is that it's a good thing as it will get America seriously going but it is qualified by the thought that America will now attend to her own defense needs frantically and tend to neglect British and Russian lease-lend. Secondly, it is thought that she'll remove much of her Atlantic patrol to the Pacific and that this, with increased British naval concentrations at Singapore, will thin out the vital Atlantic life-line precariously.

Regarding the dominions, it's too early yet for any reasoned summary but here's what's available:

Prime Minister John Curtin announced today that "Australian troops are at their battle stations," while Army Minister Forde announced that all forces' Christmas leave was cancelled. The Commonwealth War Cabinet is expected to make a war declaration against Japan later today with Curtin saying, "This is the gravest hour in our history." The only other significant likely internal development is a crackdown on Aussie middleeast troop shipments with renewed agitation for the return of a large proportion of those already there on the "Australia First" slogan.

Page 2 -- London cable no. 3433

There's no official pronouncement of any sort from New Zealand yet but London New Zealander's reaction is almost exactly the same as the British outlined above.

Ottawa cables say the Dominion forces were instructed to engage the Jap enemy wherever found and submission to His Majesty the King for formal war declaration is due later today. Canada also announced that Pacific coast defenses are out on full war footing and a new chain of air bases on the American Alaska border are equipped with radio guide equipment and now in operation. Canadians' reaction here is that the Jap menace is not regarded so formidable at it was regarded a year ago. They are also glad it will quell American isolationism which latterly has been particularly irritating to them.

The South African general reaction is the same as London's and I expect they'll move directly behind the Commonwealth. Also that it will minimize internal disputes and throw dissentients more directly behind Smuts. Most significant reaction is that with the Mediterranean closed to shipping, the Cape route has become of paramount importance. Hitherto, this was not seriously menaced but Jap entry may do so and so bring South Africa nearer the war center.

Meanwhile, the Canadian Royal mounted police are now rounding up Canada's 23,000 Japs which are mostly concentrated in British Columbia. It is further estimated that there's 8,000 Japs in British Borneo Straits and Malay, about 3500 round in Sydney and 2600 in British India and Ceylon. There are no Japs to speak of in South Africa as the immigration law is closed to the entry of Japs and Chinks. It is estimated that there are about 500 Japs in Britain. Apparently the war declaration completely surprised the Jap embassy here from Charge d'Affaires Kamimura down. Says press-secretary Matsui, "We have heard nothing at all from Tokyo. We will have to go back, but how? Everywhere is a battlefield and it's

Page 3 -- London cable no. 3433

going to be very difficult to get back."

The Netherlands East Indies, after the war declaration announced "A state of danger from air attack" and invited the RAF to station aircraft at points supporting the NEI airforce at Ambon and Kupang on Timor Island to assist the NEI aircraft and observe air approaches which also concern Australia.

LONDON CABLE NO. 3434

From S. Laird to D. Hulburd - Dec. 8, 1941

Immediately after the clear reception of Roosevelt's speech, the BBC announcer said, "I think you would now like to hear 'Ballad for Americans'". Then they played a Paul Robeson recording.

LONDON CABLE No. 3435

From Stephen Laird to David Hulburd -- December 8, 1941

Herewith review of local lead editorials today: Best was young Michael Foot's in the Evening Standard: "The whole world is in flames. A battle rages across the seven seas, and every great nation is at war for its life. No corner of this planet remains immune. Perfidy stripped of the thinnest disguise has decreed that no single home and no single human being shall escape the scorchings of this conflict .... The early contest will not be easy for our Allies. The generous material aid which they have given us will be required partly now to save America's existence. A huge fresh strain will be imposed on our sailors and our ships. The next six months will be hard. We shall need all the Dunkirk spirit and more ... The biggest battle is still the battle in Russia for the simple reason that Berlin is still the first lair of this beast which is unloosed among men .... The world is one and the war is one. All the hopes, and now all the energies of the vast majority of the human race, are securely attached to our cause. Believe that the ambitions of young America, that the sacrifice of Soviet Russia, that the long agony of China, that the courage of conquered Europe, that the will of Britain which for one whole year held the pass of freedom, believe that all these great facts can be set at nought by this latest shallow piece of trickery, and you may believe too that the pillared firmament is rottenness and earth's base is built on stubble."

Says the News Chronicle: "If it were not that Japan were the pioneer among aggressors we would say that the Emperor had learnt his part from the Fuehrer to perfection. No one can welcome the extension of indiscriminate slaughter to another wide area of this suffering globe. But if it had to happen it could have happened in several ways less favorable to allied interests. If Japan had struck at Siberia she might have put just that extra strain on the Russian war machine that would have broken it. If she had struck at Britain the free nations would have waited in suspense to learn America's verdict. But Japan has struck at America direct. America is in the war ... All the doubts and questionings that have assailed the government and people of the United States these past protracted months are swept away. The question is resolved for them. They are in the war -- and the war is indivisible .... From today onward such a combination of industrial output and moral determination is forged as makes certain the complete destruction of the aggressors."

The Daily Mirror says: "Hitler's pressure, Hitler difficulties have convinced them (the Japanese) that it is now or never in the division of loot and the search for living space. Were the Axis to be destroyed the Japanese vision of imperialistic expansion must vanish forever. The Axis is suffering severely. Japan is called up in hope of righting the balance. No doubt this last of the hungry jackals is only too willing to support the other robbers. Yet her plunge is a signal of despair as well as a symptom of madness...."

Daily Mails: "...Hitler's methods of unprovoked aggression have been not merely copied, even to the timing of a weekend spring. They have been improved upon with a devilish malignity ... Isolationism dies in the waters of Honolulu. The war which its exponents sought to avoid leaps at America's frontiers .... The Axis powers now dare the might, the resolve, the resources, and the valour of the most powerful nations in the world. In such an array of forces there can be but one decision, long and bitter though the pathway to it may be .... All doubts resolved, all pettiness swept aside, they (Americans) will now find, as we did ourselves in such a crisis, the essential greatness of soul of a people determined to be free."

The Times editorial was dull plodding resume of portents pointing toward the Pacific war, finally rouses itself to say; "....Japan has decided upon war, and she now finds herself faced with forces which, in the long run, she will be powerless to resist ...."

Daily Herald foresees: ".... The Japanese attack will have the effect of

page 3 -- London Cable No. 3435

pushing American production to the peak much more rapidly than would otherwise have been the case. But it will also require yet a further diversion of supplies which were destined for Britain ... Greater than ever, therefore, is Britain's need to organize her own production without delay to the limit of efficiency ..."

Daily Express on the whole was most pessimistic, concludes with "... America is fighting for her own life. Arms workers of Britain and Russia must be ready to provide from their own factories some of the weapons they had expected from America..."

The Telegraph's dull, on the lines of the Times, includes this interesting phraseology: "Now the die is cast and the United States is compelled to take action as a belligerent."

The Daily Sketch outlined the formidableness of the opponent, including: "... Japan is no mean antagonist. Her people can easily be whipped up into a fanatical hatred of the white man and to a frenzy which will make them exceedingly difficult to defeat..."

LONDON CABLE NO. 3436

From Lael Laird and Dennis Scanlan to D. Hulburd - Dec. 8, 1941.

Re Allied governments and U. S.-Japanese war:

Short, goat-bearded Polish Information Minister, Prof. Stankslav Stronski, stated early to a TIME reporter, "Today when the war which Germany started against Poland in September 1939 has become a world war in the fullest sense of the word, there is no one among the Poles who does not realize the importance of that fact which has now assumed such proportions that the problem of the independence and freedom of Poland is not an isolated question but it is the same problem of the freedom of mankind against the forces of aggression, plunder and slavery. ... Poland took up today a position together with all her allies against Japan as she before took up the position against all the allies of Germany ...(recapitulation of German defeats in Russia and Libya) ...it was Germany who has put to Japan the demand 'now or never'.

"Although we are very far away from the theatre of war in the Pacific, we realize that the war in the Pacific is the result of Germany's failures and I think that the cause for which we fight which is common to us and to the Americans has gained a mighty ally who will decide the war in victory for us."

- - -

Here is the TIME exclusive message from DeGaulle:

"To the people of the United States: France, the real France, will fight alongside the great American republic, the British empire, and their allies, against their new enemy who, with the help of treason, has already taken Indo-China. The French Pacific Possessions New Caledonia, Tahiti, New Hebrides, who have already joined Free France, place all they possess at the common disposal in this war for liberty."

(For the colonies mentioned, see LIFE packet 717, TIME packet 366, also LIFE packet 688 for pictures and notes on Dargenlieu who is "Free French High Commissioner for the Pacific Possessions" and is ex-provincial of French Carmelite order. Dargenlieu was a naval officer in the last war, became a Carmelite monk after the war, then at the armistice, joined DeGaulle.)

The following is not for publication before Wednesday:

The Free French will declare war on Japan tomorrow following a National Council conference this afternoon.

For New Caledonia: Inhabitants have formed their own home guard called "La Milice Civique de la France Libre" and Australia has helped to fortify the new harbor defense works including giving heavy coastal defense battery whose New Caledonian gunners were trained in Australia.

- - -

Norway held no special cabinet meeting. Foreign Minister Trygve Lie gave TIME the following exclusive statement, "The Norwegian government and the Norwegian people fully share the indignation of the American people aroused by the Japanese aggression. We are convinced that the great American democracy will come out of the war victorious and that Japan together with the other militant aggression states will suffer a final and decisive defeat. The fight the U.S. has now entered upon constitutes one of the most important links in the common fight of the democracies against fascism and barbarism and the victory of the U.S. will also mean victory for all other free peoples. We Norwegians feel a deep sense of gratitude for the sympathy which the American president and the American people have shown for our fight for freedom. We are convinced that the common fight and the common sacrifices will strengthen the friendship between all free peoples and form a basis for international cooperation after the war."

- - -

Yugoslavia's young King Peter heard the news of the war over the radio in his room at Clare College Cambridge, hot footed to London this morning to keep in touch.

Page 3 -- London cable no. 3436

Yugoslavia's short, grayish Foreign Minister Dr. Momcilo Nincic stated for the press, "The War with Japan represents one logical step in this conflict between the two worlds which are waging an eternal struggle: the world of force and barbarism created by evil forces and the world which believes in good and is working for the progress of humanity and for the equality of men and all the peoples."

"The way in which Japan has committed brutal aggression shows her up as a worthy ally of Germany and Italy and does not surprise anyone. It represents yet another proof of how important and urgent it is to destroy those regimes whose aims and methods are barbarous.

"But the latest aggression of Japan will only result in arousing the American people, I am convinced, and uniting them so that their inexhaustible resources will be mobilized to the fullest extent and will make possible the victory of civilization over barbarism." This message and more will be broadcast by Yugoslavian representative over BBC to Jugoslavia at 9:15 this evening.

- - -

The Belgians held no cabinet meeting as the procedure for/this contingency was entirely outlined in advance. The Belgian government has told its Tokyo ambassador to leave Tokyo with the British and American.

- - -

The Netherlands' Queen Wilhelmina's declaration of war will be broadcast over the Radio Orange to the Dutch people by Prime Minister Gerbrandy at 7:45 tonight. The announcement of the state of war, following the cabinet meeting at 1:30 this morning, was "Not formal" as the formal declaration is awaiting the Queen's proclamation.

LONDON CABLE No. 3427

From Stephen Laird to David Hulburd -- December 8, 1941

If you are shifting the cover to Grew: last October Grew (off the record) told me something like this: "My mission here is ended. The military group taking power here speak a language all their own and argue from premises impossible to comprehend. It is my belief Japan is completely capable of national Hara-kiri, that is, rather than be defeated in a ten years' war of attrition with China, rather than turn north and chance defeat by the despised Communists I think Japan may prefer attacking the greatest powers in the World, Britain and America. Britain and America have always been thought of by the Japanese as great and powerful countries. The Japanese military mind would consider defeat by these powers glorious and honorable."

For Grew finding a fake airbomb in his swimming pool, see our letter from Japan to Mr. Hulburd last October.

LONDON CABLE No. 3429

From John Osborne to David Hulburd -- December 8, 1941

U. S. Naval officers here under Vice-Admiral Ghormley shifted from mufti to uniforms today. Army officially hasn't shifted yet, but some individual officers are in uniforms. Baggy-eyed Ghormley, who is former chief of Navy's warplans division, didn't sleep all night, worked through today with a weary staff.

The Embassy and other U.S. military offices were buzzing all night behind blacked-out windows. Most of the activity was just officers who wanted to know what's what. So far there's been no rush of orders to home.

FYI: General Lee, U.S. Chief Military attache here, will be glad to see you in New York or Washington, but hopes his Christmas visit won't be publicized as he wants to rest privately with his family.

The only direct effect, aside from navy uniforms, against U.S. militarists here so far is the receipt of certain orders to carry out pre-planned administrative procedures regarding information, communications, etc.

Unnumbered London Cable

From John Osborne to David Hulburd -- December 8, 1941

In the Savoy, Dorchester, pink-walled Suivis, and other spots where Americans enjoy expense accounts, they are playing and singing "Over There" tonight. Also Tipperary, There's a Long, Long Trail, etc. Britishers were vastly pleased at first, but today, especially after Roosevelt speech not mentioning Germany, Churchill's with a minimum mention of the U.S., and his and London press reminders that the U.S. now must supply itself, there's a dark undercurrent of apprehension for effects on Britain, Russia and the Battle of the Atlantic. Churchill noticeably was not smooth, not happy when he referred to the "gap" looming in U.S. aid to Britain. Indications already are that this has been a subject of high quarters' discussion.

Graebner feels that with all regard to America's pressing present need we should point out that only balanced perspective and careful joint weighing of each comparative need can prevent the Jap war from immeasurably aiding Hitler. No official decision is known yet on readjusting lend-lease flow, but it is assumed that aircraft and vital ordnance items will almost, or entirely, cease to arrive here for a while.

MANILA CABLE

From Melville Jacoby to David Hulburd -- December 8, 1941

Press Wireless lost contact with the United States.

War feeling hit the populace about noon time when there were full runs on banks, grocery stores, gas stations. All taxis and garage cars were taken by the military, clogging transport systems. Our own planes overhead are drawing thousand of eyes now, while they didn't earlier this morning. The High Commissioners office still holding hurried meetings, while Mrs. Sayre's Emergency Sewing Circle called off this morning's session.

Downtown were building managers' daylight meetings to make basement shelters hurriedly. They found an acute shortage of sandbags over all Manila while Quezon's palace bought the remaining supply of 20,000 bags to reinforce Malacanang shelter. There was a frantic rush this morning to tape all shop windows in town for the first time.

Philippine scouts, riding in big, special orange buses, fully equipped with new packs and uniforms, rounded up a majority of Jap nationals. They took 500 Nips from Yokohama Specie bank and countless others to concentration camps after surprise raids.

Soldiers raiding the Nippon Bazaar in the center of Manila found twelve Japs barricaded inside. They broke down the glass doors, capturing them, found a thirteenth Jap hiding under the counter.

Police inspecting Jap nationals, many of whom appeared with knapsacks packed with tinned goods, etc., found large rolls of bills in the sacks, also a few firearms. Jap women, though not wanted, came with their husbands. Police found one old, but much used set of harbor charts in a Jap building searched.

The general military situation is still flexible, hard to analyze. You have press association reports which are all available until this evening.

Shipping from Manila has been halted. The French steamer Marechal Joffre, in the harbor, will probably be taken.

Reportedly the U.S. legation in Peking has been taken by the Nipponese.

MANILA CABLE

From Melville Jacoby to David Hulburd, December 8, 1941

10 a.m.

Manila has not yet digested the fact of war. Balloon and toy salesmen and vendors on the streets with extra editions are just appearing as fully equipped soldiers are appearing. Small groups of women in hotel lobbies are beginning to collect children at their sides. All this is happening, simultaneously taxi drivers comment: "Not serious--not the Japanese Government's doings -- only the Japanese Military's small mistake in Hawaii."

It is confirmed now that Davao was bombed at six thirty this morning, also Forthay and Baguio where all civilian emergency officials are remaining, also TA.

MacArthur's headquarters were the grimmest place at dawn this morning when the staff was aroused to face war, send troops to their battle stations. Extra headquarters guards arrived around 9 a.m. as officers began donning helmets, and gas masks while grabbing hurried gulps of coffee and sandwiches.

Newsmen were waiting around headquarters deluging the press office. Hart's headquarters were quiet. Airforce headquarters were the scene of most bustling, helmeted men poring over maps, occasionally peering out windows to the sky.

There has been no air alarm in Manila City yet but it is expected by the minute. Rumors are flying very thickly everywhere. It is nearly impossible to get an operator on telephone calls. The High Commissioner's office is blocked off by military police. The whole thing has busted here like one bombshell, though, as previous cables showed the military has been alert over the week.

There is no censorship as yet but the voluntary basis is adhered to.

Rumors are flying very thickly even among informed people. Attacks and defense have not yet taken a definite pattern, however, the Davo bombing possibly signalizing a blitz landing attack.

The Bangkok's radio silence and lack of reports are leaving us cut off from action anywhere else in the Far East.

MANILA CABLE

From Melville Jacoby to David Hulburd, December 9, 1941

The Philippines overnight assumed a war basis with censorships, round-ups/ of aliens, rationing, continual blackouts, evacuation of populated areas. There is a feeling among the populace that there is a long siege in view. The appearances of ack-acks on the parkways, wardens, Red Crossers, brought real live war to Manila. The Filipino and American general populace are just getting the experience of war, far behind even the Chinese children in Chungking, who can distinguish bomber and pursuit sounds, and well know the difference between flash of ack-acks and searchlights. However, in a few days more at this rate, the locals will soon become seasoned veterans of bombings and automatically go for cover instead of watching the "show."

Bleary-eyed Americans are still jovial. It is an oddity to see horse-drawn calashes with Americans rolling in front of the swank Manila Hotel, while all taxis are requisitioned for military usage and gas stations are closed temporarily following yesterday's rush. Life is going on surprisingly normally in the daytime considering the frequent wailing of loud sirens which are still not familiar to the populace. There is a terrific run on groceries and other supplies, especially good concentrates, bandages, iodine, flashlights, kotex. Many stores with bare shelves are closed. All Japanese shops are closed while the Chinese are labeling their shops with signboards reading "Chinese."

The military have already effected a carefully aforeplotted scheme of requisitioning all essentials, even film.

Optimistic signs of the formerly lax Civilian Emergency Administrations are the air wardens helping to direct traffic and avoid panic, cooperating under "advice" from MacArthur's headquarters. Though people are still numbed by the actual attack by the Japs on American soil, they are slowly coming out with grim

Manila, Dec. 9, 1941   Page Two

determination. The smoothness of the Japanese blitz tactics in the air still amaze even ~~xxxxxxxxxx~~ informed people. Though it is militarily unwise to give out detailed information, the Japanese, despite attacks ranging from Thailand to Honolulu, are managing to concentrate their superior aerial forces against the Philippine strategic points. It is obviously a Japanese plan to cripple our striking power, eventually landing according to blitz plans as accomplished in the Far East very recently.

Though the constant unconfirmable rumors persist that the Japanese are landing hither and yon, there is still no real indication of where they will strike hardest. However, my previous messages point out one very likely spot.

It is the United States' policy, despite reported temporary losses of the island linking the Philippines with Hawaii, to hold out in the Far East to the last man, meanwhile striking harder and harder against Japanese bases with material at hand. It is already critically obvious that the entire ABCD strategy leading to the Philippines defense must depend on new and stronger Pacific supply lines. It is foolish to draw over-early conclusions. However, continual daily and nightly exchange visits between Hart, Sayre, and MacArthur, point out the seriousness of our position. Incidentally, Hart and MacArthur are in closest cooperation. When Hart left MacArthur's office this morning, MacArthur escorted him arm in arm to his car. Hart commented on the large passageway under the old wall in MacArthur's office, joked that it is better than anything he has to go in during raids.

Due to lack of adequate communication with other Far East points being blitzed, the U. S. Far East Command is treating the Philippines as a separate defense problem momentarily while U.S. Naval forces alone, but undoubtedly also with the British, are striking powerful blows in the vicinity of the Gulf of Siam.

Naval and military activity are a very close military secret now, even aerial losses from yesterday's and today's battles, one of which was seen over Manila, were

Manila, Dec. 9, 1941

not revealed. It is reliably known that Japanese planes shot down over the Philippines have been from air-craft carriers, also from Formosan bases. Some observers, impressed with the Japs' excellent tactics, accuracy, etc., suspect not only Nazi planning, but possibly Nazi planes of Heinckel type and pilots. The foregoing, however, is absolutely unconfirmed.

The Japs have mixed high altitude bombing, dive bombing and strafing round in all major attacks.

Wire from Wm. S. Howland, Nashville, Tenn. to D. Hulburd - Dec. 7, 1941.

The news came first to Nashville by radio. All three stations, WSM, WLAC and WSIX had flash bulletins of the first attacks. All three have been breaking all programs all afternoon for bulletins.

Most Nashvillians were at dinner when the news came. Many heard it by radio on autos. Because many did not hear it as apparently dead listening time just after church, there was not a big rush on phones then. The Tennessean came out with a swell extra at 4:30 standard time.

The general reaction when people first heard the news was "What are we going to do about it?" That was heard on every side. There was not much indication of amazement that Japan had attackdd but everyone was asking what the American Navy was doing. I have some more good quotes which will send shortly.

I honestly believe that Tennesseans generally are greatly aroused. They always have been among the first to fight for the country and I heard no pacifistic comment tonight. Indication of how seriously people are aroused is that recruiting stations in Nashville have been jammed with call for men wanting to enlist.

Also the Union station was jammed with soldiers who had been on weekend leave rushing to get back to their post at Camp Forrest. All were vigorously expressing eagerness to get at the Japs. Some quotes on this coming later.

When the news came, Nashville and the middle Tennessees were enjoying a brisk, sunny Sunday. Churches were well filled. Most people were on the way home. Sunday dinner was what most were looking forward to. There were no football games and movies do not open until mid-afternoon.

Conversation at all dinner tables centered on the news. Again, general reaction was what America was going to do about it. Tennessean slammed a hot editorial and cartoon in the first edition from which quotes are coming as follows:

"Like a gangster whose ego has broken all bounds, the Japanese have decided to stake all in a desperate challenge to the U. S.

"The Rising Sun they hope is to shine over the teeming millions of the Asiatic world and even beyond. But in reality that sun is destined to set. The war that Japan has started will be ended by the U. S. on its own terms.

"There can be no compromise with the Japanese. They have staked their own fate on the sword and the sequel must be victory or Hari kari.

"And though we shall win we may as well understand at the beginning that it will not be an easy way. But we can say here and now that the sun of Nippon has reached its height and will rise no more."

Wire from Wm. S. Howland, Atlanta, Ga., to David Hulburd, December 8, 1941

Atlanta was just getting up from Sunday dinner to make the most of a sunny, warm afternoon following a cold Saturday, when the radio broke the news of the Jap war. The big station, WSB, jumped out first with a flash from the AP at 2:30 Eastern Standard Time. The flash came at a station announcement time just before the Chicago Round Table program opened. This was broken later by NBC for more bulletins. WSB cancelled the Tony Wand (Wons ?) show and also its transcribed Chilean Nitrate program to give war bulletins. The station immediately went on a 24-hour basis. Another big station, WGST, broke the news on CBS World Today program. The CBS program, Spirit of '41, was on when the flash came from AP but the station waited for CBS to break the news. The other two stations came in with the news shortly thereafter.

The Atlanta JOURNAL came out first with an extra at 4:40 P. M. The CONSTITUTION also extraed a few minutes later. Both were somewhat caught with their pants down but kept running extras to meet demands from nearby towns. Both said it was one of the heaviest runs in history.

Telephones were more jammed here than in Nashville, probably because of the time difference making the people here through with dinner. The phone company had to call in extra operators for both local and long distance.

All the movies broke their programs to make announcements of the war and to allow Army officers to call soldiers to their Post. The biggest picture showing was "Two-Faced Woman" at Loew's. Also showing were "Birth of the Blues" at Paramount, and "International Squadron" at the Roxy, which had a good many soldiers in the audience.

General public attitude was surprise at the manner of attack, followed by what the Atlanta JOURNAL aptly describes as "quietly infuriated." Some quotes following:

End

Wire from W. S. Howland, Atlanta, to David Hulburd, Dec. 8, 1941-2:50 P.M.

SECOND ADD ATLANTA WAR REACTION.

Most spectacular single incident of Atlanta war reaction was closing last night of famed Wisteria Garden Restaurant on Peachtree Street in center of downtown shopping area. Following orders issued by Lindley Camp, head of State Defense Corps, and of Mayor Roy LeCraw that all Japanese nationals must go to residences and remain there, the restaurant closed. Its proprietor is Sada Yoshinuma, a Japanese who has contributed to China relief funds, was perplexed. Said he "I was advised to close and that's all there is to it. I want to cooperate." Many Atlantans, coming downtown for justly famed steak dinners at Wisteria Garden, were perplexed by sign Closed Today which hung on door. The few who were in the restaurant early quickly ate and left.

Closing of this restaurant caused more comment than any other local reaction, as in Nashville, soldiers on leave in Atlanta appeared to welcome news that there was something to prepare for. This was very noticeable at the movies. For example, at Rialto one soldier shouted "Oh boy, this is it," when announcement of war came; and a sailor said "That's what we've been waiting for."

One Atlantan, Sydney H. Banes, whose son in law is Navy officer at Wake Island wired Knox "Allow me to suggest that special Ambassador Kurusu be held in custody until all officers and men of our Navy now at Wake are released."

Following are brief quotes from newspaper editorials:

The Chattanooga Times headed its editorial "WE ARE ATTACKED."

From Times editorial: "The Japanese could have had peace. It is doubtful if any American desires war with Japan. We shall have unity now. The America First Committee will speedily undergo an amazing metamorphosis. It is a terrible thing to be at war again. Now that it has come, we can be glad that we have the chance

Page 2 -- Howland ADD Atlanta War Reaction - Dec. 8, 1941

the men and women in 1917 and 1918 gave us -- the chance to preserve for ourselves and for others what they helped preserve for us, a free people and a Free country. God grant that this time we can win both the war and the peace that comes after it."

Ralph McGill in his One Word More column in the Atlanta Constitution "It is important to keep in mind that war is for the purpose of hurting the other nation, if we don't take off the gloves, if we don't begin to kill as many Japanese as we can, the war will be fumbled and drawn out. It is inconceivable that we should have been caught so asleep. The scrap iron, the oil, the gasoline and the materials we sold Japan in an effort to appease her out of the European war are coming home and killing American citizens, soldiers and sailors."

The American Journal editorial says "War having come to America, we have no other course and no other will but to meet it unflinchingly and to wage it to such a conclusion that the aggressor never again can menace the kind of world we stand for and on which our security depends. We are now one people with one faith, one hope and one baptism of danger and devotion to our dear country's cause."

Those are main points of reaction and newspaper editorializing. As indication of desire of soldiers to get back to posts, Dixie Limited train on which I returned from Nashville, was one hour late account putting on extra cars to handle soldiers from Nashville to Camp Forrest.

Checking further and standing by. Want any reaction to President's speech?

Wire from Wm. S. Howland, Atlanta, Ga., to David Hulburd, December 8, 1941

Add Atlanta war reaction.

Here are some sample quotes:

John Tyler, student, said, "Undoubtedly the Germans prompted the Japs, but I think we should go after Japan and whip her as soon as possible. I only wish I were 20 years old. I'd join the Air Corps so quick it would make your head swim."

John T. Akin, druggist, said: "I think we ought to give 'em everything we've got and clean 'em up quick."

Ralph Tilly, YMCA clerk, said: "I don't like it. I think it's dirty. The Japs pretended to be here on peace missions and stabbed us in the back."

Miss Jo Compton, a stenographer, said: "I want to know what Lewis and Lindbergh think now."

Danny Zell, student, said: "The Japs were damned fools."

Luther Singleton, famed dirt track auto racer, said: "It's like taking a dose of salts. We knew we had to do it but kept putting it off. Now let's get it down and over with. It won't be so bad after all."

Dorris Greene, aviation cadet from Rhode Island, said: "We ought to hop right to it and knock Hell out of them."

Negro population displayed particularly strong unity. A sample of the following quote from O. C. Moore, "Colored folks are good fighters when you get 'em stirred up. Maybe the little yellow men don't know that but they are going to find out."

Generally, quotes were of the same tenor as those in Nashville. More coming.

End.

Wire from Bill Howland, Atlanta - to David Hulburd - December 8, 1941

Add to war reaction:

As details of damage to the Navy xxx were revealed, the general public reaction here in addition to the mountain of anger against the Japs, is the question of how the Navy got caught with its pants down so badly. I heard that xx on all sides on the street during lunch hour. The stores were practically deserted while the President spoke.

Wire from Bill Howland, Atlanta - to David Hulburd - Dec. 8, 1941

Add to war reactions:

Here is a quote from Sergeant Alvin Cullom York at his Tennessee Mountain home, as reported by the Chattanooga Times: "We got to put up a united front and give those folks a lickin' right away. We should take care of the Japs first and then take on the Germans."

The Nashville Tennessean quotes him in an obviously ghost-written story as follows: "I say, on to Victory America. With Senator Wheeler and all Americans, I say, 'Give Them Almighty Hell!'"

First to declare war on Japan in the south was Local Union No. 1442, United Brotherhood of Carpenters and Joiners at Chattanooga which Sunday night issued an official declaration of war "on the Japanese Government and any other Government that may be allied with her against the United States."

All over Atlanta in business offices, groups gathered to hear the Roosevelt speech. Business was practically suspended during that time.

To David Hulburd
From: William S. Howland, Atlanta

Dec. 8, 1941
4:12 A.M.

Following additional info reaction to war. Checkup radio stations shows that WLAC broke in on CBS Philharmonic Orchestra program with first United Press bulletin at one twenty nine Central Standard Time. WSB broke in on NBC University of Chicago Roundtable about same time with flash, WSIX broke in on MBS Fort Dix program with Trans-Radio flash at one thirty six P. M. Central Standard Time.

All three stations said tonight they had been deluged with phone calls all afternoon and night.

WSB said it had interrupted/its own programs at least one hundred times with flashes and that NBC had been also breaking in frequently. Further check shows telephone company pretty well deluged with local calls. Heavy jams on long distance calls to St. Louis and Chicago. One hour delays were reported on calls to Chicago. A good many calls were placed to San Francisco which almost made it impossible to get through. Also there were numerous calls to Honolulu and Manila, which the phone company could not get through, presumably because of official jams, but no censorship on calls yet.

Western Union reported deluge of cables to Honolulu and Manila, which accepted for delivery if and when. Also jammed with hysterical wires to boys in camps, asking if any danger of them being transferred to Oriental front.

As wired previously, immediate reaction was what was the U. S. Navy doing.

Here are some quotes:

Mayor Thomas L. Cummings: "Those dirty b-----s over here with an olive branch in one hand and a dagger in the other."

John I. Suzuki, a Japanese graduate student at Vanderbilt University and former squadron leader of the Japanese Air Force against the Chinese: "If possible, I will not go back to Japan. I will stick to my religion and principles. I have been a Christian several years. I will not carry arms for my own or any other country for my life."

Of twelve other Japanese students at Madison College, which is seventh day adventist institution here, only two want to go back. Names available if want. Other ten say America is their home.

Private Estel Berry of Cody, Wyoming, 168th Field Artillery at Camp Forrest: "I'm eager and ready to go any time Uncle Sam sends me."

Sergeant Kennet Nelson, 129th Infantry at Camp Forrest: "We'll wipe 'em off the map in quick time, if the Army will send us over immediately. I'd rather be in Japan fighting than spend another 18 months in camp doing nothing."

Corporal William Quinn, of Illinois, in 124th Field Artillery at Camp Forrest: "This is something we'd like to tackle."

Leon Smithson, a cab driver: "We ought to go over there and wipe them off the map."

Assistant Attorney General Frank H. Taylor of Tennessee: "My stomach had a hollow feeling after I heard the news broadcast. I guess the best thing for us to do is to get into it immediately and wipe them out."

Congressman Atbert Gore was at a family reunion far up in the hills when political reporter Joe Hatcher of the Tennessean telephoned him the news. Gore hastened to Nashville, bulldozed American Airlines into putting him on the early morning plane to Washington. Said he: "There is no question but that Congress will act at once and I think the vote will be unanimous."

Grim realism added to Nashville reaction when radio and movie theatres broke programs to issue call for men of the 4th Depot Group of Army Air Corps, homeward bound from maneuvers to Patterson Field, supposedly camping overnight in the suburbs, call was for them to report at once for immediate departure on forced journey with no stops except for gas.

As wired, further check shows most dramatic and important local incident

Wire from Fill Calhoun, Chicago, Ill, to David Hulburd -- December 7, 1941

The Sun at 7 p.m. came out with a "War Extra No. 2" which was virtually the same as No. 1 except for fresh bulletins and a new banner "Japan War on U.S." The thought occurs that inasmuch as the Herald American ran the first Hawaii attack news as a regular peach edition and without the "extra slug, the Sun in one way can claim, in its first week of existence, having beaten all other Chicago papers with an "extra" in the biggest story yet. The Tribune for reasons I wish I knew, held up their plans for an extra and didn't come out until the regular time at 7 p.m. with a "Metropolitan" edition of tomorrow's paper. The Tribune bannered "Japan attack U.S." and above a column of war bulletins ran the following editorial:

"War has been forced on America by an insane clique of Japanese militarists who apparently see the desperate conflict into which they have led their country as the only thing that can prolong their power.

"Thus the thing that we all feared, that so many of us have worked with all our hearts to avert has happened. That is all that counts. It has happened. America faces war through no volition of any American.

"Recriminations are useless, and we doubt that they will be indulged in, certainly not by us. All that matters today is that we are in the war and the nation must face that simple fact. All of us, from this day forth, have but one task. That is to strike with all our might to protect and preserve the American freedom that we all hold dear."

Incidentally, note the Tribune's big scoop about U. S. war plans followed the Tribune's previous blasts about Roosevelt and his map of Nazi plans which the Tribune poopooed because any country naturally has war plans. Now where is the Tribune again?

The radio definitely broke the war news to Chicago as it was more than two hours before the first war paper, the Herald American, hit the streets. Off the record,

Chicago, Dec. 7, 1941 -- Calhoun -- page 2

Chicago Times men listening to the radio, also watching the press association tickers after the first flash, report that the radio was 20 minutes ahead of virtually every bulletin. C.B.S. which may have been beaten by the N.B.C. first flash, says New York will have to announce times and programs CBS interrupted, but I was listening to the Chicago Round Table when the argument over Canada's war effort was snapped and a brief flash read of the Hawaii and Manila Bombings. Thereafter on the next program, New York Philharmonic, was broken up, one time by an announcer so excited or inept that he twice pronounced Philharmonic as Philharminic, apologizing only for the first slip. There was an added rush of telephone calls as friends called friends, but no jam up of lines.

The first flash came just as Chicago home dwellers and suburbanites were digesting the roast beef and mashed potatoes of Sunday dinner which traditionally starts at one p.m. Many cancelled visits and plans to go to the movies to sit by their radios awaiting later bulletins. It seemed to me the radio took an unearthly time getting background together and any color into its news casts, but it was the retelling the people long before the newspapers.

First comments almost invariably were: "Well, it's here, or "Those Japs must be crazy."

Typical comment from a formerly Isolationist mother was: "If Hitler had just let the Japs alone this would never have happened. How terrible for the Japanese -- it's mass suicide."

Another mother, interrupted by the news while playing rummy, said: "We're in it and we'll just have to make the best of it." From younger men generally came this comment: "Well, we've got to whip the whole world -- and we can do it." What I'm trying to drive home is that no where did you hear comments about the possibility of anything but a U.S. victory. Some said "What an insult to the President when he was trying so hard to get things settled peacefully."

was jamming of Union Passenger Terminal and bus stations with soldiers from big Camp Forrest, seventy five miles distant, hurrying to report back to post without getting orders. All seemed in excited mood, anxious for action against Japs.

City is in an excited mood tonight, but actually appears relaxation of tension of past few days and apparent relief that now the U. S. has an objective for all its military preparation.

Leaving for Atlanta where will begin checking reaction upon arrival and wire by mid morning.

------

was jamming of Union Passenger Terminal and bus stations with soldiers from big Camp Forrest, seventy five miles distant, hurrying to report back to post without getting orders. All seemed in excited mood, anxious for action against Japs.

City is in an excited mood tonight, but actually appears relaxation of tension of past few days and apparent relief that now the U. S. has an objective for all its military preparation.

Leaving for Atlanta where will begin checking reaction upon arrival and wire by mid morning.

Chicago, Dec. 7, 1941 -- Calhoun -- Page 3

And many were the comments here, as probably different from those on the West Coast, that "it really is too bad for the Japanese people." Whether rightly or wrongly, people seem to believe all the so-called experts' claims that Japan has only two bath tubs in the navy, no money, no oil and all Japanese fliers are so cross-eyed they couldn't hit lake Michigan with a bomb.

Another lovely comment which also indicates how the war news first came to those who bought newspapers, was a fat woman at Michigan and Randolph. She approached a newsstand where the boy was shouting inaccurately "U.S. declares war on Japan," and apparently paid no attention to what he was saying. "What's this" she asked when she saw the big headlines. We're at war, lady, for crying out loud." "Well, she said, what do you think -- who with."

From all sides one first comment was: "This may be just what we needed to get us together and stop all these strikes and funny business." No matter what drivel they have been fed the people occasionally seem to hit down to fundamentals as exampled by comments such as: "Now we'll start turning out something.... Watch us go now. We'll turn out planes now or by God we'll know the reason why."

The Midwest, in my opinion, has known very well that they weren't doing half enough and that we were playing at business-as-usual.

Summing up comments and what they mean comes three main points: 1) Japanese attack has got people mad because they think this is a dirty deal pulled while the U.S. was trying all peaceful ways for a settlement, 2) they don't blame the Japanese people so much as they do "them warlords" and the Nazis egging them on, 3) they are glad in many ways that a break came the way it did because now we have God and everybody on our side and boy, just watch us go. The city, as such, was just getting ready for a good after dinner belch when the war news came. The temperature was 37 above, nippy and overcast with threat of snow that is now falling tonight. The usual wind was revealing legs in silk and nylon on Michigan Boulevard, torn up Loop Streets were beginning to fill with window-shoppers and matinee crowds. Newspapermen were spreading rumors about what was going to happen with the new Sun cutting into Chicago circulation and advertising. Copies were tweeting their strangely shrill whistles, bookies were wishing the newest gambling investigation would get over with, drunks were beginning to show up on South State Street and on North Clark where there is one place which advertises: "2 Big Shots of Whiskey and a Cold Bottle of Beer - 10 cents".

Chicago, the Godless and ungoverned had finished dinner and was wondering what the (censored) to do with itself when the news came. There was a pro-football game between the Chicago Bears and Chicago Cardinals, where, before the game, the orchestra played the "Star Spangled Banner" and the audience, as usual, rose and actually sang it. By half-time the Herald American's extra was out and there was a rush from the stands to buy it with word spreading through the whole place that "The Japs are raising hell and attacking Hawaii." The audience buzzed and papers passed along the rows. It was like Podunk High Schools suddenly walking on to the field to play the Bears. Theatres, having no sense of the theatrical here, interrupted no programs and matinee crowds learned about the news when they came onto the darkened streets.

The biggest single development here is, of course, that the Tribune has pulled in its horns and that for all intents and purposes Isolationism and America Firstism is deader than a bombed soldier at Hickman Field. I tried to reach General Wood 15 minutes after the first flash but his telephone is "temporarily disconnected." I presume he'll come out with a statement tomorrow a la Wheelers. The Jap attack was all that was needed to cut the ground from under America First's feet. It will be ridiculous to talk Isolationism in the next few days, dangerous to your own health in a few more after that. Some one just phoned to say the Tribune has a banner reading "My country, right or wrong."

Wire from Strother(Detroit) to D. Hulburd - December 7, 1941

The news that war was on, reached Detroit via radio. CBS had a flash at 2:29 and then led off The World Today with a Washington announcement at 2:31. An NBC flash broke the Chicago Round Table of the Air. The reaction was an unsurprised "Well, there it goes". It was a clear crisp day after a succession of murky ones, and an unusually large number of people were out riding with car radios turned on. Many of them caught the tail end of the bulletin or oblique references later, and newspapers and radio stations had a flood of calls between 2:30 and 4 o'clock. Movie houses were playing to capacity crowds, including many workmen with pockets bulging with cash from paychecks fattened by defense overtime. The Michigan Theatre was playing Fibber and Molly in "Look Who's Laughing" and had a long queue in front of the box office. Theatres didn't announce the outbreak, but new arrivals brought the word, and it spread swiftly. Many outgoing patrons stopped at the office to ask if the news was true. Station WJR in the Fisher Building has a big bulletin board in the lobby. A throng gathered at once and the concensus was "Well, I hoped it wouldn't come, but they asked for it and now they're blankety-blank well going to get it."

Men who called newspapers were generally both angry and cheerful. "Here we go. Happy landings", one said when told the news was true. One fellow was good and mad. "Why those Japs." Sitting down in Washington talking terms and then -- whambo! Some women callers burst into tears when the news was confirmed. "Oh gee, gee now he will probably get shot", one said as she hung up. Several men asked newspaper switchboards where they could join the navy. A large proportion of callers wanted to know if the U.S. had also declared war on Japan. Some asked how far it was from Los Angeles to Hawaii and others how many ships in the Japanese Navy.

Attorney General Francis Biddle was addressing 1,200 Americans of Slavic extraction at a metting of the Slav-American Defense Savings Committee in the Masonic Temple.

Strother -- Page Two

He interrupted the speech and made dramatic announcements. "I have just received word that Japan, who only yesterday announced its peaceful motives, has bombed the harbor at Manila." Governor Murray D. Pat Van Wagoner and Detroits young Mayor Edward Jeffries were with Biddle. Virtually every newspaper man in town was attending the Newspaper Guild's annual bingo party at the Book Cadillac Hotel. Shortly after 3 o'clock messages for various ones to report to their offices began coming in and most of the working newsmen among the 1,000 people present left. The Detroit Free Press was the only paper to extra tonight, however, and the Free Press as a morning paper had little difficulty in hitting the streets at 6:45 and again at 8:40. The Detroit News and the Detroit Times both plan to have extras out tomorrow morning around 7:30, but they couldn't round up printers etc. Sunday afternoon.

The Chinese Merchants Association went into meeting tonight. They were trying to find out why. There are at a least thousand Chinese here, but almost no Japanese. Hotel lobbies tonight are strangely deserted, and managers guess everyone has his ear glued to the radio. The radio stations are breaking in often with bulletins and with messages for all soldiers and sailors to report to their stations. This seemed to bring the gravity of the situation home to the listeners. There are no editorials yet. The most important immediate reaction here will be a redoubled precaution against sabotage defense plants.

Wire from Sidney James, Los Angeles, to David Hulburd --
December 8, 1941 -- 6:21 a.m.

When the newspapers finally took up the play it was a hey day for them too. On the third floor of the imposing stone pile in downtown Los Angeles that is the Times office, AP man Ted Gill was settling down to another routine Sunday of work when the bell of the printer rang its frantic flash warning at 11:30. He ran across the room with word of "the news" to News Editor Nick Williams, who immediately called Managing Editor L.D. ("LD") Hotchkiss. Hotchkiss, entertaining guests in the suburban quiet of his home at La Canada, ordered an extra. An hour later Times and Hearst's Examiner waived an agreement not to hit the street on Sunday before 3:15 with the first Sunday edition. The Times hit the street downtown at 2:10 with four inch block letters screaming "War". The Examiner beat it to the streets with "U.S. at War", by a few minutes.

Commented news editor Gill, remembering that last emergency extra in Los Angeles announced the fall of France on a Sunday, "If it's real big it always happens on Sunday. Ordinarily the Times would have printed 25,000 copies in its first edition, but up to five o'clock its succession of extras had totalled 150,000, and they went like hot cakes. Its normal daily circulation is only 220,000. As night fell the editorial writers of the Times and Examiner came on and caught up with events. Under a head of "Death Sentence of a Mad Dog" the Roosevelt hating reactionary Times began "Japan has asked for it. Now she is going to get it". It ended with: "This is a time for every American to show his colors. It is a time for coolness and courage. It is a time to sink without trace not only the enemy abroad, but the enemies within. Let there be an end of internal dissension, and end to the foolish if well-meant isolationist obstructionists, above all, an end to the efforts of disloyal self-seeking labor misleaders to hamstring our arms program."

Wire from Sidney James, Los Angeles, to David Hulburd --
December 8, 1941 -- 6:21 a.m.

Hearst's Examiner, which is anti-Roosevelt and has also fought the U.S. foreign policy said: "The U.S. is at war with Japan, and will conduct the war with every resource at its command and with the grim determination and unswerving loyalty of the American people. "This conflict is of course undesired and unwelcome." "But it is accepted with complete confidence of ultimate victory." "And it is entered with complete national unity."

We'll send along tomorrow the editorial comment of the Daily News which didn't get out an extra. more coming.

-end-

Wire from James (Los Angeles) - 12/7/41 - rec. 12:34 a.m.

Southern California never awoke to a less war-like day Before noon the thermometer climbed to eighty, and a fickle, caressing breeze played up and down the coast, moving now/from the North, now from the Southwest, and even at times from the direction of Japan. It was as handsome a day as any day in June ever was. It was perfect for swimming in the Pacific, for golf, for riding, for picnicking or for any midsummer Sunday recreation. The "Little Worlds Championship" between the Hollywood Bears and the Columbus Bulls professional football teams at Gilmore Stadium in Los Angeles seemed singularly out of tune with the lazy weather. It wasn't a day for physical combat even on the field of sport. The talk until "the news" came was mostly about how the UCLA Bruins had managed a surprise 7-7 tie in their traditional game against the Trojans of USC the day before, and the incredible shellacking the Texas Longhorns had given to the Oregon Webfoots. The front pages of the morning papers had suggested no better topic for discussion among sports-loving Southern Californians: "Roosevelt Sends Note to Mikado","San Quentin called hotbed of reds," "Belgians' Leopold weds commoner," "Finnish ships in U.S. ports taken over," "Litvinov vows Russians will continue battle," "U.S. stalling, says Toyko." The more devout were at their places of prayer while "the news" was being made across the Pacific. At Temple Baptist Church they were hearing bespectacled Dr. "Dad" Brougher discuss "The Power of Personal Influence." At First Congregational Church energetic Dr. James W. Fifield Jr. was preaching the truth that "Waters Find their Levels." At Angelus Temple Aimee McPherson was singing through a production called "One Foot in Heaven." At First Methodist Dr. Donald H. Tippett was talking about "The Bright and Morning Star." The Rev. McKinley Walker at the Annandale Methodist Church was taking his theme from the single word "Courage"

(End first take, more coming)

James (Los Angeles) - 12/7/41 -5:38 p.m.

War Add:

The sum total of immediate reaction in Los Angeles was highlighted by the exclamation that was uttered in various forms and added up to what one householder reduced to: "Why the dumb bastards" such was the overall feeling. The action itself seemed incredible but what it meant--war with Japan-- had long been taken for granted. More than one person was heard to say with resignation and a kind of finalty: "Well, this is it". To continue with the thread of "the news" coming to Los Angeles, the point must be made that the radio was the Paul Revere in the picture. After the immediate facts of assault were broadcast it was radio that saddled the ether waves and gave the door to door call to arms. Typical, from that point on is the KNX log of broadcasts for local consumption. Broadcasts were sandwiched in between the newsbreaks which filled most of the air time. At 12:38 KNX broadcast that all army and navy furloughs had been cancelled, and all were urged to report back to their posts immediately. At 12:50 the San Pedro Naval Base announced cancellation of all leaves, at 1:22 the sixth California State Guard was called to immediate duty. At 2:31 all city policemen and firemen off duty were called to work. At 3:30 the public was urged to stay away from aircraft plants and flying fields. At 5:54 all civilian and military personnel of the Fourth Air Corps headquarters at March Field were ordered to report immediately to their duty stations. Interspersed were such announcements as these: motorists were asked to assist men in uniform returning from leaves to Camp Roberts. All members of the Sheriff's emergency reserve were asked to report to the Royal Palms Hotel, 360 Westlake Avenue, Los Angeles. In San Diego all plant special police were called to duty at Consolidated's 40 million dollar plant, and all unofficial traffic was diverted away from the plant. All personnel of Navy recruiting stations were called to duty. All offices will be open continuously. Unlimited war time recruiting. All male citizens over 21 were asked to report to

James (Los Angeles) - page 2 (5:38 p.m. take)

their nearest fire or police station to volunteer for aid in an emergency. All city firemen and policemen who were off duty were ordered to report for emergency duty. All firemen and policemen are placed on two-platoon duty. xxxxxxxx All aircraft warning stations ordered fully manned for 24 hour duty. Col. Charles Branshaw, Chief West Coast procurement officer, ordered the public to stay away from the defense plants, asked citizens to stay at home unless it was necessary for them to be out, since traffic officers were needed for duty elsewhere. Governor Olson called all members of the California State Council for defense to meet with him at the State Building in Los Angeles Monday. And so it went. Radio station switchboards were lit up like Christmas trees without a break. A check with the three networks revealed that 95 per cent of those calls were from unexcited citizens who merely wanted to know when their favorite commentator could be heard again. One hysterical woman screamed over the telephone to a KNX operator that "your station ought to be ashamed of itself broadcasting all this terrible war news" but those calls were few and far between. There was some trouble early in the day from small fry municipal executives requesting the stations to make hysterical warning announcements. For instance, an unidentified man at the harbormaster's office called KNX telling them that "you better broadcast all over town that the Navy is going to blast the hell out of every boat they see, large or small, in the harbor". These calls were checked immediately with the Army and Navy who squelched them. Donald W. Thornburg, CBS vice president in charge of West Coast operations rushed back from a week end in Delmonte; Fox Case, in charge of special events broadcasts for the Columbia Pacific network was hustled out of town mysteriously late this afternoon to set up supplementary listening posts up and down the coast. CBS fervidly trying to make arrangements with the military authorities to get two announcers to Honolulu immediately. CBS sent a special policeman to their transmitter building at nearby Torrance.

James (Los Angeles) - page 3 (5:38 p.m. take)

A special guard, one man, was placed outside the master control room in the CBS building. Those, however, were the only precautions they took. Visitors were allowed to crowd through the lobby and gawk at the Christmas display and "the news" apparently didn't bother audience-show addicts who swarmed into the several CBS radio theatres for Sunday night feature shows. At NBC's pale green Hollywood Radio City, separated from the CBS building only by the Palladium, popular jitterbug haunt doing good business as usual, it was a different story. They took "the news" more seriously. They supplemented their normal special police force with hastily called Pinkerton men, Los Angeles policemen and two FBI agents. All tourists were barred from the building after 2:00 p.m. The guard in master control room in the main lobby was boarded off. A special guard was placed around their far eastern listening post in North Hollywood. A NBC engineer, came face to face with the barrel of a policeman's gun when he tried to report to work at the Engineering Room at 4 p.m. had to be identified before he could get in. But there was no evidence that NBC had any more cause than other stations for alarm. Even a small band of IATSE workers who have been picketing the Radio City building for a year because NBC wouldn't recognize their maintenance man's union, called off their picketing for the first time today. So it wasn't strange that the NBC publicity department looked pretty silly when they issued the following statement about 7:30 pm: "It ("The News") was a great shock to our stars (Jack Benny, Victor McLaglen, Edmund Lowe, Basil Rathbone, Nigel Bruce, Irene Rich, Edgar Bergen, all Sunday night features) they all went on without a break." Generally speaking people went about their usual Sunday night routines without outward evidence that "The News" had overwhelmed them. As a wiseacre reported in a gossip column some months back, "If Los Angeles ever had an air raid the people probably wouldn't pay any attention to it. They'd think it was just another Hollywood preview."

James (Los Angeles) - page 4 (5:38 p.m. take)

But they weren't just being blase, they were simply gradually accepting a fact that they had been long expecting--only they had never expected it to become a fact on so fine a Sunday. (More coming)

(end)

Wire from Sidney James, Los Angeles, Calif.
to David Hulburd -- December 7, 1941

Add War:

At Hollywood's El Capitan Theatre skittish Edward Everett Horton played to a full house matinee in a revival of "Springtime for Henry." At the Music Box, Hollywood's new, review "They can't Get you Down" entertained a sizeable "bargain" matinee crowd. At the Theatre Mart "The Drunkard" hooted and slapsticked its way well into a ninth year of entertaining Los Angeles audiences. And the movie audiences turned out normally for a Sunday afternoon of Cinema entertainment. "Citizen Kane" went into its eighth week at The Hawaii. "One Foot in Heaven" was at Warner's Hollywood. Abbott and Costello in "Keep 'Em Flying" played at the Hollywood Pantages and the RKO Hill Street (downtown) theatres. The big elaborate Paramount Theatre in downtown Los Angeles, showed Charles Boyer and Margaret Sullavan in "Appointment for Love", while on the stage, a road show of the musical comedy "Meet the People" entertained customers. And at Grauman's Chinese Theatre in Hollywood, the morbidly curious, tipped off by the Legion of Decency's campaign against it, crowded in to see Greta Garbo and Melvin Douglas in "Two Faced Woman."

When "the news" did come it didn't hit Los Angeles with a bang. It leaked in to the super-curious and the shut-ins, who even on a perfect day can stay by their radios. It got around at first almost by word of mouth. "Did you hear the news?" neighbor asked of neighbor. It spread limpingly, not like a fall brush fire in the Hollywood hills. There was no hue and cry on the public streets where the outdoor loving were bound for their Sunday pleasures. It moved through backyard gardens, across golf courses, into bars where more convivial citizens were braving some more of the same to rehabilitate themselves from the rigors of the night before, and finally to the beaches of the fateful Pacific. Typical was the way it came to a group of paunchy Hollywood newsgatherers and press agents:

A pint-sized moppet, proud of a piece of news he didn't understand completely, stepped up to the sidelines and said "hey, did you fellas hear about U.S. and Japan?" The goings on in Herbert's drive-in bar in the San Fernando Valley was typical of the casual acceptance of "the news" by the run of the mine Angelenos two hours after it was out. As bulletin after bulletin broke into the regular broadcasts, a Franck Symphony, a sermon, a swing fest, the occupants of the small barroom fell into a jocular mood. "You guys with the Japanese gardeners, how do you feel now"? cracked one. A stocky, medium-sized blond youth and his taller companion became the butt of numerous bad jokes. It was apparent that the blond youth was about to be drafted and that the other recently had been released from army service under the new draft law, but was subject to recall. There was a resounding guffaw when the already flash-tortured Franck Symphony ended and a saccarine-voiced announcer blurted: "Do your Christmas shopping early." Then an over-painted female, slightly in her cups, sitting at the end of the bar, giving no sign she had the slightest idea of what the hell was going on, told (loudly) the story about the "destitute prostitute". At a booth, five men played hearts, talked vaguely about the war situation. Brightest remark from this group: "Do you suppose Hitler had anything to do with this".

Typical of the small working man's reaction is the remark of a waiter at Romanoff's restaurant, in the middle of the afternoon. "I don't want to think about it. It's too hard to believe". Even the theoretically more-informed classes were apparently lacking in any real comprehension of what the hell it meant. Charles Einfeld, vice president and head of all advertising and publicity at Warner Brothers, hearing the news as he came in off the Hill Crest Golf course at 2:00 p.m. had only this to say; "I'm dazed".

The Los Angeles rich play-girls and play-boys week-ending at Palm Springs, hearing the news by accident in mid-afternoon (because of magnetic disturbances caused by the surrounding mountains it is impossible to get radio programs in Palm Springs until well after dark) were blase. A young aviation officer from March Field spend-

page 3 -- Sidney James, Los Angeles, December 7, 1941

ing the weekend at the Springs' El Mirador Hotel, got a hurry call from Headquarters to report back for duty. He had to cancel his dates in town and so the word spread through, leaked slowly by telephone gossip until nightfall when people began to gather at bars. Not singular were the remarks of one pretty, black-haired socialite resort girl when she heard the news. "Everybody knew this was going to happen, so why spoil a perfectly good Sunday afternoon worrying about it." A little later she remarked, "They couldn't have bombed Pearl Harbor. That Admiral I met in Coronado is in charge and he is a perfectly lovely person".

For the first few hours after "the news" broke you couldn't raise long distance or the telegraph services. By early evening the Southern California Telephone Co. asked all radio stations to ask civilians not to make any unnecessary or purely social calls because all telephone facilities were needed for military and municipal purposes. By mid-afternoon, the outlets for the major radio chains were fully staffed and humming. Mutual's KHJ broke into "Hollywood Whisperings", a Hollywood gossip program, at 11:45 to break "the news" to their listeners. "The news" came to CBS listeners at 11:30 over local KNX during Columbia's European Roundup "The World Today". NBC listeners here, tuned to local KECA, heard the news about the same time when the University of Chicago Round Table Program was interrupted for the Flash. More coming.

-- end --

Wire from Sidney James, Los Angeles, Calif.
        to David Hulburd -- December 7, 1941 (12:34 p.m.)

War Fourth Add:

After all these excited local break-ins--for now every Radio in the City was turned on -- it is no wonder that by evening there was evidence of hysteria. By this time movie theatres were breaking in for flash news on the screen and newsboys were hawking extras everywhere. Finally every radio station began broadcasting intermittantly at the request of the Chief of Police and the Sheriff who had been swamped with calls from hysterical citizens: "There is no immediate cause for alarm."

Wire from Sidney James to David Hulburd, Los Angeles, Calif.
December 7, 1941 -- rec'd 7:47 a.m.

We are breaking in here to give you a cogent observation from LIFE's Peter Stackpole who spent some time in Hawaii on assignment recently. Having recently returned from a month's cruise with the U.S. Fleet in Hawaiian waters, I returned to the mainland with the opinion that I had just seen one of the world's best protected bases. I had believed the encouraging boast of navy personnel that, due to certain devices for detecting the presence of enemy ships and planes, no enemy craft could approach the Oahu area without first being detected and intercepted before it ever reached the shore line. Tonight when I hear reports of heavy damage to Hickman Field, Ford Island, and the possible sinking of two battleships in Pearl Harbor, I can begin to realize a few of the possible reasons for our force's apparent failure to meet the attack quickly.

The fact that a second wave of Japanese planes was able to reach the base confirms the fact that damage must have been heavy and the job of mustering flying personnel and getting them out to the air bases must have taken hours. Saturday night in Honolulu is not unlike that in any large American town. Sailors and officers usually enjoy a weekend shore leave. Officers include most of the flying personnel and they are allowed the whole weekend ashore without having to report back to the ships at Pearl Harbor until early Monday morning.

This means that though many of the ships were well manned with sailors, large numbers of officers and fliers were still ashore. Because of a decided housing shortage, the whole Honolulu-Waikiki-Pearl Harbor area is jammed with defense workers, sailors and soldiers, who, due to the regions bad transportation have relied on old rattle trap cars for which they have paid a high price. Oahu's undersized highways have thus become jammed with cars, serious traffic problems have developed. To make matters worse, the average officer prefers to spend his weekends in Waiki, which is about 20 miles from Pearl Harbor, separated by downtown Honolulu.

page 2 -- Sidney James, Los Angeles, Dec.7,1941 (7:47 a.m.)

To cover this short distance one can usually expect to remain in transit from an hour to an hour and a half, whether he takes a crowded bus, a taxi or his own car. The latter would be quickest. Sunday mornings were the only periods when I don't recollect having heard the constant drone of planes overhead from army, navy and marine bases. Ironically enough, the only plane which actually met the attacking Japanese when they came in was a private ship whom the Japanese didn't bother to shoot down.

Taking for granted that the Island's defense system was taken by surprise, possibly because of an over-confident feeling among its defenders, we can best judge the extent of military damage by coming reports of how many Japanese planes and ships our forces were able to sink during this fateful Sunday. The fact is that it is traditional in the service to get blind drunk on Saturday night. The Japs must have been counting on this, apparently they were right. End Stackpole. More coming.

-- end --

Wire from Sid James, Los Angeles, to D. Hulburd - Dec. 8, 1941.

7TH ADD

The hottest spot in this area is Los Angeles harbor and specifically, Terminal Island. Earliest radio broadcasts told of the rounding up of all this area's some 3,000 Japanese. Despite repeated instructions to all civilians to keep away, many carloads of curiosity seekers headed down Sepulveda Blvd. for the harbor. On their way, they saw the huge B-19 at Mines Field, probably wished it was in Hawaii with a load of bombs. As they passed through Hermosa Beach, they saw visible evidence of preparedness: camouflaged anti-aircraft guns manned by alert gunners. When they approached the harbor, they were politely but firmly turned back by a swarming force of policemen and soldiers. No one was allowed near the Point Fermin area where the army's concealed coast artillery is placed. Even residents of that area were escorted home and practically put to bed by soldiers.

Unable to get near the harbor, many inquisitive drivers went up the steep hill west of San Pedro, got a good look at the harbor. The whole area was quiet and motionless. Below them the red tile roofed barracks of Ft. MacArthur reflected the setting sun. The only sound came from the loud speaker of the football game at the fort. The only moving objects in the harbor were a few odd sailboats and the returning Catalina Island boat loaded with weekenders.

Earlier in the day, all the vessels had been ordered away from the pier and by this time all the big ships and commercial boats were at anchorage. Across the inlet from San Pedro, Terminal Island's huge refinery tanks stood out against the low, brown shacks of the Japanese fisherman behind Terminal Island was a huge backdrop of Long Beach buildings and behind this the dome-shaped signal hill oil field whose crowded derricks made it look like a huge pin cushion. Down at the Terminal Island ferry landing, two busy army intelligence men, supported by policemen and armed soldiers were busy searching every car for alien Japs.

Already that day they had interned over 300. Each boat-load brought a few more. The bewildered Japs were placed in a makeshift chicken wire detention camp near the entrance to the ferry. Self-conscious rookies occasionally followed the giggling Japanese across the RR tracks to the lavatory. A young Jap boy was making a steady journey between the pay phone and his parents inside the detention station. An elderly Jap complained bitterly when the officers took his new Buick and placed him in the camp.

But there was no violence. Across the inlet on Terminal Island, everything was almost too quiet. Soldiers patrolled the streets in pairs. The main street of Fish Harbor usually very gay on Sunday night, was almost dark. One Jap restaurant was open. In there, an old bald Jap was screaming to anyone who would listen that he has been in the U.S. since 1906. His three children were working quietly. Occasionally they would interpret his jumbled remarks.

A one-armed sailor was making sweeping statements about the harbor's defense. An American commercial fisherman was complaining because the Navy had kept him from going out of the harbor that morning. "How do they expect us to make a living? I'd sneak my boat out but they've got enough dynamite in that harbor to blow the whole Jap navy to bits. Hell, I wouldn't try to get a canoe through that net." It all seemed calm and quiet but these 3,000 Japanese are sitting right in the middle of our biggest west coast harbor. There Japs could drop a match and set a million dollars worth of gasoline on fire. And another match would take care of three or four shipbuilding plants. Japanese district of Los Angeles, largest colony of Japanese outside Asia, loosely called "Little Tokyo" looks almost as vulnerable to fire bombs. It lies just a few blocks from the Civic center, is bordered on other sides by skid rows and factory districts. There live about 3,800 of Southern California's approximately 60,000 (to be checked) Japanese. Of these, about 2/3 (more rather than less) are Nisei -- born in America.

Page 3 -- James - Los Angeles - 7th Add

If you had happened to wander down into little Tokyo today that is what you might have seen. You would (if you came from the better part of town) have passed the civic center, there seen policy officers, sheriff's officers, recruiting station men from army, navy and marine corps (they were all ordered to their posts for the duration over radio in apparent expectation of sudden large enlistments), just plain citizens in as busy a mob (on Sunday) as the center sees on the busiest weekday.

You wander down into the Japanese section and note that workmen are busy on tall ladders, growing out of truck, raising Christmas garlands (with a gay Santa Claus) across First Street, near Los Angeles St. You might notice that the Christmas decorations extend from near the entrance to the Yokohama Specie Bank to the Tojito Trading Co (with its window filled with Christmas gifts). You might also notice that both Los Angeles St. and First St. were filled with double lines of traffic each way, that on each corner were two policemen. If you were aware of things as they used to be you would know that policemen work in pairs only when when there is imminent danger, that traffic is thick on weekends and week days in that part of town.

You might talk to one pair of cops. He says: "The God damn fools. I've worked in this district for years. I like these nice clean people. They're a damn sight cleaner than those lousy wops and spiks cafes a few blocks from here. But these damn fools Sunday drivers have to come down here to have a look at it. Maybe they expect a bomb or some Jap to cut his guts out in the middle of First St. They are the same guys who would drop their water if a single bomb dropped, but would come out later to look at the hole without sense enough to worry about when the next bomb was going to drop. And the same guys would help lynch a poor bastard Japanese who might be trying to earn a living down here selling his countrymen's junk. We gotta protect the Japs against the Americans, not the other way around.

But FBI and Naval Intelligence (who for years have had dossiers on every Japanese in the district) are picking up some 14 of them, herding some 300 more into a corrall at Terminal Island. If you chance to take a cab the driver might tell you, "I

Page 4 -- James, Los Angeles - 7th Add

live next door to a Japanese family -- nice people too. Hell they're said to give more tips than any white man."

Easily the most intelligent source of Japanese information in Southern California is the Los Angeles Daily News, of which Neisi Togo Tanaka is the English Language editor. So if you had a chance to walk into the editorial rooms of the Daily News tonight (between English Linotype and ending cases of Japanese characters, among which soft-slippered, slick-fingered Japanese character-slinked) you would have walked immediately into a tiny room which looked as though it couldn't hold all it held. Here where all the leaders of Japanese thought in Southern California, ready and willing to agree with anything which would "please" allow them to go on living life they had been living. If you were lucky you would have chance to overhear the whole group (representing every honest Americanized Japanese group) vote to accept a statement phoned from San Francisco by Saburo Kido, national president of the Japanese American citizen League (leading patriotic Japanese group).
The statement read:

"The National J.A.C.L. has offered the facilities of its entire organization to the government in this great crisis. We are pledged to an unequivocal repudiation of Japan and bend our energies now to the common objective of an American victory and a defeat of Japan. I am confident that Americans of Japanese ancestry will respond with true loyalty to America and that we shall have cause to be proud of their record. I am also confident that all their parents, who are non-citizens, because the naturalization laws have prevented from becoming citizens, will stand by us and faithfully abide by the laws of good Americans.

"We recognize the need for unity and are confident of our usefulness to America to this common defense of our shores.

"This sort of statement does not necessarily represent the entire Japanese colony in Southern California.

You might remember that some 600 representatives of Japanese business were here (such business at Matsui, Matsubishi) that the less than 1/3 of the others were born across the Pacific, that, after all, these people believe in their country, might want to support it, that they might be forced into action by threats against their relatives in Japan.

"You might also talk to them and learn they are almost more American (again the 2/3 we can account for) than most of your own ilk. Typical of them is young Joe Masaoka who has a horribly flattened nose, low-growing black hair, slant eyes. He also has an honest face, a perfect English accent, a college education (Utah), a fear of occidental "hoodlums" who might choose to attack his kind.

"Masaoka and I watched the family Sunday, radio-listening cars go by all day by his people's stores whose owners only wanted to sell their goods in order to buy an American sort of Christmas for their children. Most of them were sensation seekers or the type of skid-row people whose only boast is they have a Caucasian face.

"This guy Joe (and he is typical of a dozen) said: "Look, you Americans have among you Irish faces, German faces (and I understand Germans fought with you against Germans in the last war, just as brother fought against brother in your own civil war) Italian faces. What's wrong with Japanese faces? I know what you say: we are Oriental faces, we can't integrate, but why not? My best girl friend went to Japan five years ago to learn dancing. You know what happened to her? She was arrested on the street for wearing too much lip-stick. She's back here now and she's going to stay. And the rest of us. I have enough money to own a car. Don't you think I like that, do you think I'd change that? That is something no one of my generation and breeding could do over there ever. Over there I'd be a coolie. Over here I can talk to you. Over here, by God, we'd fight our own nation and that isn't being unethical because really we think they are just trying to get for themselves something we (as citizens of America) have already got. We believe enough in that so we'd fight Japan.

Page 6   James -- Los Angeles - 7th Add

"Off to some sort of war this week went some 2500 (local estimate of number of Japanese in the U. S. army). This figure should be checked, but according to local sources represents highest proportionate representation (by two and ½ times) of any racial group in the U. S. and according to local knowledge, not one has/ever been guilty of major infraction of army rules. The navy will not take Japanese. Only this morning ten huge army trucks went to the center and posed for pictures while Japanese members of the Japanese shrubbery Association loaded them with shrubs they were donating to Camp Roberts."

Hollywood note: By the time a bright three quarter moon was high in one of Los Angeles' better Chamber of Commerce heavens, they had accepted the fact. "New news" was driven home by things like an early evening report on movie boxoffices throughout the country. The report said revenue had dropped from 15 to 50% with the hinterlands and neighborhood houses reporting biggest slumps. Apparently the working masses, accustomed to Sunday night escape at the movies before "blue Monday" chose to stay at home with their ears glued to the radio.

Things like Producer Joe Pasternack's Japanese gardner walking into the Pasternack living room at 6 p.m. announcing flatly: "I no work anymore." FBI agents stating a preliminary investigation of Hollywood shenanagins, as an aftermath of the Bioff trial, got orders to forget about glamorland for the moment, were all over the country over 40 trunk lines reserved exclusively for their use. At Ciro's, Hollywood's top night spot, usually pack-jammed on a sunday night because of a weekly charity show, attendance was half of normal. For the first time, the evening opened with a rendition of "The Star Spangled Banner". On a half dozen tables in the gaudy, green and red draped cafe, portable radios had at least one ear of the diners. Ciro's charity supporters sat on their hands when Noel Crorath, a dark, sloe-eyed entertainer sang a song entitled, "I'm an International Spy", didn't crack a smile when he said, "Here's one written in B. H. (before Hitler)."

One note at least warmed their hearts. Commedian Bert Wheeler announced that he wished to sing a song, written this afternoon by musician Lew Pollack and lyricist Ned Washington. He explained he had been driving up Sepulveda Blvd. just after two o'clock when Washington overtook him in his car, hailed him to the curb, said he had an inspiration, was about to jell it at Pollack's house. The inspiration, which Wheeler sang for the Ciro audience: "It's here at last -- the die is cast -- America.

<u>Chorus</u>

The flag flies high -- so do or die -- America
Let's stand together today in that old American way
Get in this fight with all your might and make those cowards pay.
Oh, we didn't want to do it, but they're asking for it now.
So we'll knock the Japs right into the laps of the Nazis.
When they hop on Honolulu that's a thing we won't allow.
So we'll knock the Japs right into the laps of the Nazis.
Every man will do all he can to knock every soldier of Japan into kingdom come, things'll hum.
They'll hear the beat of a million feet of people who'd rather fight than eat.
And here we come, here we come.
I'd hate to be in Yokahama when our bombers make a bow.
For we'll knock the Japs right into the laps of the Nazis."

Earlier in the evening, army MP's scoured the town, let it be known flatly to all restauranteurs that no drinks were to be served to men in uniform. And to cap off Ciro's charity evening, a blonde, blushing lieutenant of the 364th infantry mounted the podium and boyishly asked all military men to report to duty at once, assured the patrons, "We have the situation well in hand. It is up to you people to protect the civilian front." He promptly sat down amid hearty applause and ordered a drink.

Wire from Holland McCombs, San Antonio, to J. McConaughy -- Dec. 8, 1941

First take:

The day was coolish and switched from gray to clear. People were lounging around homes and apartments. Some were nursing hangovers from Saturday's football games and Saturday night's jamboreeing. And their gals were cleaning up after picnics in Brackenridge Park, getting ready to visit the zoo and "take pictures." The smart set was getting in naps before later cocktailing. Some were headed for a polo game, others for rides in park and country. Many had gone to ranches and ranch parties for the weekend. Downtown streets were quietly full of ambling salesmen, soldiers, girls, school kids. Lines were beginning to form in front of picture shows. Out in wooded Brackenridge Park, kids were riding the ferris wheel and flying jenny, babies were being held in swings, miniature trains were tooting and whistling as kids were whirled by adoring parents. Other kids were riding ponies around a little sawdust circular ring. Still others were riding burrows (free) down fenced lanes in the park. Here and there down the downtown streets among San Antonio's polyglot population you'd see a carload of Japs, Chinese, Negroes, Mexicans, Italians, Germans, Bohemians, Poles, even Hungarians. The main streets were pretty full of wistful-eyed window shoppers. Some of the folks at home were eating, lounging, listening to the University of Chicago Round Table Discussion. These were the first to hear a cut in. It was a flash from WOAI newsroom. This was about 1:35. Into Batheh Batcherlor House stormed a member who had just heard the flash on his car radio: "Those s.o.b.'s have done it." This man was getting ready to go hunting, and blurted: "To H. with hunting quail, I got a notion to go out and hunt Japs." Another man at home had just finished a quarrel with his wife, though he had gone to lie down on the couch and pout. She went in another room and pouted. Then Kaltenborn came on. This was the first news in that home. After the first few statements, the quarrel was forgotten, both joined in listening, commenting with force, even held hands in excitement, began calling friends, jabbering, cussing.

Men in the San Antonio Light heard it over the radio at 1:45, called the AP Bureau at Dallas who had not heard about it, "We woke them up," say Light men. The Light had an extra on the street at 2:15 and kept crews on hand all Sunday. The San Antonio Express (morning) had to round up a crew, got out an extra at 5:00 p.m. Folks weren't so surprised that happened. But they were completely flabbergasted at the way it happened. One guy called me and exclaimed: "Are the bums crazy? Do they think they can make a frontal attack on the U.S.?" Another said: "There's something behind all this we don't know about. If we were so much on the alert as they claim we are out there, how in H. did they get in to bomb Pearl Harbor? It's the most fantastic thing I every heard of."

Except for my friend going hunting, folks didn't seem mad until later when reports came about specific loss of life. Some people heard it at one-thirty over the World Today, cut in for a newsflash, program. Others listening to small stations had record-programs interrupted.

Wire from Holland McCoombs, San Antonio - to J. McConaughy, Dec. 8, 1941

Second Take:

We went downtown at 5:30 Sunday p.m. The streets were crowded with soldiers and civilians but except for an occasional "Damn those Japs," and newsboy cries of "War Extry" things were pretty calm. Soldiers seemed more interested whether they are to get Xmas leave than anything else. In front of the Majestic Theatre where they are playing "Skylark" with Claudette Colbert, was a long line of soldiers and civilians. Just in front of us was a pretty, calm, self-sufficient young Japanese woman with a cute little 2-year-old girl. Folks didn't seem to mind and she was perfectly at ease while newsboys kept shouting right in front of her face, "War Extry!" "Japs Attack U.S.!" etc. She bought her ticket right in front of me, walked into the show which was constantly interrupted with announced flashes and when a newspix of Kurusu flashed on the screen and the audience hissed him heartily, she actually cheered news announcements of Japs attacking Pearl Harbor. By this time folks were getting a bit war-feverish. By nightfall San Antonio police had begun rounding up Japs, investigating them and have already outlined their behavior, requiring them to report to the police regularly.

Corpus Christi Naval Air Training Station was the first military post in this territory to order all men to their posts. Third Army Headquarters ordered all men to war uniforms, to report to their commanders. M.P.s flocked downtown, joined forces with the police on rounding up anybody who looked suspicious. Extra guards were thrown around San Antonio's great army supply depots, airfields, machine shops, etc. Telephones to all army posts around here were jammed. If the Japs were coming across the Rio Grande it wouldn't be possible to advise some army posts by phone. Phone service in these posts is always lousy, now there just ain't any. Officers were stationed at the home of the Jap consul in Houston. The San Antonio Light ran a sort of full page call to arms, headed "United Nation Marches to Victory."

McCoombs, San Antonio - Dec. 8, 1941

Filipinos in Dallas were afraid to go out on the streets, asked Dallas people to please learn "differences in our races." They say they are being mistaken for Japs. As the President's speech comes on here in San Antonio, 10 women are now standing in the rain on the streets weeping because of the loss of American lives. / One of the Things that got me most when news was coming in on the radio, was how we'd listen to this world-stirring drama, then be switched back to Bulldog Drummond, The Shadow Face, etc. and were we supposed to shudder? We felt a bit disgusted at the attempt of fear through the sugared, hush voices. Then when we got a newsflash of the bombing of the Hickman barracks with the loss of lives, we were (switched) to Catholic Hour dedicated to and talking about Peace. We felt like saying, my God, if that's a recording, take it off, simply out of respect for the times; if it's spot stuff, why don't somebody tell the Reverend what' has and is happening. This morning there were larger crowds at mass than usual. At one six o'clock mass were dozens of officers in uniform. People were renting and buying radios. One radio shop reported it rented out fifteen receiving sets last night.

(More Coming)

End

Wire from Holland McCombs, San Antonio, Texas to James McConaughy - 12-8

Add Jap War (Third Take)

The spotter we have in headquarters third army (lodged in a downtown office building) just called and reports that guards have been placed on all floors, even in elevators. A tunnel between that office building and downtown hotel have been closed.

In Orange, Texas, K. Suski, representative of Jap Steamship Lines for 16 years, offered to surrender to police. So did Jap K. Kishi, 35-year resident of Orange.

Officers of Third Army headquarters hurrying from office to office with grim expressions and working under tense pressure. Firemen and police leaves cancelled Sunday. This morning San Antonio arsenal (containing tanks, guns, ammunition) correlated its radio with that of San Antonio police and doubled guards. This morning's San Antonio EXPRESS carried an editorial headed: "Stand by the Nation." First sentence: "Treachery has been characterized as the most infamous and detestable of all the vices to which human nature is subject." Further: "From out of a smokegascreen of Japanese treachery -- laid in this nation's capital during the two weeks past -- emerges war upon the U.S. . . . The U.S. is at war with the Axis partner of Hitler and Mussolini -- as Nazi Germany had schemed and desired. Stand by the Nation."

Deserter, Jap soldier, in 45 Division is being held in Camp Barkeley stockade and refuses to tell court martial where he has been for the past two months of A.W.O.L... more

                                                       End

Wire from Holland McCombs, San Antonio, Tex.
       to James McConaughy -- December 8, 1941

Add war (fourth take): Dallas police picked up six Japs, say they are now holding them for immigration. El Paso has sworn in a hundred deputies to augment the police force. Border Patrol reports adding men, increasing vigilance along the border. Home Defense Guard at El Paso is furnishing patrols for bridges and other vital points along the border and guarding 100 miles of Southern Pacific Railroad.

Recruiting offices opened in San Antonio at eight this morning, were swamped with young men wanting to enlist. The attitude of soldiers this morning is roughly expressed by the observation of one Texas private: "Well, let's have a war." A soldier draftee from New York says he was out playing football with the men of his company when he first got the news. The game didn't even stop. He said: "The Texas boys seemed to be happy about it. The Eastern boys were more concerned."

Two officers and two privates when asked: "Well, what are we going to do now" gave exactly the same answer: "We'll whip 'em." Out at Fort Sam Houston enlisted men in all shapes of dress and undress gathered in the "day rooms" to hear the President's message, seemed to realize what might mean to them, were cool, collected and so far there's been very little conversation between them about the war or its portent. This afternoon's San Antonio Evening News editorialized:

"An act of basest treachery unworthy of a nation calling itself civilized and has all the earmarks of having been Made in Berlin ... The amazing and almost incredible fact was that the American defenders were taken by surprise and allowed the raiders to get within bombing distance..."

This nation is shocked, certainly; but in coming out of the impacts of the first shock, it is rising up in wrath to strike back... Looking ahead even for a day, what could the Japanese have expected to gain from that initial advantage? They must have gone mad. This is an act of desperation -- a way to commit national suicide (this is also the opinion of lots of people we've seen and talked to today)...

"Orders have gone out to army personnel that they are not to make any comments whatsoever and everything in this area is to be released directly from the office of the Commander of the Third Army.

Most significant evidence of war here is the general tightening up on the whole army front from headquarters of the Third Army on down. Officers must wear uniform on all occasions. Young Lieutenant just in office is griping about having bought a new civilian suit, and now wants to sell it, says, "It'll be a h. of a long time before I'll wear that suit."

This is the end of the first spurt, but will keep on the lookout for anything specially worthy and will wire when we come across it.

Wire from Holland McCombs, San Antonio, Tex., to James McConaughy 12-8

Add Jap War:

Radio Station KTSA has put up a bulletin board in the lobby of the Gunter Hotel as people are crowding around reading bulletins as they are posted. Now since things have sort of simmered down, people seem to be glad that a definite break has been made and that we have good "causus belli." There seems to be a general toughening up of sentiment. Majority figure Japan is in for destruction or some such, and that Well, they asked for it."

End.

Wire from Hammond (San Francisco) to D. Hulburd - December 8, 1941

Herewith answers to your questions. More to come on 1) developments on both sides of the bay and outlying counties where many war industries are located 2) color, San Francisco and Transbay and country. 3) General roundup unduplicated by wire services.

1) How news came to San Francisco: The radio was the first to announce with KSFO (Columbia) and FKRC (Mutual) coming on about the same time with a first one-line flash that Honolulu and Manila were being bombed, Manila bombing unconfirmed. KSFO was tuned into CBS coast-to-coast hook-up on "The World Today," a drinks roundup of drink world's capitals. New York interrupted "shortly after" program began at 11:30 A.M. KFRC got a phone flash from the local AP at 11:32, read the same one-line flash over the air at 11:44, interrupting "Strings In Swingtime"..sustaining musical program from Hollywood.

NBC stations KGO and KPO were cut in on by New York sometime after 11 but did not log time.

Telephones were taxed by innumerable calls everywhere. Lyle Brown, Division Manager of the Pacific Tel & Tel, says long distance facilities were particularly taxed. He is requesting the public to refrain from making anything but the most urgent long distance calls. Radio station switchboards were flooded with people asking for more info, asking if they'd heard aright.

KSNO went on the air after an hour or so asking the public not to phone in, that news would be broadcast as soon as they got it. NBC and CBS each estimate that they received "Several thousand" calls between noon and 8 P.M.

Newspapers: The Chronicle newsroom received the first flash at 11:29 A.M., which would be a phone call from the AP downstairs.

The first papers hit the street at 2 P.M. with the presses running steadily since. The Examiner got the flash between 11 and 11:30. Oscar Gardiner, Ass't. City Circulation Manager, says the Examiner hit the street at 12:45 with the first Steve Early flash. Ed McQuaide, Ass't. City Editor, however, says the first edition was at 2:09. No one on either paper has any circulation figures. People are gobbling them up as fast as they roll however. The Chronicle carried a topline of four-inch letters WAR:

2) It was like a rubber band breaking, a rubber band which had been stretched out for a long time," said Benjamin Fox, special officer, who stood on Market St., San Francisco's main drag from noon to eight P.M. "Ever since I was a kid, we've been expecting something like this. Now it's come and it's a good thing and I think almost everybody thinks so."

"I think Japan had a Goddam well struck her neck out a little bit too far this time," said E. W. Mallery.

"That's my honest opinion and I think that Japan's neck is going to get nipped off."

Generally the reaction in San Francisco, most Japanese-fearing city in the United States was first: surprise, stunned surprise. Then indignation. Then a smiling sense of relief, confidence that the Navy which has been itching to get at Japan for many years, would take over and "Blast/goddam that country off the map."

Although local defense councils were flustered into action finally, there was no fear that bombs would start dropping on the coast. Most people viewed the war as a naval engagement, nothing to touch the home shores. Officialdom, however, rushed to man the barricades, special guards were ordered for defense plants and special anti-sabotage patrols were instituted or supplemented.

A sum-up of attitude would be "They've got a lot of guts. They're asking for it and now they're going to get it, really."

A service-station man, "Boy, this is important to me. It means maybe I go to war. I used to be a marine."

A motorist in the service station: "I just heard about it. Down the street

I almost ran over a ~~bri~~ Jap on a motorcycle. Maybe I should have hit him. That would be my contribution.

3) Will be covered in supplemental material following immediately.

4) Mayor Angello J. Rossi proclaimed a state of emergency for the city, setting aside emergency funds to pay for civilian defense directors, calling on employee, employer groups to "Forthwith terminate their existing differences during the present emergency and end all disputes so that San Francisco may present a united front and so that every citizen may work for the one end, the safety of our country."

Previous to the Mayor's proclamation, ~~drink~~ John F. Shelly, President of the San Francisco Labor Council (AFL) and State Senator had announced a meeting of all AFL striking unions to compose differences with employers. Strikes current in San Francisco: 16 hotels picketed in strike against 26 members of the San Francisco Hotel Association; The Department Store Employes Union is picketing three stores, including the city's largest, The Emporium. Berkeley workers in the park, street, corporation yard and garbage departments had scheduled a 240 hour work stoppage for Monday; welders, (CQ) cutters and helpers union (independent) seeking a breakaway from AFL crafts, had threatened a nation-wide strike on the basis of four grievances of San Francisco ship yards. Berkeley, opening wedge in CIO's national drive for organization of municipal workers, was called off. So was the welders strike. Rossi called the Monday meeting unions, employers in local strikes, to seek a settlement. Important development: A terrific civilian response to a hitherto lagging drive for 25,000 volunteers 12,500 air raid wardens, 10,000 auxiliary firemen and 2500 auxiliary cops. In the last two weeks of registration of the drive only 3200 people signed up. Tonight no one knows the exact total on the day's registration but Civil Defense Headquarters estimate conservatively at least 1500 signed up, probably more. An operator on 24 trunk lines at the

Fire Department Headquarters said she had handled 3000-4000 calls herself. Many are just fearful and asking for miscellaneous information, but many are asking imperatively where and how to sign up for civil defense work. The swamped operator wailed: "I hadda call for help". Sampling of 54 fire stations and 10 district police headquarters, which are the registration points, reveals 49 persons signing up at one fire station in an hour, 60 at another. Consensus is that on an average 60 to 70 persons signed up at each registration place. That would mean better than 4000 people-and they're still queued up all over town waiting to sign up.

Unable to get a 24-hour total until 9 Monday morning when Fire houses and police stations tabulate and report to headquarters. The registration was held up to an average in the Japanese section where there are a lot of Negroes, poor white people; in the North Beach which is the Italian section and in the Potrero district which has a heavy settlement of white Russians.

5) Editorials San Francisco Examiner: With the nation at war every industry becomes a defense industry. There is no room for strikes. Both for the good of the labor movement and as a patriotic gesture, the hotel and store unions should call off their strikes. Anything that hampers business, hampers the nation in its defense and San Francisco has now become a key point in the war. This is no time for debates about the open or closed shop: no time for pickets to be parading the sidewalks when Americans are being killed by bombs. There couldn't be a better time or a better reason for calling off the strikes. San Francisco Chronicle Editorial "By the act on Japan, America is at war. Time for debate has passed and the time for action has come. That action must be united and unanimous. 'Politics is adjourned'. Whether between parties, faction or economic groups. From now on America is an army with every man, woman and child a soldier in it all joined to the one end of victory. If war had to come, it is perhaps well

Hammond -- Page Five

that it came this way, wanton, unwarned in fraud and bad faith, virtually under a flag of truce. We can not know how long this war will last, how wide it will range now what it will cost us in toil and sacrifices and in treasure. We do not know that whatever the cost we will pay it and that our reward will be to hand down to our children the free America which our fathers bequeathed to us." American unite; There are no edits in the other paper so far. ▮▮▮▮▮▮▮▮▮▮▮▮▮▮▮▮ said (not to be quoted) "Where the hell was our Navy?"

Nathaniel J. L. Pieper, San Francisco FBI chief said: "As far as Japanese nationals are concerned, we received instructions from the Attorney General to take certain Japanese aliens into custody for the immigration department."

Twenty-eight were arrested up to one A.M. and an attendant in the immigration station said "One or two more are expected." Pieper wouldn't say how many were arrested, how many to be arrested. In Santa Clara County, where Permanente Cement Plant and Henry J. Kaiser's famous magnesium plant is located, Sheriff William Emig said "One Jap arrested, three in question. Pieper said the legal status of the Japs is in doubt, waiting instructions from the Attorney General. The U. S. attorney was unavailable for comment.

Generally speaking, Pieper said: "We are fully mobilized and ready for anything, cooperating with Army and Navy intelligence, and working on prevention sabotage. So far no cases of sabotage are reported."

Police: Chief Charles "Charley" Dullea, bluff, gruff and self-assured, says there has been no trouble at all in Jap town, no outbreaks no violence. In addition to four regular beat patrolment from the Northern Station Dullea dispatched a special detail of 35 uniformed men, 15 plainclothesmen to Jap town this afternoon about 3. Cops are principally keeping traffic rolling, diverting it from Post-California streets, Steiner-Laguna streets (four blocks each way) area where most of San Francisco's 5000-7500 Japanese live. A few civilian curiosity-seekers poking around early in the evening to see what's doing, and were told to keep moving. Japanese stores were open, life going on as usual.

The police department has an entire personnel of 1400 subject to immediate call. No days off. Everyone is working 12 hours on, 12 off. This is the tail end vacation season so no one is on leave.

Dullea says there are no restrictions on civilian movements.

100 San Francisco cops have been detailed to the FBI.

Dullea acts as though the situation were well in hand, says belligerently that "We're working with federal agencies on this to prevent any trouble, any outbreaks by an irresponsible people."

WIRE RECEIVED FROM (San Francisco) SUEHSDORF -- TO DAVID HULBURD - Dec. 8, 1941

San Francisco was crisp-cool, bright, clear, sunny today like an autumn football day in New York. Felt like any other Sunday, relaxed, calm, quiet in early morning. Kids playing in street, Italians in Suchsdorf's North Beach neighborhood going to 11 A...mass at Saints Peter and Paul Church (where Di Maggio was married) as usual. Atmosphere was clear, bay glinting with silver of sun on water. A few sail boats pushed out from yacht harbor in the Marina. Day quiet in entertainment field. No football. Some football talk of University of San Francisco's 26-13 licking by Mississippi state at Kezar Stadium Saturday and of Oregon's 71-7 blasting by Texas at Austin. Pedestrians and motorists clogged streets moderately no more than usual for Sunday. Later in the day there were perhaps more official olive-drab army cars rolling around than usual. And the idlers in the streets were talking up the situation. As you passed by you could hear people unburdening their individual knowledge of Japan's navy's strength, our own changes etc. A man explains vaguely to a woman something about the fleet's big guns; small boys and high school adolescents talked loudly, assertively, with gestures and explosive laughter on air raids and where they'd be when they came.

Movies showing: United Artists showing Wanger's Sundown; palatial Fox showing Garbo's "Two-faced woman," Paramount, Crosby's "Birth of the Blues." Fox west coast theater string of seven including Fox and Paramount -- announced once between early evening shows that members of companies K and L of the California State Guard should report immediately to the Armory. But other theaters made no announcements; no interruptions. United Artists suggested that service men leave name and seat location if personal calls should come in. Several did, from enlisted men's families who heard intermittant broadcasts from 12th naval district etc. to report to stations.

Radio: following news bulletins, government agencies began calling at all networks to have emergency announcements read. They began shortly after 12 noon. First

2.

on air was Alameda Naval air station, following them. Though not in this order, came 12th naval district, ninth corps area, San Francisco fire department, coast artillery units attached to San Francisco harbor defenses. All messages ordered service men to report to their stations or headquarters immediately. Simple message (ordered by Captain W. K. Kilpatrick, twelfth naval district chief of staff, at 12:30 P.M.): "attention all officers and men, twelfth naval district and Alameda naval air station: Report to your stations immediately." Alameda air station phoned networks at seven P.M. to cancel its announcement because all men had reported. Networks estimated they broadcast news flashes or emergency announcements every ten minutes since noon. Most regularly scheduled programs were hash, a few minutes of this, a few of that, an announcement, then another butchered program.

The Philharmonic concert was absolutely riddled.

Net works on 24 hour duty now for an hour after local fire department announcement was broadcast, blatant, bovine, fog-horn department siren blasted intermittently over the city.

People: radio, newsmen, communications services generally pally, full of chatter, eager to talk about the war. Rollicking would seem to be word for radio stations where cheerful bedlam reigned. "Modern design news bureau" cracked KFRC mutual news room early in evening. Radio men asked as many questions as they answered, flapped the jaw generally on the still lean diet of news. Usually lackadaisical police department, on other hand, all business, all efficiency, refusing to answer anything over phone and demanding that reporters present themselves at a hall of justice with credentials if they wanted information. Collared at the hall, the chief and his minions were their old, generally cooperative selves. Details AP reception direct Honolulu story: San Francisco Associated Press located second floor Bastard-Gothic Chronicle Building Fifth and Mission Streets. Clyde Gilbert Bartel (cq), 42, seven years San Francisco AP, now Sunday cable editor, says office had gotten Steve Early flash Washington and he was busy answering civilian calls for information and making

AP business calls to member papers when operator cut in with info overseas operator on wire with Honolulu call. As Bartel remembers it, this at about 11 a.m. he dashed into Buffy Little AP photographers room across hall to take call. Bartel heard voice, cool, but little keyed with excitement saying: "This is Burns, Eugene Burns. We're being bombed." Bartel said: "Yes, I know you're being bombed and so is Manila." Burns said: "Yes? Well, they're over us now and the attack is still going on." He gave his story in about five minutes. "Be sure to call us back, "Bartel said at end. "Yes," said Burns. Bartel roared back to office, batted out his first story by 11:28, Burns called back about noon spoke ten more minutes with additional details. A third call was coming through but before connection was made war-navy department censorship had gone into effect and Burns unheard from. Bartel says Burns calls came in clearly although both were shouting at each other. Occasionally circuit would fade like shortwave radio from Europe. But generally intelligible. No boss could be heard behind Burns voice. Bartel struck that Burns whom Bartel unknows doing routine job in best newspaper tradition. Unhurried. No dramatics, no gags, no stammering, strictly business. Bartel too pressed by time to think of own reaction.

United press was lucky. The office was closed. James Sullivan, bureau manager, had dropped in, however, to do some routine work after attending church in Berkeley and before the afternoon crew came on. The telephone rang: "This is the overseas operator calling. Just a moment while I complete the call." Sullivan jumped for the radio wire, only ticker in operation on dull Sunday morning, there saw the Early flash from Washington, got back to the phone to hear Mrs. Frank Tremaine, wife of up man in Honolulu say: We are being bombed, they are fifty planes over the city." She didn't identify as Japanese. Sullivan then went to work like crazy. Sullivan thinks call came about 10:45."

CORRECTION AND SUBSTITUTION IN WIRE FROM SAN FRANCISCO (Suehsdorf) TO DAVID HULBURD, RECEIVED 12-8-41.

Please disregard paragraph on United Press getting flash (Page 3, last paragraph) and substitute the following:

"James A. Sullivan, Bureau Manager, got the first flash when the telephone broke the dull Sunday routine. Most staffers were out of the office. Operators said: 'This is the overseas operator, hold on while I complete the call.' Then Sullivan heard (about 11:45 A.M. he recalls) flash bell on the teletype, dashed over to the ticker and read the first flash from Steve Early. He went back to the phone and talked to Mrs. Frank Tremaine, wife of UP man in Honolulu. She said, 'We are being bombed. About 50 bombers are coming over.' She couldn't identify bombers as Japanese."

End

Wire from Hammond (San Francisco) to D. Hulburd - December 8, 1941

Color add: I was up in the country when the news broke. It arrived via radio, party line telephone. The first word was from a Hawaiian boy working at Hagel ranch, who walked up announced unhappily: "Well, they just bombed Honolulu, the sons of bitches." From then on news arrives sporadically as various peoples drove up, plus what we learned from the radio. Our first reactions were almost of relief-- tremendous pressure building up for weeks finally resulting in an accomplished fact. People in the country were disbelieving at first, then resigned, calmer than in the city, perhaps they feel they are protected by distance from vital military objectives.

The weather was warm, sunny, typical California winter-springtime with the hills turning green after the first rains. All roads, ferry out of town were jammed with Sunday tourists (this before the news broke); roads were equally crowded later.

Returning to the city, the first thing noticeable was the blackout on the Golden Gate bridge, no lights showing even at Toll Plaza, collectors dropping cheery well-trained "Good evening" for brusque "Thanks." The gate bridge ramps were also blacked out, although the presidio through which they pass was still showing lights. One ramp was partially closed off with police guarding it. (Later it evolved the blackout was a mistake-someone thought he heard Japanese planes, and ordered lights switched off. The lights came back on later).

The San Francisco-Oakland Bay Bridgeport remained lighted, but regular state highway patrol units were augmented by armed companies of the California State Guard (volunteer organization inaugurated after the National Guard units were called to active service.) A hundred men were guarding the Oakland side approaches, Toll Plaza, and the bridge span through the tunnel on Yerba Buena Island, site of the naval receiving station and Treasure Island. On the other side of the tunnel, San Francisco units pick-up patrol, guard dirt and fifty street approaches. They were also stationed along Embarcadero guarding state-owned belt railroad, wharves and warehouses. Altogether, about four hundred guardists on the San Francisco side. These men were ordered on duty from state adjutant general's office, Sacramento, officer of DAT at San Francisco Armory (guard headquarters) said exultantly: "We dare anyone to get in (Embarcadero warehouses, etc.). They wouldn't get two feet:" The general impression driving through all parts of town -- war was still not an actuality to San Franciscans. They were talking about bombings, ship sinkings, etc. but it still was distant, unaffecting them personally. The most striking evidence of this was at the city's hospitality house for soldiers, and sailors. It was jampacked with gay, laughing, cheery men and gals. Although we were told there were only about one-third of the usual Sunday night crowd there due to leave cancellations, there were still fully five hundred on hand. The hostess said many men were writing letters, sending wires, but that was the only difference from the usual weekend. She was swamped with telephone calls from men wanting to know what they were supposed to do, friends trying to get track of others, but those at the dance apparently were unaffected by the situation. Apparently, the news was too big to penetrate in such a short time or else they were expecting it for so long that its final coming didn't make such difference one way or other. The bus was due to leave for Tiburon Naval Base at midnight but was put forward to eight. The sailors were irritated at leaving the gals rather than worried or apprehensive.

Jaltown section on the city was blocked off to all traffic for several hours this evening (making it seem a complete isolated settlement) since the police were expecting trouble. However none materialized. The cops said they were sent out with orders to expect anything, patrol in twos until relieved. They are expecting to be put on a 12-hour duty although not ordered so far. The shades in all Japanese homes were drawn, a few shops continued to be open but the majority were closed. There were few Japanese on the streets except for the curious around the Hotel Aki from which the FBI took the manager earlier, and the Fuji Transfer company across the street where the FBI men were going through the files after packing the owner off to the Hall of Justice. A candid expression of the sergeant on duty: "Why in hell couldn't they have waited until after Christmas." One little Jap came streaking out of the hotel in a great stew, said he was out fishing all day, came back to see a girl, and the FBI held him for questioning all afternoon with others found in the hotel. The majority of the Japanese we saw were either sad, bewildered, or else trying to appear unconcerned, slightly belligerent or tyring to appear nonchalant. The only ones outside the Japanese consulate, somewhat outside the borders of the Japanese section, were a cop, and two curious girls. The cop said no crowd had been up there probably because few people knew he lived there. The fire in the afternoon brought considerable attention, however. The cop said the FBI went over the debris ash by ash. One of the gals said she noted with interest three new trunks arriving at the Consulate last Wednesday.

"I thought something was up then".

The waterfront was dead in the evening, except for the usual crowd of tourists at Fishermens Wharf. Chinatown was crowded with the usual Sunday mob, Japanese owned stores (of which there are many) remained bravely open. Only serious Chinatown crowds were around ideographic newsposters in the windows of Chinese newspaper.

Night owl Beaneries were not even bothering to turn on news broadcasts, radios were giving out their usual swing record programs.

Wire from Arnold Aslakson, Minneapolis, to J. McConaughy, Dec. 8, 1941

News first broke on the radio about 1:30 p.m., WCCO, CBS station. Sandwiched between the Spirit of '41 broadcast from an eastern naval base, and a World Today news roundup, WLOL Mutual broke at 1:35 into "This is Fort Dix." WTCN, NBC broke the "Voice of Experience" at 1:36. KSTP, NBC sandwiched at 1:29 between the MacAlester College musical program and Chicago Round Table on "Canada: A Neighbor at War." There were dozens of calls to the radio stations asking "Is it true; will the boys home on Christmas leaves have to go back?" One asked: "Is it another play? (Apparent reference to Orson Welles); several women who called KSTP choked up. One said she had a boy in Pearl Harbor. Another one had a boy in Honolulu. Number 1 couldn't believe her ears. A man who phoned WTCN exploded: "Why those sons of bitches!" Radio switchboards were not jammed, however, apparently because of fast radio followup of the first flashes. We are unable to check the phone company on traffic yet. But several people, 50 of whom I called at random, told of running to friends' homes or phoning friends the news.

The St. Paul Pioneer-Press extraed at 4 or 4:15, the Minneapolis Morning Tribune at 4:30. The Trib had two extra pages in the first extra, upped it two pages more for each extra up to the fourth.

Curtis Edwards, WTCN announcer: "I didn't think they'd stick their necks out. I didn't think they'd have the guts." A young newspaper man (not I): "Oh, are they a bunch of damn fools." A painter and decorator: "Oh, oh. We're in it. I didn't think it was going to happen -- yet. We got to go at 'em." A retired realtor: who described his views as modified America First, though not an A.F. member: "How in the hell could we get caught napping like that? To think they were able to come over our base at Pearl Harbor is beyond my comprehension when we know how treacherous those Japs are. I'm disgusted." Draft-age men to each other -- several such conversations: "Well, we're in it. Our number's coming." Bakery Stock Clerk: "Well, it won't last long. They asked for it. We tried to

Aslakson, Minneapolis, Dec. 8, 1941   P. 2

be white and they turned on us like rats." Shoe salesman's wife: "Oh. It's happened. But Japan will take a beating." 16-year-old: "Japan must be about out of supplies. But glad I'm not 17 yet."

An investment secretary and his wife: He: "The U.S. will declare war now." She: "Do you think so, really?" He: "I wonder how long they'll be able to hold out. Will the Russians attack Japan now?" A credit man who said he wanted to "go get 'em" after the Panay: "I think we ought to declare war on the whole Axis. But how could they get caught napping at Pearl Harbor?" A bank auditor: "That bunch of double crossers." An Architect: "It's here at last. Might as well get it over with." Two neighbors to whom he passed the news phlegmatically just said thanks. They went to turn on their radios. Numerous others "hadn't thought much about it," "expected something, but not so soon." A majority expected an attack on Thailand or the Indies. Not Hawaii or the Philippines.

You can't help thinking that people are now more aroused, but it is too early to use any superlatives. Three walked on Christmas-lighted Nicollet Avenue, main shopping street, for half an hour. We saw many little knots of people gazing in windows as if nothing extraordinary. There always 20 or so in front of Powers Department store on the corner watching the animated display of the three wise men, shepherds, manger scene of "Peace on Earth." They listened to the music, remarked at the display, walked on.

When the news first broke, there was a chill rain, turning to wet snow by evening. Many were at dinner, others reading Sunday papers. There was no football. Movies."Keep 'em Flying," Abbott & Costello, at the Orpheum: "Suspicion," Grant and Fontaine, in "Shadow of the Thin Man," "Ladies in Retirement" at the others; no major theatres broke the show with the announcement. But the movie business slipped one-third as people stuck to their radios.

The Pioneer Press editorialized: "The Axis powers have brought the second World War to the Western Hemisphere, the Axis Powers that have recklessly launched

Aslakson, Minneapolis, Dec. 8, 1941   P. 3

this terrible war will find this country better prepared than they have imagined. The spirit of the American people under such provocation is equal to all the cruel sacrifices that this bloody business will impose."

The Interventionist Minneapolis Morning Tribune: "We must realize, each and every one of us, that this treacherous attack is not a detached incident which involves merely Japan and the United States. But on the contrary, an integrated detail, a part of the pattern of Hitler's world war plans... The fight, plainly, is not with Japan alone. It is with the entire Axis partnership of gangster nations, with Germany and its scavening satellites wherever they may fling down their challenge to us."

Through G.V. Cannon, president of Minnesota Marine Veterans Club, went a telegram to FDR: "300 World War Marine veterans in Minnesota request the privilege of service in a suitable classification to relieve younger men." Police Chief Edward B. Hansen asked for 100 extra police (Minneapolis force now 100) to guard defense plants and utilities. The Navy doubled guards at all naval equipment plants. The local America First Executive Committee said: "Japanese attacks, must, of course, be resisted." A group of state and local leaders of the Defend America and Fight for Freedom Committees wired the Minnesota delegation: "It is now clear that this is our war," and called for a declaration against Germany.

Maybe you missed this: Immediately after the first announcements of war, one network, I think it was CBS plowed merrily through the "good news" program with John B. Kennedy, telling the good news of how America is healthy, never ad-libbed a line to tone it down. Terribly incongruous.

<u>End</u>

Wire from Aslakson (Minneapolis) to J. McConaughy - December 8, 1941

Add Japanese side lights - Minneapolis: Local telephoned calls estimated up about twenty percent necessitating about thirty additional operators. Long distance calls are up as much as 45 percent.

Wire from Ben Avery, Phoenix, Ariz. to J. McConaughy - Dec. 7, 1941

News of the attack on Pearl Harbor hit Phoenix at 1 p.m. via the Phoenix CBS station KOY interrupting the CBS program "The World Today" at 12:30 p.m. Mountain time. I was the only person in the Arizona Republic newsroom and was immediately swamped with telephone calls. The telephone company reported no trouble. We hit the street with an extra at 4:45. All of our staff were scattered around, some playing golf, some out joy riding and the news editor was in Tucson.

Remarks of some Phoenicians who called to ask if the report was true:

"Well, I'll be damned. What is our army doing -- have you got anything?"

"What's this I hear about Japan declaring war? -- Have you got anything on the game between the Chicago Bears and the Cardinals? Aren't you getting anything besides that war stuff?"

Many of them, when advised about the war just said, "Well, I hope we blast them off of the face of the earth," or "How many of the yellow so and so's have we killed?" There also were a number of calls from relatives of servicemen in the Pacific asking about certain ships. Arizonians definitely were aroused. There are about a thousand Japanese farmers in the Salt River Valley and for weeks Arizonians generally have commented "If those Japs want to start something they'll sure find a fight" and opinion is general.

The news hit Phoenix on one of the quietest Sunday afternoons I've seen. The weather was warm and sunny and most everyone was out riding around, playing golf or just lolling on green lawns, almost no one was downtown, just a few scattered cars and an occasional pedestrian. Many were out in the country. The news ended the siesta hour though for within a short while crowds were gathering around sidewalk radios from Lord knows where. Many were in theatres. There were no football games. Phoenix' two big theatres were well filled. The Fox was showing "Keep 'Em Flying" but did not interrupt the program. The Orpheum interrupted "International Squadron" an RAF picture and absolute silence followed the announcement for about a minute, then the audience buzzed.

Page 2 -- Ben Avery, Phoenix

Dime theatres reported the same effect after making the announcement. Governor Sidney P. Osborne heard the news at his desk in the Capitol where he was catching up on his correspondence and immediately called H. R. Duffey, in charge of Phoenix FBI office, then summoned the Arizona civilian defense co-ordinating council into an emergency session at 4 p.m. The meeting was held to issue all council members to stand by for orders if needed in the event of an attack on the Pacific coast and general evacuation of coast residents to Arizona. After the meeting, the governor issued a statement asking all Arizonians to keep cool and do nothing until orders were issued and to leave everything to regularly constituted authorities.

Huge dams on Salt river already were under guard and have been for months. No editorials are available but am airmailing a special delivery with a picture of by-standers holding copies of the Republic extra, watching a wandering organgrinder with his monkey perform on a downtown street.

Wire from James Bell, Topeka, Kansas, to David Hulburd, Dec. 7, 1941.

War came to Topeka at 1:30 PM on a quiet, warm, 56 degrees, sunshiny Sunday. Most Topekans had finished big Sunday dinners and were napping on their sofas. First flash over Columbia's WIBW came at the end of the Spirit of '41 program. I got it over NBC Blue network while listening to the Great Plays series. I was in the bath tub. The second bulletin in re the attack on Manila made me sick. My parents, brother and sister are in Manila. My wife turned pale and said, "There it is." My telephone rang a few seconds later. I was called to help issue an extra and write "What it's like over there" story. Daily Capital switchboards were jammed immediately. One man, with distinct rural midwestern accent, asked: "What the Hell's going on out there? Has Uncle Sam declared war yet? Why in Hell hasn't he? How old do you have to be to get in the Army and Navy?" Others wanted to know if it were true. One mother, with a son at Pearl Harbor, choked up when told that Hawaii had been bombed and said, "Maybe they'll kill my boy, but I know he will be avenged." The telephone company says lines have been unusually busy since first flash. Several persons have attempted to put in calls to Honolulu and the Philippines, without success. The Daily Capital's 4-page extra hit the street just before 7 P. M. Kansas City Star had its extra in town an hour and a half later. Thousands of persons were waiting to get copy of CAPITAL. They went like hotcakes. People drove in from the residential districts to get them.

There was no hysteria. Everyone was interested. No one was very excited. My wife's first expression, "There it is", was common phrase. I would say that Topeka is taking the news with grim determination. Most Topekans, I believe, didn't think it would ever happen. When it did, they took it calmly. There are isolated cases of panic. One woman called the Capital frantically saying that a Jap plane had just dove on her house. It turned out it was a private plane flying over the city at high altitude. Capper and Ratner, with radio addresses coming up, had to change their texts in a hurry. Both pledged their wholehearted support of the President. Alf Landon, in a telegram to Roosevelt, said: "There is imperative need for courageous action by the American people. The Japanese attack leaves no choice. Nothing must be permitted to interrupt our victory over a foreign foe. Please command me in any way I can be of service."

Capper said, "Japan's attack means war and we will see it through. I will support our President."

Junior Senator Clyde Reed, ill in Parsons, left immediately for Washington by plane. Capper returning by train. The news came when many Topekans were in the first afternoon show at movie houses. No pictures were broken into to give the flash. The biggest crowds were at Bob Hope's "Nothing But The Truth." I saw them come out. They were laughing and gay. When they heard the news, their faces sobered rapidly, then they went away quietly. One man said, "Guess we'll have to lick the sons of bitches." An indication that Topeka is taking the news calmly is that all theatres reported nearly normal attendance at night shows. The people are not aroused in the usual sense of the word. They are quiet, calm and determined that the U. S. will win.

Three members of the local Navy recruiting office staff have requested sea duty. I've talked to several dozen persons and none express regret that war has come. All feel it is necessary. The feeling is this:

Right or wrong, we are in this thing now and we've got to win. No use singing the Star Spangled Banner or shooting Jap restaurant owners. We're ready to do whatever is asked of us. Poor old Capper is broken hearted. He wandered about the Capital news room with a long face. I believe there were tears in his eyes. He kept saying: "It's too bad, it's too bad." Later in the evening when preparing to leave for Washington he was brighter and more determined. "I will support the President - it's the one thing left to do," he said. The only sporting event in process was State Field Dog Trials, (hunting). The news took the kick out of the dog lovers sport. The afternoon, which started off spirited, ended rather flat. "I guess our hunting will be confined to those God damned slant eyed bastards from now on," said one sportsman. In Topeka, I would say the single most important development of the day was the joining of Capper and Landon behind Roosevelt. Landon's statement was the most sincere he ever made. When I talked with him I got the impression that he would gladly do any job the President required of him. CAPITAL won't have editorial comment before Tuesday morning. Will wire digest of State Journal's editorial Monday P. M.

            End

Wire from James Bell, Topeka, Kansas, to David Hulburd - 12-8-41

Editorial comment of Topeka STATE JOURNAL:

"As a people we must travel a long and difficult road before the U. S. again finds itself at peace with all nations. No one knows the terrible toll we may be called upon to pay for our weakness in those years when we depended for security upon the pledged words of other nations, including the one which attacked us without warning Sunday. But, however difficult the course may prove, we must travel it. Whatever the cost in blood and sacrifice, we must move swiftly to pay it. This is our war. We must win it."

This, I believe, is an extremely good summation of Topeka's general attitude. The city is at work today, but jobs are suffering by the lack of interest of employes. Navy and army recruiting offices report tremendous upsurge of enlistment. The sun is shining, it is warm, and two short hours ago, the U. S. declared war.

End

Wire from Harold Boyle, Portland, Me. to J. McConaughy - Dec. 7, 1941.

Portland, Me., a big new naval base for the Atlantic fleet, is just recovering from the shock of the Reuben James sinking after that ship left here for Iceland, received news of the Japanese bombings with more excitement than is common to the Yankee temperament. The news first came by radio (Columbia chain). The newspaper office was bombarded with telephone calls asking "Is it true?" "Does Associated Press confirm it?"

A cold but sunny afternoon here with little going on in a city still somewhat under the influence of the old blue laws except for theatres open. Most excited were about a thousand sailors on shore leave from boats just back from convoy duty. Many expressed real concern over the report that the U.S. Oklahoma had been hit. Several in the newspaper office commented that they had mates on the Oklahoma.

The most common statement in middle-class circles, "Now we can be unified; no more strikes; let's get down to business. Entrance into European war next." A small isolationist group here, followers of Congressman James Oliver, who is an outright isolationist, changed its tune. One: "There's no answer to this one. Give them (the Japs) as good as they send."

General reaction here, from bus drivers to a few wealthy: "A typical, underhanded way of acting. Americans are through taking it lying down." Typical Yankee reaction: "They stabbed us in the back."

Very few Japanese in Portland; this city, which is a no. 1 defense site with naval base, two large shipyards and four army posts, interested in reaction of west coast to talk of bombings, blackouts, etc. Portland is the nearest Atlantic port to Europe and expects similar reaction in the case of war with Germany.

My honest opinion is that the news affected many the same way as in 1917. People are serious; no wisecracking or grumbling about meddling. Said one newspaperman: "I feel sure of one thing. Up to today, I wondered whether we were another France; too soft. What I have seen today convinces me that American

Page 2 -- Boyle, Portland, Me.

(At least Maine people) can fight in the old way."

Quote from lead editorial in Portland (Me) Press Herald, largest newspaper (morning) in Maine in Monday issue:

"No better proof of fundamental Japanese treachery, of which the country has been hearing for many decades, could be found than the foulness of conduct that launched attack upon this nation while it was earnestly trying to seek a peaceful settlement of the Far Eastern question. In 50 years of public life, Sec. Hull said he had never known a document so filled with "infamous falsehoods" as that delivered on Sunday to him by the Japanese emissaries in this country. Of that we shall hear more today.

"The issue is between democracy and despotism. It is we democratic powers against world slavery. It is the U.S. against Hitler, his satellites and stooges. If the congress has the guts which an American congress ought to have, it will refuse from this day to blink at duty. It will recognize verities. It will declare war upon every enemy of peace and decency. We must not only furnish the tools; we ourselves must help finish the job."

Wire from John Durant, Boston, Mass. to David Hulburd - Dec. 8, 1941

In Boston, five days of unseasonable warmth and fog lifted and a sharp, cold wind needled down from the North across clear skies in which the fiery sun was preparing for the final plunge into the West. Boston was pervaded by Sabbath calm with folks, after a hearty noon meal, slouched in their chairs beside the radio, in movies, Sunday driving in the country, or visiting neighbors. There were few people on the streets. All was quiet. Then electrification came at 2:29 as local radio stations announced, "Unidentified planes, presumably Japanese, have just bombed Oahu."

As newspapers, the BOSTON GLOBE, POST, heard the radio report, immediately confirmed by news ticker, editors ordered bulletins and slapped them on bulletin boards fronting Washington Street by 2:45. Pandemonium reigned at BOSTON RECORD where the 4:30 P.M. edition was being made up. The RECORD put a special war edition on the street at 3:18. Small knots of people with coat collars turned up stopped in front of the newspaper row of bulletins, passed on. It was too cold for more than - "why those bastards of Japs."

The four biggest Boston movie houses did not break the program to announce the Jap invasion.

One of overtones of thought I am beginning to pick up is----From now on, England has got to come second and the United States first in regard to production of our planes, tanks, etc.

Editorials in Boston Papers:

HERALD: "America's period of "blood, toil, tears and sweat" is at hand;" POST: "This attack in one instant has destroyed the disunity which has been disturbing America. The causes of this war can be left to the historians to evaluate. The twilight of peace is over;" GLOBE: "United as never before, we will meet this challenge"; RECORD: "We are all Americans now, united, strong, invincible."

Page 2, - John Durant - Boston.

As people clung to their radios, announcements came piling in -- Report for duty at once; Navy recruiting stations will be open at 8 A.M.; all manufacturers of defense materials are to take immediate precautions against sabotage; Metropolitan police ordered to 24-hour duty to protect Boston's water reservoirs; John McCormick (?) Majority House Leader, receives a telephone call from Roosevelt, and his wife at Dorchester home hastily packs his bag for his return to Washington; extra guards rushed to Charlestown Navy Yard; Ex-Governor Curley wrapped up the Japanese decoration presented to him by the Japanese Embassy in 1917 and mailed it to the Japanese; at all power plants were detailed guards; Civilian Defense workers were requested to stand by for instant action; at Newton, hundreds of people were in the midst of anti-air raid practice when the news came and they simply kept on with their rehearsal with grimmer sense of reality; Mayor Tobin spoke, Governor Saltonstall called out the National Guard. One sad note is that Boston still has no air raid warning siren.

Immediate public reaction in the following order was: unbelieving astonishment that the Japs would have the nerve to attack Oahu, wrath at the treachery of the Japs, spontaneous recognition that we are united in the common goal to lick the Japs.

The most important developments were the speed with which the people were notified for events and mobilized for emergency via radio, and the unquestionable and immediate reaction of "at last we are united."

For quotes of the man on the street, I like best the fellow who said to me, "That settles it, we're united now." A waitress - "There's been too much talk and not enough action. Let's get going." A schoolteacher - "Let them have it, they asked for it." A Sailor - "It's me or them - and I'll make damn sure it's not me." A shopkeeper - "This is one war the U.S. will approve of." Everywhere you went it was the same, united at last, go out and get those Japs.

End

Wire from John Durant, Boston - to J. McConaughy - Dec. 8, 1941

Telephone calls in New England were up 25% after the announcement of the Jap invasion Sunday, and recruiting stations here report today a big rush. Before the Navy and Marine recruiting station in the Federal Building opened at 8 a.m. there were 41 men, ages 17 to 43, waiting outside the door to join up, and the offices have been swamped ever since. The Army reports that the number of recruits is "10 times normal." A grandfather/and a son, all of the same family, came to the Navy recruiting station here, and there is an excellent chance that all three will eventually be accepted for Coast Guard and Navy service.

Wire from Clayton Fritchey, Cleveland, to J. McConaughy - Dec. 8, 1941

There is a good angle here on the impact of the Jap attack and how all conflicting opinion on the Far East instantly crumbled before the reality of actual war. Yesterday and today 80 delegates to the Institute of Pacific Relations met in Cleveland to thrash out oriental problems and find the best course for the U.S. to pursue. Many of the nation's greatest authorities on the Far East are in confab, along with congressmen, prominent industrialists and such journalistic experts as Hugh Byas and James R. Young, both Tokyo correspondents.

News of the attack broke at the start of Sunday afternoon round table. There was dead silence for two minutes. In those 120 seconds, 80 different opinions were resolved. It was unanimously agreed, as one delegate put it, that "Japan has handed America its long-needed unity on a silver platter." The Institute met here under the auspices of Cleveland's Foreign Affairs Council, directed by Brooks Emeny. Everything was done in a very swank way. Delegates and guests gathered at the Cleveland Country Club Saturday, had lunch, cocktails, dinner, spent the night at the club, then started over again Sunday morning. No speeches were allowed; all back & forth discussion. Among those present: H. F. Angus, Department of External Affairs, Ottawa; Dr. M.S. Bates, Nanking College, China; Robert F. Black, president of White Motors Co.; Kurt Bloch, research director, Institute of Pacific Relations; Congresswoman Frances Bolton, Edward C. Carter, secretary-general of the Institute; Gordon K. Chalmers, president of Kenyon College; Sir Shanmukkhan Chetty, Indian Purchasing Mission; New York; Congressman Robert B. Chipperfield, Frederick V. Field, chairman of the Editorial Board, Amerasia, New York; Congressman Bartel J. Johkman, Congressman Karl Mundt, Count Sarlo Sforza, former Italian Foreign Minister; N.A.C. Slotemaker de Bruine, director of the Netherlands Information Bureau, New York; Congressman John Vorhys; delegates also included half a dozen bank presidents, economists, heads of rubber companies,

Fritchey, Cleveland, Dec. 8, 1941   P. 2

editors, prominent lawyers, etc. Almost a complete cross-section of people. I never saw a greater mixture of men and women and never heard greater mixture of opinion -- until the radio flashed out the stunning news. If one blast from the radio can unify a group of arguing professional experts it ought to be able to unify everybody else. Most of the Congressmen mentioned above are regarded as isolationists, but not one dissented from quick consensus that America's course had been set.

It is understood that everything said at these conferences is off record, but after a radio bulletin had come in, the Chairman of the meeting finally broke the silence by turning to one isolationist Congressman and asking what answer America would give to the Japanese attack. The reply was: "Our answer is probably being given by the American fleet right now." Applause.

An interesting fact is that not one expert present had foreseen such a drastic offensive. Up to the moment the news broke, the overwhelming opinion was that Japan had no wish to fight U.S., that the peaceful solution of all Pacific problems was possible, and the Japs were too intelligent to commit "national suicide" by going to war.

The only speaker to come close to the mark was James R. Young, who said the action of the Japs had nothing to do with "Government" or "Intelligence" or anything else. Japan, he insisted, was being run by a gang of gangsters in the Army and Navy who were responsible to no one. These "gangsters" he maintained, would do anything to perpetuate themselves in power, no matter what the certain consequences to Japan. Young brought a portent to the meeting. Four days ago he suddenly received through the mails, a file the Japanese had kept on him since his arrest in Tokyo. There was no note of explanation; just the file. Sent from the New York Japanese Consul. There was an air about the incident of someone cleaning

Fritchey, Cleveland, Dec. 8, 1941

out papers before moving. Young also told Congressmen present that in Washington there was available to them Japanese war plans which had been seized three or four years ago. These plans, he said, called for the identical operations which the Japs followed today. If what Young says is true, then the Germans didn't plot the strategy of this attack.

Hugh Byas pointed out that the Japs had struck the same kind of surprise blow at Port Arthur against Russia, and recalled the story of how the Jap ambassador went to the Russian Court Ball while an attack was being carried out without knowledge of the Russians. Byas said he had thought in the present situation the Japs would try to keep the U.S. divided by pursuing the war in such a way as to put us in the position of helping British imperialism.

In an effort to explain the seemingly insane attack, one Institute official said the State Department had received a story to the following effect: the Japan war lords knew they could not win in China, but could not afford to admit and withdraw. A defeat by the U.S. and Britain combined would cause no loss of face. Therefore, the best solution was a short war with the Allies and quick surrender.

General excitement here was slow getting underway. The first flash came over radio station WGAR at 2:30, just as the World Today program began on Columbia system. Station managers here tell me that listeners didn't seem quite to grasp the news at first. Phone calls were nothing like the Orson Welles war. When World War II broke out, it had been preceded by an hour-by-hour radio build-up for several days. This one, of course, broke out of the blue.

More from Cleveland later.

End

Wire from Clayton Fritchey, Cleveland, O. to James McConaughy - Dec. 8, 1941

PLAIN DEALER says: "Once more this nation is called upon to protect its own destiny and that of free people everywhere. There will be no faltering, and again, by the Grace of God, no doubt as to the outcome."

CLEVELAND PRESS: "The Japanese found us slow to wrath. They will find us mighty in wrath. They found us unwilling to strike the first blow. They will yet find us striking the last blow...America salutes the President, who fought so nobly for Pacific peace, and who now leads us in the just cause of self defense. America salutes the armed forces, who have never lost a war."

CLEVELAND NEWS: "This war will not end when Japan is defeated, but when the Axis is smashed, whether that takes one year or ten."

Mayor Frank J. Lausche has wired Roosevelt that all of Cleveland is marching at his side.

An American Legion broadcast appeal this morning asked all home and building owners to display the American flag every day from now on.

Radio bulletins cleared the streets of auto traffic last night. This was the lightest traffic casualty list for Sunday night in many weeks.

The only current labor trouble in this area was immediately settled. Four striking units at Great Ravenna Shell Loading Plants called off pickets this morning. The plant is back in full production. The Cleveland Civilian Defense Council met at 11 A.M. Anti-sabotage forces at all industrial and utility plants were immediately increased and priorities established on civilian use of police forces.

Says Arthur P. Gustafson, attorney for Cleveland chapter of the America First Committee: "I'm terribly shocked. I'm hoping we are so situated we can put an early end to this war. It looks like the only way to end it is to demolish Japan. I trust our Naval and Air forces are sufficient."

End

Wire from Grey(Portland) to J. McConaughy - December 7, 1941

Portland was warm Sunday, sky bright above with a haze fringing the city. It was good golfing weather. At Mount Hood, skiers had fresh snow. Church-going Portlanders were listening to sermons when the White House flash came at 11:30 am PST Newspaper readers were sunk in the funnies or scanning the headline, "F.R. makes Final Plea." Home radios were tuned to "Chicago Roundtable"(NBC red), "The World Today"(CBS), "Swingtime Strings" (Mutual) when network newscaster cut in. Listeners sat up shocked, turned up radios, telephoned neighbors.

By evening, the telephone company had increased their switchboard crew nearly 50%, long distance lines were jammed, calls to Chicago were delayed two hours; to San Francisco two hours; to Tacoma--Fort Lewis--one hour; all Seattle circuits were in constant use. At 7:55 pm PST, the Pacific Telephone & Telegraph Company bought radio spots to ask that citizens use long distance only for most urgent business. Extra guards were placed around telephone buildings.

The "Oregon Journal" had the first of five extras with UP bulletins on the street at/2:15. The Oregonian (whose AP Sunday wire ordinarily opens at one o'clock, today opened at 12:30) was out with the first complete paper at 3:30. At 7:30 pm I asked a one-legged newsboy, standing on a downtown intersection on crutches peddling extras, what people were saying, "As a matter of fact," he replied, "I've just been too damned busy to talk to them about it."

To most Portlanders, the news was incredible. None had expected the Japs to get close as Hawaii, which is closer than New York to Portland. When one lad rushed out of his house to tell a congregation leaving Church, some said: "You're fooling." Once convinced, most Portlanders were calmly furious, determined. They said, "Well, they asked for it--now we'll give it to them." "They ought to take every Jap and throw him into jail, American or not." "Let's find Lindbergh and ask him about it." "I'd rather play with a rattlesnake than a Jap anytime." High school boys said, "Well, we'll have to fight now." A Soldier on leave drawled to his buddy, "We'd better polish up our shootin' irons." One soldier on Sunday afternoon walked about the Portland business district carrying a portable radio going full force. When telephone lines got crossed, a strange man's voice broke into two housewives' conversation to talk war with them. Finally, they all just listened to his radio blasting news into the telephone. Sugar buying picked up in open grocery stores. Newsreel Theatre inserted a Navy short "The Battle" in the program.

The great unhappy question Sunday afternoon was "Where were our Navy patrols? How could the Japs get that close to Hawaii?" Newspaper executives, extra reporters moved into newspaper offices, glumly hovered about the copy desk to read incoming bulletins. Headline writers dropped the polite form "Japanese", made it "Japs". Oregonian newsmen cheered when the wire editor read an unconfirmed bulletin Jap carrier was sunk. Men called Lindbergh, Wheeler sobs, but inevitably returned to the Navy question. One said "The Navy was caught with their pants at half mast," another, "What makes me sore is that this was the last great nation that had a chance to surprise the Axis, and here they pull the same thing on us Germany pulled on the rest," another, "We oughta be bombing Tokyo.

When a reporter telephoned the news to Portland's acting Japanese Consul Y. Oka, he snapped, "It is just a wild rumor. I have had no word at all. I have just heard what is on the radio; I don't believe so. I don't believe so at all. I think it is just rumor. I think it is just wild rumors, very wild rumor". Shortly he was burning papers in the Consulate stove. Smoke filtered into the eighth floor corridors of the Board of Trade Building. Police threw a guard around that office and the Consul's home. Oka told newsmen between 1000 and 1500 Japanese have been trying to leave the Portland area. American-born members of the Japanese American Citizens League, admittedly facing hard times, told newspapers they hope the fairness of the caucasian Americans would ease their lot as citizens.

At Oregon shipbuilding Corporation's vast plant beside Willamette River,

Mrs. Henry Kaiser christened the SS Thomas Jefferson at 3 pm Sunday while shipyard workers cheered it down skids. Launching guest, Oregon Governor Charles A. Sprague, hurried from there to Oregonian office, sat down at the City Editor's typewriter to peck out wire to Roosevelt .. "1..We must not rest until menace of Japanese aggression in the Pacific is definitely ended..."

Governor Sprague Sunday night proclaimed a state of emergency for the State of Oreg Oregon, precise meaning to be clarified Monday.

Sunday night's wildest rumor here was that San Francisco was being bombed. The region's military and civilian defense forces sprang into action quickly. Bonneville Power Administration doubled guard around the dam, power plant, scatter substations. Portland's city Water Bureau ordered out Bureau employees to guard pipe lines, reservoirs; city bridges were placed under armed guard. At Vancouver, Wash. ALCOA operated its new reduction plant Sunday night with yard lights blacked out. All ships in Columbia River ports Sunday were frozen in port area by navy order.

Editorial quotes: Oregon Journal--"Attack on Hawaii and Philippines, Sunday, wx was cold, calculating-- and insane. It was planned, suicidal betrayal of peace conversations. To President Roosevelt's personal peace appeal to Emporor Hirohito, it returned a brutal insult of murderous violence.."Now we know the worst, now we can have at an unpleasant task and have done with it as rapidly as we may".

Oregonian--"...Japan, as an empire, is about to go down beneath the waves of the Pacific. America will destroy her--and America suddenly united, whose great strength is xxtxxngx as strength of ten through righteous sense of unspeakable outrage... her material dreams will be angled and quite wreckage at bottom of the area. America pledges it. America believes that in that undertaking it carries banners of God."

Wire from Gray (Portland, Oregon) - 12/8/41 3:30 p. m.

Blackouts ordered for tonight at Columbia River's mouth and Gray's Harbor (Aberdeen Hoquiam). May cover entire North Pacific Coast area, including Seattle and Portland

COPY of telegram from Michael Griffin, Louisville, Ky. to McConaughy, Dec. 7, 1941

WINN, NBC, broadcast news 1:30 during program "Great Plays." WGRC, Mutual, at 1:33, during Serenade for Sunday; WAVE, 1:43 during Chicago Round Table, WHAS, Columbia, 1:42 during old fashioned revival hour. Following its beat WINN swamped with phone calls. All stations had to hire extra operators. Bell Telephone Company here reports big pickup of local calls following first flash, but emphasis on long-distance calls after news Japan had declared war. Manager thinks parents calling sons at camps. Courier-Journal extra out 4:30, first since Hitler invaded Poland. Paper had to call printers who were attending union meeting. Papers sold biggest on record, as fast as presses could print at start, according to Jasper Rison, circulation manager. Press roll on first extra 43,000, all sold in Louisville. Total sale of two extras preceding first night edition nearly 70,000 in Louisville alone -- unprecedented here.

First reaction here stunned surprise. Noon newscasts carried no hint, newspaper stories Sunday here indicated Japs backing down, afraid of U.S. A taxi driver thought about announcement a second or two, then said: "Is this going to hurt this country?" Two Fort Knox officers dining in a hotel turned to each other, asked: "What is it, a gag?" When one of them realized report on level he groaned: " Nuts, there goes my trip to Sugar Bowl." Mr. and Mrs. Harry Preston informed by a reporter while they were window shopping on Louisville's 4th Street, principal thoroughfare. Small, blonde, extremely youthful Mrs. Preston bit her lip; husband, tall, slim, also youthful, stiffened. Neither spoke for an instant. "This is a big surprise." he said. "But we have resigned ourselves. Our boy Robert (23) is with the Atlantic Fleet or was last we heard."

Fort Knox soldiers strolling the streets with girls were surprised, but apparently pleased. "I didn't think the Japs had the nerve," said Sergeant R. McCallum. "But we're ready for 'em." Most civilians took it with their mouths

Page 2-- from Griffin, Louisville - Dec. 7

open, had nothing to say at first. This was followed by strong irritation that Japs could have attacked Pearl Harbor and got away with it. Everybody showed exasperation. "What was Navy doing?" "How could an airplane carrier get that close?" were typical angry questions from every type of citizen.

Louisville citizens just getting ready to enjoy what they call "a pretty day" when news broke. Sun was shining, air crisp and cool. Most people at Sunday dinner or getting ready for automobile rides. Downtown streets populated mostly by soldiers and their girls. Sunday traffic, heavy here since Defense effort started year ago, at its quietest, movies doing brisk business, no standout films, none interrupted to give news fearing it might cause commotion, according to managers.

Obviously took a matter of an hour or two for news to soak in, but this warlike community plenty mad now.

For months defense plants here have been strongly guarded, so no extra details put on following announcement, but at Knox extra guards thrown around all utilities. "We're already guarded to the hilt, so guess we'll just go on making powder," said Lieut. Col. R.E. Hardy, Army Engineer in charge of Indiana and Hoosier Ordnance Works (DuPont Powder Plant, Bag Plant at Charlestown, Ind.)

"Somebody is crazy in Japan," said Maj. Gen. Jacob L. Devers, Chief of Armored Force at his Fort Knox office. "I don't see how they can hope to accomplish anything by this attack. As for us here, this thing will of course speed up our whole program of preparation. It ought to bring an end to all these foolish strikes for one thing. I don't plan to do anything about calling men back to the Fort immediately, but if this thing is as serious at it appears to be, we may have to cancel holiday leaves. It may also bring a halt to discharges of men over 28-year limit and, conceivably, we might begin calling back some of those already discharged and placed on reserve. That, of course, is up to the War Department."

Page 3-- from Griffin, Louisville -Dec. 7

Civilian Defense Committee here called meeting for Monday night with Mayor. Veterans outfits began offering services if needed.

Herbert Agar, away since last spring, dictated lead editorial to Courier via telephone from New York: "War has chosen us. There is no more excuse for doubting that barbarism has come back into our world.... And we must face the terrible truth that the end will not be found in Japan, or on the wide wastes of the Pacific. The end will be found in Berlin.... America will now unite to beat Japan. America must now unite to finish the job by beating Germany, the source of all our woe."

Wire from Robert Hagy, Pittsburgh, to D. Hulburd - Dec. 7, 1941

PITTSBURGH AND THE WAR

The strangest development here involved America First assembled in Soldier's Hall in Oakland Civic Center, three miles from downtown Pittsburgh. Senator Gerald P. Nye, tall, dark, handsome North Dakotan, spoke to 2500 ranked and filers (capacity) from hall-wide platform above which Lincoln's Gettysburg address is spread in huge dark letters against a dirty buff background. I was assigned to cover it for the Post Gazette, and just a few minutes before leaving the office flashes and bulletins came over the AP wire on the Hawaii and Manila attacks.

I arrived at the hall just at 3 p.m., the time the meeting was scheduled to start and found Nye in a two-by-four room backstage ready to go on with the local officials of the Firsters. I shoved the pasted-up news at him. Irene Castle McLaughlin, still trim wife of the dancer killed in the World War I, another speaker and Pittsburgh chairman John B. Gordon, clustered around the Senator to read. It was the first they had heard of the war and Nye's first reaction was: "It sounds terribly fishy to me. Can't we have some details? Is it sabotage or is it pen attack? I'm amazed that the President should announce an attack without giving details." Cool as a cucumber, he went on to compare the announcement with the first news of the Greer incident, which he termed very misleading.

I asked him what effect the Jap war should have on America First, whether it would disband. He replied that "If Congress were to declare war, I'm sure that every America Firster would be cooperative and support his government in the winning of that war in every possible way...but I should not expect them to disband even if Congress declared war." Nye and the others then paraded on to the platform as if nothing had happened. Although the news had come over the radio, apparently nobody in the audience knew anything and the meeting went on just like any other America First meeting with emphasis on denouncing Roosevelt as a warmonger. Mrs. McLaughlin expressed concern for America's wives and mothers, her voice catching as she referred to Vernon Castle's not coming back, dabbed a tear from her eye as she sat down.

The next speaker was ruddy, ruralish Charlie Sipes, Pennsylvania State Senator, locally famed as a historian. Routine America First stuff until, in the midst of an attack on Roosevelt for trying "to make everything Russian appealing to the U. S.", he cried: "In fact, the chief war-monger in the U. S., to my way of thinking, is the president of the U. S.", while the hall, decked in red-white-and blue balcony bunting and "Defend America First" signs was still full of roaring approval, a white-haired, heavy set man stood up from aisle seat well to the rear. The man, although nobody knew him and he was in mufti, was Col. Enrique Urrutia, Jr., Chief of the Second Military area (Pittsburgh District of Third Corps area) of the organized reserve. "Can this meeting be called after what has happened in the last few hours?" Co. Urrutia, infantryman, 31 yrs. in the army, burst out, livid with incredulity and indignation. "Do you know that Japan has attacked Manila, that Japan has attacked Hawaii?"

Apparently the crowd took him for a plain crackpot heckler. They booed, yelled "Throw him out" and "War monger"; several men near Urrutia coverged on him. According to Lieut. George Pischke, in command of detail of 10 policemen assigned to keep down disturbances which usually mark America First meetings here, the committee's blue-badged ushers "tried to man-handle" the colonel. Cops were in quick, though and Lieut. Pischke escorted Urrutia out of the hall (through a blizzard of "war-monger" shrieks and reaching women's hands) at the latter's own request. "I came to listen", he told me in the lobby, purple with rage. "I thought this was a patriot's meeting, but this is a traitors' meeting." Inside, sipe, a cool hand, tried to restore calm, said soothingly "Don't be too hard on this poor bombastic man. He's only a mouthpiece for FDR. Then Sipe went on with his speech.

A couple of other people addressed the crowd. Finally came Nye. Still no word from leaders about the war. Nye started at about 4:45 p.m. for nearly three quarters of an hour he went through his isolationist routine. "Who's war is this?", he demanded at one point (referring to war in Europe). "Roosevelt's" chorused the rank and filers. "My friends," said Nye callously, "are betting 20 to 1 that if we don't stop in our tracks now, we'll be in before Great Britain gets in." Howls of laughter. A few minutes after this, I was called to the telephone. The city desk had a bulletin on Japan's declaration of war and asked me to get it to Nye. On a piece of copy paper I printed in pencil: "The Japanese imperial govt. at Tokio today at 4 p.m. announced a state of war with the U. S. and Great Britain." I walked out on the platform and put it on the rostrum before Nye. He glanced at it, read it, never batted an eye, went on with his speech...

"It is Nazism to do any thinking here in America," and so on. Nye started to speak around 4:45. I gave him the note at about 5:30 for 15 minutes more, he continued his routine, "I woke up one morning to find that we had 50 ships less -- that President had given them away despite laws forbidding it." "Treason" yelled some. "Impeach him" yelled others. Finally, at 5:45 more than two and a half hours after the meeting started, Nye paused and said: "I have before me the worst news that I have encountered in the last 20 years. I don't know exactly how to report it to you but I will report it to you just as a newspaperman gave it to me." Slowly he read the note. An excited murmur swept through the packed hall. Nye continued: "I can't somehow believe this. I can't come to any conclusions until I know what this is all about. I want time to find out what's behind it. Previously I heard about bombings in Hawaii. Somehow, I couldn't quite believe that but in the light of this later news, I'm sure there's been many funny things before. I remember the morning of the attack on the destroyer Greer. The President went on the radio and said the attack on the Greer was without provocation

but I tell you the Greer shot first. That was the incident the president said was unprovoked and that's cheating."

With that, he disposed of the new war, but more or less upset and flushed in the face, he didn't do much more than flounder through five or six more minutes of stuff about America's prime duty being to preserve democracy lest "victor and vanquished alike fall" and communism "grow in the ruins". Loud applause. "Keep your chins up", said Senator Nye and sat down. Benediction, a couple of announcements and the meeting was over. Plowing through his fanatical followers, I gave Nye a third piece of intelligence -- that Roosevelt had called a 9 p.m. meeting of the cabinet and congressional leaders. I knew he was scheduled to talk tonight at the First Baptist Church (pastor of which is pacifist) and I asked him if he intended to fly to Washington. Flustered, grim-lipped rosy faced, sweating, he muttered, "I must, I must try...", and strode quickly out of the hall talking to somebody about plane reservations..Whether he couldn't get a plane or what, he nevertheless ended up keeping the church appointment, announcing he would take the train to Washington later tonight. At church, before 600 people, he was grim, bitter, defeated. "I had hoped for long that at least the involvement of my country in this terrible foreign slaughter would be left more largely to our own determination."

Then he reviewed events leading up to the war, accusing Roosevelt of "doing his utmost to promote trouble with Japan". Inferring that we were already at war with Germany, he declared: "I am not one to say my country is prepared to fight a war on one front, let alone two." Then several people laughed at a reference (out of habit?) to "bloody Joe Stalin". Nye said coldly: "I am not making a humorous speech." But on the Jap attack he said: "here is a challenge. There isn't much America can do but move forward with American lives. American blood

but I tell you the Greer shot first. That was the incident the president said was unprovoked and that's cheating."

With that, he disposed of the new war, but more or less upset and flushed in the face, he didn't do much more than flounder through five or six more minutes of stuff about America's prime duty being to preserve democracy lest "victor and vanquished alike fall" and communism "grow in the ruins". Loud applause. "Keep your chins up", said Senator Nye and sat down. Benediction, a couple of announcements and the meeting was over. Plowing through his fanatical followers, I gave Nye a third piece of intelligence -- that Roosevelt had called a 9 p.m. meeting of the cabinet and congressional leaders. I knew he was scheduled to talk tonight at the First Baptist Church (pastor of which is pacifist) and I asked him if he intended to fly to Washington. Flustered, grim-lipped rosy faced, sweating, he muttered, "I must, I must try...", and strode quickly out of the hall talking to somebody about plane reservations..Whether he couldn't get a plane or what, he nevertheless ended up keeping the church appointment, announcing he would take the train to Washington later tonight. At church, before 600 people, he was grim, bitter, defeated. "I had hoped for long that at least the involvement of my country in this terrible foreign slaughter would be left more largely to our own determination."

Then he reviewed events leading up to the war, accusing Roosevelt of "doing his utmost to promote trouble with Japan". Inferring that we were already at war with Germany, he declared: "I am not one to say my country is prepared to fight a war on one front, let alone two." Then several people laughed at a reference (out of habit?) to "bloody Joe Stalin". Nye said coldly: "I am not making a humorous speech." But on the Jap attack he said: "here is a challenge. There isn't much America can do but move forward with American lives. American blood

and American wealth to the protection of our people and possessions in the Pacific."

Leaving the church, another Post-Gazette reporter caught him, asked what course he would prescribe for the nation finally he gave in completely. The fight gone out of him except for enough to make one more crack at Roosevelt. "We have been maneuvered into this by the president," he said, "but the only thing now is to declare war and to jump into it with everything we have and bring it to a victorious conclusion."

Page 6 -- Add to Hagy, Pittsburgh

The weather is fine, sunny and clear and brisk (in the thirties).

Many people were downtown with children looking at the Christmas window displays at Kaufmann's, Gimbels, Horne's and other department stores.

Everything is calm. There is no evidence of street excitement in the afternoon. You wouldn't know war had broken. "Calm prevades the city on the war's outbreak," was the Post-Gazette's two-column Page 1 reaction story headline.

When the Post-Gazette, the only morning newspaper came out, extras sold fast even though most people had the news by radio. The Post-Gazette came out at 6 p.m., an hour and a half before the usual bulldog time. The Press run, on an extra 110,000 instead of the regular bulldog run of slightly more than 50,000. The normal circulation of all editions is 225,000 to 230,000. Now expecting a total run tonight of a half million.

The Post-Gazette editorial comment: "...wanton attack ... there is no doubt that the U.S. armed forces will give a good account of themselves. There must be redoubled effort at home to see that they have the weapons and equipment which they need. Certainly this challenge must galvanize the entire nation to immediate and effective action. Since Japan has elected to fight, it is perhaps as well that she chose to attack the U.S. directly. Nothing could have united the American people so immediately and completely."

Sunday night crowds were as big as usual in the busy city. Hotel lobbies were quiet. Newsmen reported seeing a railroader grab an extra at Pennsylvania station, take one swift look at the banners and say quietly to no one in particular, "Goodbye Tokio". "Well, that settles it," was common comment. Most people appeared to be stunned briefly, then stoical rather than aroused, determined but not excited. A middle aged newsy at the corner of Penn Ave. and Tenth St. said, "We'll know how to fight this war -- I was in the last one."

The nearest thing to excitement outside the newspaper offices and radio stations was apparent in the city's dinky little Chinatown, just one block in size. The usually stolid Chinese padded up and down Third and Second Aves. shaking hands with each other. Slapping backs, smiling happily while the youngsters hopped about them in the sunshine.

Swiftly moving into action to protect this "stock room of a far flung arsenal" against they hardly knew what, top city officials held a tense, serious half-hour meeting starting at 7:30 p.m. around Mayor Cornelius Decatur Scully's big oval conference table on the fifth floor of the City County building (correct proper name). Department heads gave the mayor, head of Pittsburgh's civilian defense council, brief, terse reports on what they were prepared to do, what they might need in money and men for fire-fighting, anti-sabotage work, etc., what steps they had already taken for emergencies. Half an hour -- that was all. "We mustn't waste any more time on discussing tonight," said the mayor finally. "There are grave problems we must meet as best we can and money will be no consideration in this emergency."

Police Supt. Harvey Scott later held a special meeting of his inspectors, told reporters he already had 150 men on extra detail guarding bridges, plants, reservoirs, main highway junctions. Both Scott and fire chief Nick Phelan said they would ask city council Monday for extra appropriations to augment man power and equipment.

Army and Navy recruiting officers prepared for a brisk business Monday mornings. Out for dinner tonight, I walked behind five apparently carefree young men who acted as if they were starting out for an evening of fun. "Well, you guys," I heard one of them say as they passed a newsstand, "What'll I do -- enlist tomorrow?" He seemed very happy about the whole business. "Why not?" said one, and then they changed the subject.

A cab driver, after reading the Nye story in the Post-Gazette told me: "That guy committed treason out there this afternoon. If I'd known what was going on out there,

I would have had a hundred drivers out there and we would really have strung that guy up." Man next to me (grabbing coffee in the greasy spoon) a laborer, said between gulps of spaghetti, "Now maybe Wheeler and Lindbergh and these other guys will shut their traps."

Wire from Hagy (Pittsburgh) - rec. 12/8/41 11:38 a.m.

Add Pittsburgh reaction:

Downtown theaters jammed Sunday afternoon and night, but unable to find any case where the show was interrupted for a war flash. The Biggest crowds were at Loew's Penn, playing Crosby in "Birth of the Blues" and at Fulton, playing Abbott and Costello in "Keep 'Em Flying."

The city's P. M. papers had extras out Monday at 7 a. m. -- Press and Sun Telegraph.

Word was spreading today of bizarre ads in lost and found column of Sunday press classified section (paper out Saturday night). Between two ads about last rat terriers appeared the following:

"Tokyo -- 8:05 p.m. -- news in English JLG4, 15D10 MEG., 19.8 M; JZJ, 11.80 MEG., 25.4M."

Farther down the column there was another: "Okyo -- 12:25 A.M.AA Children's Hour. JZJ, 11.80 MEG., 25.4 M; JZJ, 15.16 MEG., 19.7M."

The press was mum on where the ads came from. GBI flooded with calls from ad spotters. Local FBI boss told me he saw no significance in the ads but admitted he had never seen others like them in Pittsburgh papers and that they certainly appeared in a strange place. He said he had turned the matter over to the Federal Communications Commission.

At 10 a.m. today, Pittsburgh police radio broadcast an alarm to pick up men in a car with Michigan license plates, and query the occupants on taking pictures of the Westinghouse Electric and Manufacturing Company plant at East Pittsburgh, booming with defense orders. A few minutes later, police radio, WPDU, announced that military police at West Point wanted three Japanese in a brown sedan, adding: "These may be the same men wanted in connection with the taking of pictures at Westinghouse." Panic, probably.

(more) 1.

Add Pittsburgh reaction (Hagy Pittsburgh) - Page 2

Army and Navy recruiting stations jammed as expected this morning. Men lined up in heavy but brief flurry of snow waiting to get in.

People here now definitely aroused as, after first shock and stunned calm, they gradually realize the enormity of what's happened.

(End)

Wire from Grover C. Hall Jr., Montgomery, Ala. - to James McConaughy -

Dec. 8, 1941

When Jean Harlow died the Telephone Exchange here literally burned up; fuse after fuse was replaced. The war flash did not jam wires nearly so much, but the calls mounted approximately a third. The flurry continued until nightfall.

Saturday night I attended a dance at the Officers' Club, Maxwell Field, headquarters of Southeast Air Training Center. Flying officers at my table agreed that the Japs were only bluffing, returned to their puerile pontifications about the dullness of British cadets in training; paucity of trainer planes. There was no sense of the immediacy of conflict at all.

Sunday I had dinner at a lawyer's birthday celebration. The phone rings. "Mr. Pickens says Pearl Harbor and Manila have just been bombed by the Japs." Everybody looked at their plates, while he turned on the radio. "I don't see why in Hell they don't let the older men do the fighting," said 47-year-old lawyer. This was a typical scene.

The war flash caught Montgomery at dinner. The weather was crystal-clear, nippy. Christmas decorations were up on Dexter Avenue, along which Jeff Davis rode to the Capitol on Goat Hill. There was a lot of talk about the Blue-Gray game in January.

A self-conscious flying cadet who wants to fly a bomber lay down on the floor to listen to radio flashes.

At a suburban tavern dozens of young people sat in booths at dusk drinking beer and whisky. I listened to the radio, but even more to personalized chatter. I saw one girl looking furtively at her draftee-fiance.

That night I watched a stenographer and a first grade schoolteacher. They indulged their escorts in close attention to radio bulletins, but they didn't care so

Hall, Montgomery, Dec. 8, 1941   Page 2

much about the details.

A drugstore waitress: "This is it." The State's purchasing agent: "something, isn't it?" Our lady Sunday editor: "Fight like hell."

Essentially, Montgomery was deeply shocked. They had thought and never doubted that the Japs were bluffing. They were deeply resentful over the treachery. Vengeance bent, confident of victory, dazzled by cataclysm, but with little second thought yet of cost. They think it's a damn good thing. There is a sense of relief, like the passing of a painful kidney stone. ~~drtyyne~~ Hop to it, get it over with.

From the Montgomery Advertiser: "Here was a different America, an America that had been surprised, but one in which surprise quickly gave way to determination. Whatever initial advantage Japan may have gained by choosing Sunday morning for an unannounced and unprovoked attack upon the U.S. bases, has been more than offset by the effect upon the people of this country.

P.S. "Sergeant York" is playing here to capacity.

Wire from Henry Hough, Denver, to D. Hulburd - Dec. 7, 1941.

Jap war query questions:

1/ The radio broke the war news one hour and one half before the first Denver Post extra hit the streets. The Third Post and second Rocky Mountain News extras are now out. Many residential areas where the extras haven't reached still don't know about the war except for persons who listen to the radios. Calls to several persons showed they hadn't happened to listen to the radio today and hadn't heard about the "dumb Japs".

2/ I was waxing the floor when the radio gave the first unconfirmed report about the Japanese attacking Hawaii. It gave me a cold chill. Everybody is interested but very few are excited except soldiers. One waitress in a popular downtown bar said, "These soldiers have just gone wild. They are getting drunk all over the place." Sunday night crowds downtown are thin always with soldiers in evidence everywhere. No particular excitement is evident and no crowds congregating as they do around Times Square in N.Y.

At eight tonight the city editor of the News instructed a reporter to query America First leaders to see what they have to say, papers and Associated Press report no newsworthy incidents in the area around Denver except for precautions to prevent possible sabotage at defense plants and mines. Mutual Broadcasting Co. outlet station KFEL in Denver received a phone call from an irate listener who wanted to know why the "Lutheran Hour" was cancelled. When told that some schedules had been upset by the war news, he snorted, "Do you think the war news is more important than the gospel?"

Telephone operators at newspapers and radio stations report not many calls which surprises the hello girls. Veterans of Foreign Wars and their ladies in formal dress holding a big banquet in the ballroom of the Albany Hotel to hear the national commander of the VFW on a talk broadcast by Mutual had made no provision for the war bulletins to be read during the evening. When I asked them about it, they said they don't think it necessary. Movies didn't interrupt programs today with war flashes, left patrons to hear about the war after they left the theatres. A big line of people waited to buy tickets tonight at the Denham theatre where Major Bowes Amateur Hour is playing. In homes, family gatherings are huddled about radios listening to war reports and exchanging opinions.

3/ Denver today was sunny and warm with most people out riding in their cars as usual on pleasant Sunday afternoons. No games were scheduled today. The Junior Civic Symphony concert at Municipal Auditorium had the usual small turnout at 11¢ per ticket.

4/ No editorial comment available yet.

5/ No important incident of development except for steps taken by police and defense forces to safeguard defense spots from possible sabotage.

To sum up, everybody is keenly interested but very few are excited, some are mad. Nobody is afraid.

End.

Wire from Clem Hurd, St. Louis, Mo. to D. Hulburd - Dec. 7, 1941

St. Louis, Mo. Dec. 7 news of war came by radio, no paper published until about 6 o'clock when Globe Democrat got on street with eight page paper. Post Dispatch and Star Times each has its own radio station which supplied frequent bulletins. Globe Democrat second extra contains disconcerting one column headline Manila Quit; Army placed on alert reading of item indicates no retreat merely typographical error quit for quiet. At Radio Station KSD of Post Dispatch a local program of Champion Buglers of Jefferson Barracks and Fort Wood had just finished program at 1:30 with Sgt. C.K. Bob Young, champion of Jefferson Barracks blowing to the colors. Few minutes after program ended news came in by AP -- an interruption was made in University of Chicago Round Table program just started. One Army major present for preceding program remarked "Darn, I just had a chance to go to Hawaii and turned it down." At KMOX, Columbia network, break was made by chain program "World Today" at 1:40. Many people called radio stations and newspaper offices for verification but switchboards of Bell Co. were not swamped. However, there was unusually heavy traffic through St. Louis on long distance calls to points west of here. Calls to Denver and San Antonio were delayed up to one hour. Extra girls were called to St. Louis exchanges, all of which are dial operated, in anticipation of rush which did not develop until 6 P.M. Telephone traffic chiefs went to their offices on hearing news on radio. Fifteen extra girls were called in to handle long distance calls, mostly to West Coast; from points east of here all calls to West Coast must pass through St. Louis or Chicago.

A few quotes: "What were those 350 soldiers doing in barracks -- were they playing poker or do they sleep until noon." "I bet those Germans told them to do it." "Roosevelt finally got it, now he will have to send that one bomber that the British didn't get over to take care of the Japs." Roland G. Usher, author of famed Pan Germanish and head of Dept. of History, Washington University, told Globe

Page 2-- wire from Clem Hurd, Dec. 7

Democrat first reports indicated to him the German Air Force took part in the attack over Pearl Harbor. It had long been his belief, he said, that Germany has been trying to bring the United States into war against Japan. At reception attended chiefly by members of moderately fashionable Pilgrim Congregational Church some of the following were heard: "They ought to blow the Japanese Navy out of the water." "They can't start bombing Tokio any too soon because look what the Japanese have been doing to China for months -- but we're a people of higher ideals and should not do that unless they force us to. We don't want to remember that we began the war that way."

People of city in general took news quietly -- few people on streets downtown. Day was cold, about 40 degrees, and sunny -- no professional football game. Big movies as follows: Fox Theatre showing "Keep 'Em Flying," Ambassador "Little Foxes," Missouri "One Foot in Heaven," St. Louis "Appointment for Love," Loew's, which postponed "Two Faced Woman" because of Archbishop Glennon's objections was xx showing "Design for Scandal." No announcement made at Loew's but large radio in lobby drew crowd of about two hundred -- little comment except for expressions of incredulity at first. At other theatres mentioned a regular news broadcast is given every three hours, Pearl Harbor news contained in broadcast at 1:38. News received in silence, but at Fox later announcement of Senator Wheeler's statement "Going to lick hell out of them" was applauded. Jefferson Barracks Air Corps replacement training center, bordering city, asked theatre managers to notify any soldiers from that post to return immediately, but no general announcement to that effect was made. Many soldiers visiting city packed up and left immediately for camps on hearing of attacks.

Quote from Globe Democrat editorial: "It is a stunning and ghastly act to undertake a major war. Only with the deepest reluctance and realistic foreboding does this country take up arms -- yet we will do so with the stanchest confidence,

Page 3-- wire from Clem Hurd, Dec. 7

grim and courageous acceptance of duty and an impregnable will for victory. God grant this be a quick and decisive war. Whatever its length or the sacrifices it entails, America is ready.

Wire from Keen (San Diego) - 12/7/41 - 12:26 a.m.

The news came to San Diego between 11:30 a.m. and 12 noon Pacific Standard Time via radio on a beautiful, sunshiny day as San Diegoans either cruising about idly in their autos, mowing lawns, trimming hedges, loafing around the house, or reading Sunday papers.

San Diego has two direct network outlets, NBC (KFSD), and Mutual (KGB). On KFSD, a play was in progress; on KGB, George Fisher, the "Hollywood Whispers" reporter, was reeling out film gossip when the first bulletins broke.

Immediately thereafter, at intervals of fifteen minutes or less, came radio announcements ordering all men of the 11th Naval District back to their posts at once. Leaves from Camp Callan and Ft. Rosecrans were canceled.

People at first seemed stunned by the news of Honolulu and Manila bombings. "Sounds unbelievable -- like another Martian broadcast," was the sentiment of some. Gradually the realization came that this was the real thing. And when the call for servicemen to return to their posts was issued, the full impact struck and spread. A large number of people knew of the event, passing word along to others personally or by telephone before the first San Diego extra hit the streets 2:15 P.M. (PST)

In the morning, the usual huge Sunday pleasure-seeking mob of service-men were swinging through downtown San Diego, frequenting bars, and other entertainment spots. For at least one hour after the radio calls started asking men to return to posts, number of uniforms didn't seem to diminish. Then suddenly they began disappearing, and by early afternoon, comparatively few service men were seen along San Diego's various pleasure rows.

The major afternoon activity/ was the pro-football game, Los Angeles Bombers v. San Diego Bull Dogs, traditional rivals and big crowd attracter. However, with servicemen eliminated and everyone else glued to radios, the crowd usually 10,000 for such a game, was held down to 3,5000. Too early for spectacular interruption of movies.

Some reacted in forced humorous manner. "Wanny buy a house cheap?" asked residents of near the waterfront, where San Diego's defense industries and navy and military bases are located, and where bombings, if any are likely to occur.

Slowly mounting anger was most typical, however. It wasn't manifested in any violent outbursts, but was best exhibited by the scene at the San Diego waterfront during the entire afternoon.

As Navy men rushed back to shore stations and ships, civilians sped to the waterfront to watch the activities. A transport was loading up at a dock; sailors were boarding shoreboats; a great throng was standing silently, glumly, without a smile, observing. That crowd, looking west across San Diego harbor, and out beyond Point Loma to the Pacific where her enemy was raining destruction and taking lives, possibly of their own sons and brothers, was the most grim, silent crowd I've ever seen. From it rose an atmosphere of determination and unity.

Sailors' wives, some with children, were there to bid husbands farewell, possibly for the last time. There were no hysterical scenes; almost all the women were sad but dry-eyed.

The average comment of the servicemen, aircraft workers and other civilians on the streets was: "It's the best thing that ever happened. Now we'll get in there and lick them to a pulp."

The major development after the news broke was the mobilization of service men. Following on the heels of that, San Diegoans by hundreds offered volunteer services to local defense council for duty as auxiliary police, air raid wardens, medical corpsmen, nurses' aides, etc. Everybody wanted to do something to help.

Not a Jap was seen on the streets here throughout the day. Harold Nathan, FBI head here, said his crew was completely mobilized and waiting for word from

Keen, San Diego, page 3

Washington. A roundup of Japanese nationals due momentarily. The exact number of Japs here is considered secret by FBI, but at the local Buddhist Temple, the Japanese Church, they estimated there were 450 Japanese families in San Diego County, approximately 2,000 people. Parents mostly aliens, and children born here. The occupation of most is farming. There are very few Japanese fishermen in San Diego, where the Portuguese and Italians have the fishing fleet monopoly.

No Jap stores have been closed yet, and no anti-Japanese outbreaks have been reported by the police. The Japs seem to be keeping under cover, and in interviews professing loyalty to the United States.

Outward signs of war -- police clearing all streets adjacent to the Consolidated Aircraft Corporation's giant plant, and other defense industries of parked autos to permit the fullest access of emergency vehicles; guards with fixed bayonets at the Naval Training Station; comparative scarcity of service men in night clubs, beer halls and shows; people clustered about radios on streets downtown. No greater restriction in people's movements than usual -- it has been very strict in the vicinity of the Naval bases. For the first time, Camp Callan, selectee coast artillery training center, forbade visitors to enter except on official business.

No editorial comment yet available. Will file more early in the morning on this and more on San Diego public reaction.

(END)

Wire from Harold Keen, Edit. Dept. San Diego TRIBUNE-SUN to David Hulburd - 12-8

Editorial comment from San Diego UNION Monday morning:

"Japan yesterday signed her death warrant as a world power when she treacherously attacked Honolulu and other American and British outposts in the Pacific . . . By this action, which equalled in cruelty and treachery anything ever perpetrated by Adolf Hitler or any other criminal in history, Japan removed herself from the pale of toleration. This spark in the Pacific, which was ignited by a fawning puppet of Hitler and probably at his instigation, sets a new blaze which may prove to be the backfire that will save the decent peoples of the world from the full effects of the catastrophe that has been raging in Europe for more than two years . . . By this act, she started a string of events that quickly will send her reeling back into the medieval age from which she was rescued by this country just a century ago.

"Despite all the criticisms that might have been directed against the Roosevelt Administration for its handling of certain phases of the international situation, there has been room for none and there has been precious little voiced over its direction of affairs in the Far East." (This is significant because the San Diego UNION is strongly Republican and violently anti-Administration).

"Japan was appeased time after time . . . For four years we kept our markets open, supplying her with materials which enabled her to wage war against China . . . Now, she appears in her true colors, wrapped in the bloody flag of an international outlaw."

Another editorial urged avoidance of hysteria.

More "man in the street" comments: "It's about time we got out there and cleaned 'em up,"--Wally Kazikowski, 13, Marine. "We've been ready for it, and now we don't have to wait any more," - Clyde B. Casebeer, 20, Marine. "The Japs are digging their own grave; we're ready to put 'em in it," - Brad Thompson, 18, aircraft worker. "We should have killed off those damned Japs a long time ago," - Eugene Smith, 22, salesman. "I'm glad it's come to a showdown and now we can teach those Japs a thing or two," - F. Bringas, 24, aircraft worker.

End.

Wire from Robert Kintzley, New Orleans States, December 7, 1941 - to David Hulburd

The flash came to Orleans families as they gathered about the dinner table or in the living room waiting for the bell. The temperature was 50 degrees, thin-blooded natives were mostly indoors, too early for most for movies. There was a feeble, pallid sun. The flash broke into local, peaked juvenile singing for Red Goose shoes on WWL, (1:44 P.M.), in Great Plays program on WDSU, dance recordings on WNOE. The first and only extra was the TIMES-PICAYUNE at 3:25 P.M. with double 8-column, 215 point banner. The PICAYUNE staff was the only Sunday crew here. Switchboard, paper and radio were temporarily congested. Most calls were on casualty identifications since there were many from here in the war zone.

People in grog shops drank beer; shows ran no flash; the general spirit was the awful realization rather than flag-waving. Civic leaders didn't find ready tongue. Association of Commerce President Robert L. Simpson said, "This is a horrible situation, but we've got to see it through." Others were of similar tenor, not blasting the Japs. The Orpheum Theatre interrupted "The Men in her Life" at 9 P.M. to announce from the stage that all service men were ordered to report to posts. About 25 arose, marched out grimly -- no demonstration. Saenger Theatre with "Sergeant York" and Loew's with "H.M. Pulham, Esq." noted nothing unusual.

The best indication that the people were aroused was the good business (no figures) Navy and Marine Recruiting Stations did when they opened after the flash. Twenty seconds after Colonel Frank Halford, in charge of Marines at Southern recruiting division, opened office in came Lyman Crovetto, 29, dice dealer: "I'm rarin' to go," and when told his married status with a son, 10, might rule him out, his face fell: "I just have to get in." He left after physical to see if his beautician-wife would sign affidavit releasing him from support. When Federal Building elevator operator told drunk prospective recruit Navy recruiting station was closed, he said, "Ah'll wait," and went to sleep on chilly steps.

Best quote from Gung-Hsing Wang, Chinese Consul-General here was: "...This will be the last time Japan has a chance to hit below the belly." He added jubilantly: "As far as Japan is concerned, their goose is overheated." He was called from bath tub to the telephone after an attache had told a reporter: "He's busy in the bath tub. What's the trouble?" From British Consul-General John David Rodgers: "It's been a terrible day, hasn't it?"

The best news action was around the iron-fenced Japan Consulate on aristocratic St. Charles Avenue. The crowd hit 2,000/ mark around 5 PM with 6 cops and 3 motorcycle patrols. Burning of Consular papers in two wire trash burners worried next door resident because of flying embers. Attaches chased unburned wind-tossed fragments about while crowd hissed. The Fire Department doused the fire, cops grabbed the wet pile over a foot high, and took it to the precinct station. Around 11 P.M./ to the handful of cops and newsmen left, Consul Kenzo Ito sent out eight cans of Schlitz and thermos of tea. One cop nabbed the beer to take home; the tea, eight cups and saucers were taken back with regrets.

PICAYUNE editorial excerpts: "The militarist gangsters at Tokyo will find they have worsened their own bad case before the bar of world opinion and weakened their military position by the foul and ineffectual blow ... Yesterday's sinister developments have aroused Americans as no previous occurrence of this war has done...The American people do not shrink from the conflict thus forced upon them."

Most important development probably was the determination to all-out smother Japan. Typical cock-sureness: "We can lick 'em hands down. They got it comin'." They mean it, but they were solemnly undemonstrative.

Louisiana State University students massed in Baton Rouge, marched to see President Major General Campbell B. Hodges, who came out in lounging robe and told them it was their duty to study hard. He envisioned a long war and said students would probably get their chance.

End.

Wire from Jack Meddoff, Buffalo, N.Y.
     to James McConaughy -- December 8, 1941

Nearby Fort Niagara troops today quietly took over the job of guarding the great defense industries of Buffalo and the Niagara frontier, supplementing police, deputy sheriffs and private guards. Workers on day shifts reaching plants of Buffalo Arms Corporation, Bell and Curtiss-Wright Airplane plants and other defense factories, found uniformed soldiers grimly on guard fully armed. The first electrifying reports of Japanese attacks broke into the calm of a bright, pleasant December afternoon, but hours passed before the sensational news reached the majority of the people, and its grave import was impressed on the public mind.

The first report here was flashed on four radio stations almost simultaneously at 2:29 p.m. and people at home or in cars who had radios turned on were stunned by the sudden news. "This is Camp Dix," and "Spirit of '41," both ironically enough were military-type programs, were interrupted as the flash broadcast on stations WGR and WKBW. Thousands in downtown and neighborhood movies knew nothing about it until they came out, and some didn't even know for hours afterward because the first extra did not hit the streets until nearly 9 p.m. Sunday, just a few minutes before the regular first-edition time of Buffalo's only morning paper, the Courier-Express. The only p.m. paper, the News, did not go extra. Buffalo and environs took it calmly, the usual Sunday afternoon and evening routine being followed and no excitement visible anywhere. A banner crowd at the American Hockey League game Sunday night, the 10,000 spectators cheering and shouting at players as if no war had descended.

Radio stations WBEN, WKBW and WGR, carrying NBC and CBS and NBS war bulletins, were on the air all night long and will remain on a 24-hour basis during the emergency. Reaction of man in the street was evidenced when I asked a number of them, picked at random.

A few quotes follow: "We should get at Japan and get at 'em quick andthen go over and get Hitler". -- William H. Moesel, 16 Floss St., Department Store salesman.

page 2-- Jack Meddoff, Buffalo -- Dec. 8, 1941

"I blame Hitler; he made Italy stab her friends in the back and now he has made Japan do it. We ought to declare war on Germany too" -- Leon Sikorski, 360 Doat Street, tailor.

"Italy and Germany told Japan to do it; we ought to get all three of 'em and get 'em good." -- Joseph Brucato, 71 Johnson St., Buffalo Athletic Club waiter.

Franklin A. Dearing, 34 Horton Place, shorthand reporter in the District Attorney's office -- "We ought to kick hell out of the Japs and then kick hell out of the rest of the gang."

John W. Caudell, 95 Livingston St., retired merchant; "I hope we knock hell out of them but don't say hell, it won't look good."

Richard Potkowski, 17 years old of 58 Harmon Street, just discharged from the 27th Division at Fort McClellan after 14 months, said: "I'm ready to go right back in now and help show the Japs where they fit."

Meanwhile soldiers and sailors, home on furloughs, crowded railroad terminals hastening back to posts. But there was no outward excitement, everybody was calm about the whole thing.

Buffalo News in a lead editorial today says in part: "America must and will strike back at Japan with all her force and determination. Whatever be the cost in blood and treasure it shall be paid.... From now on our war effort must be total. No half-measures will suffice."

Courier-Express also made a war lead editorial saying in part: "...The war is on. It is not a war of America's seeking. In no American mind can there be any doubt about the ultimate outcome of this war.... Japanese Empire has signed its own death warrant as a world power. But in signing their country's death warrant the Japanese war lords have given a temporary reprieve to their model and mentor, Adolf Hitler."

page 3-- Jack Meddoff, Buffalo -- Dec.8, 1941

When the first radio flashes broke Sunday afternoon, more than 2,000 Girl Scouts were singing a Christmas program in Kleinhans Music Hall and offering a silent prayer for a Happy Christmas all around the world, all unaware of Jap attacks.

Newspaper switchboards, normally quiet Sunday afternoons were deluged with calls from anxious parents and relatives of men in the Pacific Fleet.

Buffalo men in their forties began volunteering to Navy within an hour after the first flash was heard. Chief Yeoman Gerald P. Milan said he got more than 25 calls at the Navy recruiting station Sunday night from men wanting to fight the Japanese. He said some told him they were way past 35 but felt physically fit and if accepted "would join up in a minute."

......

Wire from Jack Meddoff, Buffalo, N. Y., to McConaughy - 12-8-41

Most interested person scanning the last war news and listening avidly to the radio is Frederick W. McMillin, Jr., of 176 Sanders Road, Buffalo, a salesman for the Federal Portland Cement Company, whose brother is known as the Navy's "dictator" of the Pacific Island of Guam -- Capt. George Johnstone McMillin, 52, who makes his home in Youngstown, Ohio. Said McMillin: "My brother is known as 'King' by the 23,000 natives of Guam - the Island - and, this is little known - is actually the property of the U.S. Navy and not of the Government. My brother was sworn in as Governor-Commandant of the Island April 19, 1940, for a two-year term."

McMillin's last letter from his brother came two weeks ago. McMillin said his brother has pointed out in letters that Guam has no natural harbors and only one landing field and there is a visible Japanese Island only forty miles away. Said McMillin: "In his last letter my brother told me of evacuating the island of all women and children six weeks ago. This left him without his family consisting of his wife and two children, Adelaide, 16, and George Jr, 14. They are in Long Beach, California, having arrived in this country the day before Thanksgiving day. Another daughter, Ruth, 21, is with her husband, Lieutenant William Mack, in China, at present. Capt. McMillin is an Annapolis graduate, 1911; took part in Vera Cruz disturbances and then was on the U.S.S. Delaware in the World War and served aboard the battleship Sacramento on convoy duty off Gibralter; was later assigned to Mare Island Navy Yard off California. On Guam Island he lived in a Palace built by the Spanish in 1600's in the capital city of Agana, population of 12,500, a modern little city. The palace is as large as a city block and its attached gardens also are a block in area. Seven miles away is the seaport town of Piti which is in command of a Marine Corps battalion headed by a Colonel. They supply the police force. There are only 53 Japs on the island but they have lived there a long time."

End

Wire from Edward Morrow, Omaha, Neb. to J. McConaughy - Dec. 8, 1941

Omahans who generally follow the midwestern custom of dining Sunday shortly after 1 o'clock, were mostly finishing dinner when the radio programs (one was Sammy Kaye's orchestra) were interrupted to bring news of the bombing of Hawaii. Half empty theatres interrupted pictures to flash the news on the screen and some customers got up and left. The show at the biggest house, the Paramount, was Sergeant York. Movie business thereafter was very light.

Telephone calls, both local and long distance, shot up as friends and relatives called each other with the news. Omaha office of the Northwestern Bell called 12 extra operators, mostly for long lines work. The World-Herald did not have an extra until 4:45. The World Herald sold 19,200 extras containing fairly complete account of what had happened. This was the entire run and newsboys were unavailable to handle more. Many of those who bought said they were going to keep the first extra, which had an 8-column "War" across the top, as souvenirs.

There isn't the faintest doubt that people here are aroused as indicated by quotes of World Herald reporters picked up on the streets.

Best came from one of three soldiers who stopped to read a radio bulletin. The one soldier whistled, said, "Boy, take your last look at Omaha for a long time. Which way's the war?"

The afternoon in Omaha, after a sunny morning, was windy and cloudy and bleak. Soon after word came here, FBI men plucked K. Hayashi, member of the San Francisco Japanese Consul staff, from a United Airlines plane here. He wanted to proceed by train but was told to stay here. He refused to go to a hotel and remained overnight in the airport waiting room.

The World Herald was swamped with calls from relatives of soldiers, sailors and civilians in the Orient and had to call three extra phone operators. Nebraska has always been a great feeder for the navy and probably has more men per capita in the navy than most.

The World Herald, which started out being Isolationist but has been wavering considerably in the last months, though it hasn't relented in hating Roosevelt, called for all aid to the President. The editorial said in part: "Japan's unannounced attack, treacherous and murderous, upon American outposts in the Pacific, has shattered the veil of illusion and wishful thinking that all too long has befogged the American mind and hindered vigorous and effective action by the government and the people of the U.S.

"We face the naked fact. No longer can it be glossed over. We are at war -- at war in the Pacific as in the Atlantic. And the measure of our unreadiness is startlingly evidenced by the fact that Japanese aircraft carriers, submarines and bombers, even parachute troops, were able to cross thousands of miles of the Pacific Ocean and reach Oahu undetected until they began shooting.

"No use now to quarrel over that dismaying and humiliating disclosure.

"From this day forward, citizens may expect the utmost vigilance and efficiency to the fullest possible extent on the part of the government and our military arms.

"Around our President, Franklin D. Roosevelt, our Commander in Chief, all citizens from today and to the end will be rallied, giving all that they have to his support and encouragement. May the God of hosts bestow upon him wisdom and strength and grace of his tremendous task."

<u>End</u>

Wire from Bob Munroe, Miami, Florida to David Hulburd - December 8, 1941

The Outstanding reaction here was first disbelief, then a rush to newspapers, radio stations to confirm, swamping switchboards already congested due to lack of trunk lines, apparently continuously tied up with government and other emergency traffic. It is estimated that more than ninety percent of callers expressing opinions said U. S. should have entered war sooner. Exceedingly vague geographical sense apparent. One man inquired seriously of radio station WIOD, "Will President Wilson speak tonight and if so, what time?"

Three Miami-Miami Beach broadcasting stations broke news at 2:23, 2:29 and 2:32 respectively. WKAT had blue network NBC show, "Great Plays." WIOD had NBC Red "University of Chicago Round Table." WQAM had "Spirit of '41."

All interrupted then and frequently throughout the day and night giving local and wire news. WQAM show involved interviewing torpedo boat crews and sound effect of boats roaring off into the distance. Termination program just fading when war bulletin flashed.

University of Miami, Coral Gables, officially ordered closed for the day, Monday, but neither of two Deans in charge during the absence of President B. F. Ashe from city would say anything except, "No special reason," and no plausible reason apparent to outside observer. University has large number of cadet fliers in training, both American and British. Guards placed around campus.

Miami Daily News, owned by former Ohio Governor James M. Box, presidential nominee in 1920 with Roosevelt as running mate, was on the street with extra edition at 5:13 PM, claiming 12-minute beat over Miami Herald, morning paper opposition. The News will say editorially Monday, "Not even the bitterest critic of the Administration can charge that the U. S. asked for this war with

Japan. President Roosevelt and Secretary Hull have treated Japan with un-exampled patience, not only throughout the last eight years, but even through the very last days and hours, when the final treachery was being compounded. In return they received the sly, sneaking stab in the back, a trick that Hitler and Mussolini hardly needed to teach the Oriental.

"Now that the war has come, there is only one weapon in the armory of American traditions: It is steel, applied with the fully flexed muscles of the vast productive organism which nerves our armed forces. We will fight with vigor and conviction, but not with over-confidence. We are faced with a brave and reckless foe, who for many years now has been piling up a store of secret armaments. Let us beware the complacency which lost the day for France and almost lost it for England.

"We will fight with perfect unity on the home front -- that is, with perfect unity of all our people who are first and foremost Americans -- for Japan's wanton attack has at last ended the unreal debate over whether we are or are not at war. The nation must now close ranks to see the struggle that has been thrust upon us through to a victorious finish."

Miami Herald said editorially, "The U. S. will fight this war in the only way it knows how to fight - fearlessly, as one, and with every resource at its command. Every humane and human interest in the moral code of our people propels us on -- to victory."

No Miami movies were interrupted for war news bulletins and no evening attendance fall off was noted. Think the people on the whole relatively calm and philosophic following first excited reactions. There were no big sports events in progress at the time. People were mostly motoring, fishing, golfing, etc., outdoors in warm December sunshine, and few interrupted their pursuits except momentarily. A member of a foursome playing bridge at the Miami Biltmore Country Club in the locker room as first news was given on the radio inquired loudly, "Where in Hell is the nine of spades?" The most frequent comment heard was, "I'm glad we're in it. The sooner we get it over with the better." Also, there was some criticism by competent military fliers re the Navy Patrol failing to spot the Japanese aircraft carriers. Radio telephone-equipped sport fishing fleet off Palm Beach, notoriously garrulous among themselves, received the war news afloat and became unnaturally quiet for the balance of the day. Coconut Grove coastguard, air base and other local military units redoubled the 24-hour guards and personnel and individually expressed eagerness to fight and unanimous optimism as to the ultimate result.

END

Wire from Clarke Newlon, Dallas to James McConaughy - Dec. 8, 1941

Twenty-five hundred people sat in the Majestic Theatre at 1:57 Sunday afternoon. They had just watched the finish of probably one of the most dramatic war pictures of the year -- Sergeant York. On the film flashed the title. Then there was a break in the sound and over the speakers came the announcement that Japan had attacked Pearl Harbor, Manila, Japan had declared a state of war with the United States. There was a pause, a pin-point silence, a prolonged "Awwwww" and then thunderous applause.

This, however, was not Dallas' first news of the opening of hostilities. At 1:10 p.m. radio station KRLD broke into its Columbia program "The World of Today" (a news program) to give Dallas and KRLD's listeners the news. From then on its phones were swamped and the station devoted more than half the remainder of the day to news breaks and resumes. Usually open until 2 a.m., KRLD stayed on all night. NBC's WFAA broke the news at about the same moment and within the next three hours the station's telephone operator estimated that 400 weeping women telephoned all asking the same question: "Do you have the casualty list yet? When will it be broadcast?" All said they had sons or brothers or sweethearts in Pearl Harbor or Manila. The men called too. They wanted to know: "Is Roosevelt broadcasting tonight? Are we in the war for certain now?" Both men and women inquired if this meant the end of all furloughs. WFAA broke into a local sustaining program with its first war news break. The title "You Might Be Right." The station stayed on throughout the night, as did Mutual's WRR.

The Dallas Journal issued three extras, at 3:50, 5:09 and 8:07 and delivered a free paper to every regular subscriber. Estimated sale: 46,000. The Dallas News issued its first extra at 5:50 and sold 20,000 within fifty minutes. Switchboards of both the News and the Journal were swamped with the same hysterical relatives of soldiers and sailors at the scene of the Japanese bombing.

Wire from Clarke Newlon, Dallas, Dec. 8, 1941   p. 2

Clyde Stewart, manager of the Dallas Telephone Company, a division of Southwestern Bell, said that his office used a larger force Sunday afternoon than had been on any "normal occasion" and the long distance calls after seven were long delayed due to the rush of business. One boy called Dallas from Camp Hulen near Houston with the information that he had waited an hour to get his call through and had called as had hundreds of others in camp because his company had been told they might be called out on thirty minute notice.

Dallas got the news as it sat, mostly, at the traditional southern Sunday dinner and took its war news with fried chicken and hot biscuits. It was a raw and cloudy day out with the temperature around fifty, unpleasantly cool for Texas autumn. There were a few people on the streets, but up and down every business and residential street the noise of radios drowned out normal Sunday traffic sounds. The concensus of a score of quotes: "I'm glad the suspense is over. Now we can get busy and get something done."

Typical: Lewis Fisher, 25, dismissed from active duty Nov. 7th because of dependency: "I'm ready to go back now that there's something to do and someone to fight.

Mrs. H. F. Dudley, housewife, husband barely over draft age: "I'm upset, but think it's better now than later. I'm ready for my husband to fight."

Charles W. Hopkins, employee of U. S. Steel Corporation: "We'll stomp their front teeth in. Japs are the same caliber as Hitler."

Earl R. McGraw, roofing contractor: "Suicide for Japan."

Roy Carter, credit man, "Not fully prepared but we can take care of it."

Mrs. Jim Stewart, housewife: "We'll whip hell out of 'em."

Most important result so far seen: Every man in or out of draft age told his friend: "Better grab a gun, Bud," and laughed, but every man and every woman seemed to have been aroused from the numbed lethargy that constantly-hammered and recurring

Wire from Newlon (Dallas) to D. Hulburd - December 8, 1941

headlines of Russia-Germany-England war have brought about. There was more of the feverishness of September 1939. The war was real, and very close once again.

Editorial excerpts: The Dallas Journal, "We submerge all differences in the common determination that we shall support the government of the United States with every resource and every effort of every citizen in this country."
The Dallas News: "The war we face is different from any war we have ever known. Our peril is far greater than before. We will win with/the full strength of America in the effort. That we will not win if we do not exert that full strength is a contingency so much to be feared that we dare not risk it." The Times Herald: "The harder we hit, the sooner shall we prove to the despots that we have the power to crush them and the sooner shall we have peace and security".

Wire from Harry Schwandner, Milwaukee, to James McConaughy - December 8, 1941

Milwaukee received its first war news in a Bulletin read over WTMJ, Milwaukee Journal radio station at 1:58 p.m. Sunday. Popular University of Chicago Round Table of the Air was interrupted to give the flash. It came as a profound shock to Milwaukee, strongly isolationist, happy hunting ground of America First Committee. Wisconsin football fans were listening to the broadcast of the Chicago Bears-Cardinals game (of interest because Wisconsin is the home/state of Green Bay Packers) when the announcer interrupted the game to give the first flash of war. The news was startling to Milwaukeeans. Thousands telephoned to the Milwaukee Journal for verification. Switchboard was jammed with calls for hours. Reporters had to wait for 15 minutes to get through the telephone jam. Radio men from WTMJ swamped out operators. Most callers asked "Is war declared? Is it true what the radio just said?" Word spread rapidly through the city, recovering from mid-day dinners.

The telephone company reported that a huge flood of calls. The city was excited. Isolationists swung over with interventionists in a "let's go" attitude.

Lansing Hoyt, chairman of the strong Wisconsin charter, America First Committee, told a journalist reporter at his home that the United States would "bomb to the ground" Japanese cities. He said: "We have been for defense all along. Now we are for offense. It looks like war against the Axis." Hoyt is Milwaukee Republican chairman and a brother-in-law of John Cudahy. Hoyt has been a leader in arranging Isolationist mass meetings in Milwaukee, at which Wheeler et al spoke. Edmund B. Shea, prominent Milwaukee attorney and president of the Milwaukee chapter, Committee to Defend America, said that all Americans should united in the common cause of defending the nation. Shea had announced earlier Sunday a series of meetings to whip up sentiment in Milwaukee against isolationism, with Senators Pepper, Murray, Ball, Lee Bridges as speakers. Gov. Heil sent this telegram to President Roosevelt:

Schwandner, Milwaukee - Dec. 8, 1941

"The news of Japanese aggression is a distinct shock to citizens of Wisconsin. I pledge you the full and unified support of our people. May the Lord give you help and strength in this hour of grave peril."

The desk clerk at Milwaukee's largest hotel, Schroeder Hotel, said that the guests couldn't believe their ears at the news. "It was like a dash of ice water," said the clerk. Walter Stern, a retired president of a flour mill, said: "I'm shocked beyond words. Well, we're ready. It is full steam ahead now." Harry M. Silber, an attorney said: "I'm so surprised that I hardly know what to say. But I'm sure we'll take good care of them." The Rev. J. R. Linsen Mayer, pastor of the Roosevelt Drive Presbyterian Church, in a middle class district, gravely told the latest war news to a silent audience of 100 gathered for a hymn sing. Then he prayed for defeat of "the forces of Japanese aggressions," emphasizing that the record showed that the United States had been attacked without warning. The general Milwaukee scene:

It was a quiet Sunday afternoon, with no big events to attract crowds. The city's main street, Wisconsin Ave., was jammed with parents and their children looking at Christmas store window displays. A raw wind whooped in from the south at 25 m.p.h., lashing Lake Michigan into whitecaps and foam. Lead clouds hung over the city, blotting out the sun. A favorite Sunday pastime of Milwaukeeans is to drive slowly along Lincoln Memorial Drive along Lake Shore through the city's beautiful parks. Thousands were doing that Sunday when their cars' radios gave them the first war flashes. Many startled listeners parked along the drive to listen to the bulletins. As word spread along Wisconsin Ave., crowds gathered in knots to exchange news. Downtown bars suddenly were jammed with pedestrians who wanted to get close to a radio. They talked earnestly and grimly. Milwaukeeans who have long felt that the United States shoud stay out of Europe's war were

Schwandner, Milwaukee - Dec. 8, 1941

fighting mad that the Japs had attacked the U.S., killed U.S. soldiers. They felt that here at last was something to get mad about, fight for.

The Milwaukee Journal and Milwaukee Sentinel extras were off the presses about 5 p.m., hit the streets about the same time. Extras sold heavily. The Journal reported sales of 66,000. Downtown crowds grabbed extras fast as newsboys offered them. Cries of newsboys, "Japs declare War on U.S.," rose above the Christmas chimes that tinkled on Wisconsin Avenue from loudspeakers on street corners. In the crowds were young soldiers and sailors on leave with their girl friends. Service men looked grim. Their girls were whitefaced, some tearful. Young men and women generally seemed grimmer about the news than the older folks.

I am rewiring, Monday, the first editorial comment.

Wire from Harvey Schwandner, Milwaukee - to David Hulburd - Dec. 8, 1941

First editorial comment, Milwaukee Journal: "We are all in it today... Guns have spoken; the only answer is guns.... For those who go where bombs fall and torpedoes cleave the waves, the task appointed is plain. For those who stay, the task also is clear, -- to back up with all we have the men we send to assert the creed of freedom, the obligation we owe ourselves and owe Island peoples whose government we have undertaken, whom we are pledged to defend. Americans stand together today in determination. We pray that the struggle may not be long continued, the cost in life and human values too great. But short or long, we are all in it -- to aid our Government with material things, with counsel, with the unfailing assurance of support, whatever the price to be paid."

Wire from Sullivan (Seattle) to D. Hulburd- December 7, 1941

Police detail in the oriental section in Seattle was doubled to guard against disorders. Police and the FBI guarded the home of Yuki Sato, Jap consul, and officers refused admission to a group of neighborhood children calling to give a Christmas present to one of the Consul's children. But Gordon Lewis, 8, son of a navy lieutenant-commander, talked his way in, handed schoolmate, Syuki Sato, 8 a toy automobile and a dimestore dive bomber. The Consul's children leaned out of the windows, talking to neighborhood children.. Said the Consul to the press: "I am very sorry, no statement." Jap stores and restaurants stayed open but the Jap quarter was almost devoid of Japs. They stayed in their homes.

There are about 6,000 alien Japs in and around Seattle. Long distance telephone communications, when war news broke, were tremendous in the Seattle area, and the telephone company had to send out for all its extra operators.

A few hours after the news broke, soldiers began leaving Seattle by bus and truck for Fort Lewis, Fort Lawton and other posts, sounding good humored but fatalistic good-byes.

The most immediate visible result of the war is prompt patrols -- police, soldier, sailor, deputy sheriffs, state police, company guards and others of defense regions, bridges guarded, Seattle 28 mile pipeline guard tripled, extra guard around water purification plant up in Cascades, light power, gas and other utilities guarded.

Remarkably fast, Rear Admiral C. S. Freeman at Bremerton, Commander 13th Naval District: Gen. Kenyon A. Joyce, Commanding IX Corps at Fort Lewis; Capt. Ralph Wood, Commanding Sand Point Naval Air Station, Governor Arthur B. Langlie, City officials, Civilian Defense leaders, all got in communication with each other and agreed on what was to be done-- protect all strategic points, calm citizens, be on alert.

The war news first came to Seattle via radio, NBC and CBS stations, between

11 a.m. and noon. On CBS, it broke into the program of the New York Philharmonic Orchestra. The Post-Intelligencer had an extra on the street 3 hours later, the Times was on the street in about 4 hours after the news was received. The Times staff, not due until Monday, all came down to work.

Telephone calls also served to spread the news. Hundreds of persons called friends. In one 15 minute period, the Times got 700 phone calls asking what papers siren was screaming for. The Times said "War declared", most frequent comment was, "Is that all?" Comment:

"Well, this spoils our day at home, my husband is being called down to the office"-- housewife.

"My husband will be working longer hours from now on, and do we need the overtime"-- wife of a defense worker.

"It's awful, what will we do? What are you going to do? We'll be bombed within a week" -- war-conscious but rather neurotic woman business executive.

"I'm going back home to my folks in Wisconsin" -- young Zoman nurse.

"And I'd have to pick a day like this to go see "The Man who Came to Dinner." -- young girl who had a Sunday afternoon date.

"Japan asked for it, and Japan will get it--in the neck" -- James Y. Sakomoto, Seattle-born publisher of Japanese-American newspaper.

At seventh avenue and Olive street, two soldiers and their girls stepped off the curb smiling, while newsboys nearby shouted and waved black headlines, in Aurora Avenue. A sailor with a bag containing roller skates, marched briskly into the neighborhood roller skating rink.

This first and immediate reaction is sobering now. As twilight falls, people are calling each other on telephones, talking its over more quietly. More intelligent questions are coming to the newspaper offices. The flippancy is nearly gone. State, city and country agencies are functioning nicely, shutting off alarm

Sullivan -- Page Three

and hysteria, but grimly getting ~~in~~ ready for the worst.

Busy here, but will file more.

When the news came to Seattle the city was basking in sunlight, day was cold. People were going to church, starting out on Sunday drives, eating late breakfasts, listening to ~~it~~ radios, reading Sunday newspapers. At the Orpheum Theatre, a line stood waiting to get in to see "Maltese Falcon" and "Target for Tonight" and other theatres were getting early Sunday crowds. Over various districts of the city, an Army or Navy plane would circle and people looked up with lovely interest.

A 12-year old freckled-faced fat boy, making change for a package of cigarettes in a neighborhood drug store, asked the customer: "What do you think of the Japs? Say, we've got to give it to them."

In homes, neighbors drifted in to talk over news; telephones kept ringing with friends on the line.

Those out driving heard the news by car radios, or noticed state patrol cars assembling around Lake Washington floating bridge, Boeing Field, Point Wells oil storage area, Fort Lewis, Sand Point Naval Air Station and other strategic points.

Four fishermen on Tolt River county north of here heard the news by car radio. They dropped all fishing for the day and got back to the city by noon to be with families.

Wire from M.S. Sullivan, Seattle, Wash. to J. McConaughy - Dec. 7, 1941

Sidelight; Marine Corps recruiting station opened at 6 tonight (Sunday) "by demand", had 78 enlistments by 9 o'clock, 3 more in office enlisting when recruiting officer called the newspaper. Navy and Marine recruiters are starting enlisting tomorrow from 6 a.m. until 11 p.m. daily.

This is late, and reactions calming down. Lots of people on the street looking at Christmas windows, buying newspapers. A line now a block long for "Maltese Falcon" and stage play "Man Who Came To Dinner" packed. No theatre interruptions, but news bulletins flash on. Service men left when the bulletin said to go to stations.

John Boettiger in the editorial called "War Comes To the U.S.": "We must now really go all out for the war effort. Now that the die has been cast, the thought of defense is secondary. It is not altogether impossible that a Jap aircraft carrier could slip through close enough to our coast to conduct a foray upon our airplane and shipbuilding plants. In this war it will be labor that has the greatest opportunity. Strikes of any kind should be wholly outlawed."

Most general reaction here was astonishment and "How do they (Japs) think they can get away with it?"

Exact position of ships out of Seattle unknown, but Alaska Steamship Co. has three vessels enroute north and several ships of America Mail Line may be in combat zone.

Would say single most important development is rush to guard strategic points on Puget Sound. Would say people aroused to belief Japan should be crushed at once.

Wire from M. S. Sullivan, Seattle, Washington, to David Hulburd - Dec. 8, 1941

TIME'S editorial -- "War has come. The bickering (of our country) has been stilled as quickly and completely as the clicking of a light. Here are the days when we of America are a united people behind our Commander-in-Chief, our President, and behind those to whom he delegates his authority. Some of us have sat smugly back in a feeling of security -- but (Japan's attack) is probably the very jolt America needed to snap it out of its lethargy."

End.

Wire from Toms (Indianapolis) to D. Hulburd - December 8, 1941

The news reached here near one-thirty central standard via radio flashes over all stations many catching bulletins interrupting broadcast of Chicago Bears-Cardinals pro football game jamming all switchboards but there are no extras at the moment. The Indianapolis Star Bulldog reached the streets shortly after 9 last night. The Indianapolis News issued an extra t at 7:30 this morning, three hours ahead of its usual time. Most people expressed themselves in moderation and noted immediate retreat from customary language of isolationists in this inland belt. The first word of conflict brought remarks like:

"No fooling, we're in it."

"Let's recess politics".

The matter was taken seriously here and there was a tendency toward panic by persons living near big naval powder deport and new ordinance plant under construction. Many took advantage of the sunshiny afternoon to motor after lunch yesterday so downtown streets were sparse and movie attendance extremely light. "Suspicion", "Sundown" and "Birth of the Blues" were showing but there were no interruptions.

If any supplemental fact of note was apparent it was the hegira of motorists to country roads. The Indianapolis Star carried a page one editorial "Japan has attacked. With no warning war is thrust upon us. Is America united? Is Indiana united? There is but one answer. Yes. Hoosier boys are at the Pacific battle front, on the ~~axinfg~~ sea and in the air. You can show you are backing them up as they fight your battles. Let old glory give the answer. The Star suggests that the flag be flown today from all public buildings & from factories and other private industries, from the stores and schools and from homes. It will thrill every heart against the trying days ahead. It will put courage and faith in victory in all of us. Not only today, but every day. Keep the flag flying."

Will follow News editorial.

Wire from William L. Toms, Indianapolis News, Ind. to David Hulburd -

Dec. 8, 1941

Indianapolis News of Charles Warren Fairbanks' family in Page One editorial says in part:

"The American people will not live in slavery. Better death in defense of liberty than life under the totalitarian heel. That is today's challenge to every American.

"The time has come to lay aside partisan, sectional and other differences. There is only one division - Americans and the enemies of Americans. And there is only one choice in this country - to be Americans all the way. It is not American to delay a necessary act of Congress, to put any private business above the public business, to lay down a tool in any defense industry. It is American to strip for the fight and drive through to a quick and complete victory.

"To the discharge of this obligation the American people address themselves, under President Roosevelt, as one man fighting for all that he holds worth while in this world.

"Hitler is attacking, indeed, but through the Japanese, as he has so long tried to do.

We must fight with everything we have. It will not be easy. But the greater our concentration and the greater our sacrifice, the sooner the victory."

End.

Wire from Wm. Vaughan, Kansas City, Mo. to J. McConaughy - Dec. 7, 1941

It was cloudy this morning when Kansas Citians went to church, but by the time they started home for the traditional Sunday dinner of the middlewest the sun had come out. It was another perfect, unseasonably warm day in a string of similar ones. The temperature was to rise to 55 degrees by 4 o'clock. Before then the news had come that Japan was at war with the U.S.

The first word came through radios and was missed by many families who were at dinner when the flash was read. A copy reader on the telegraph desk of the Kansas City Star, down for an early trick, caught the flash from the Associated Press and sprinted up a flight of stairs to the studios of station WDAF. At 1:33 p.m. the news of the first White House announcement went on the air, interrupting the Chicago Round Table. At 1:39 Station KMBC broke in on the religious Round Table, a panel of Kansas City pastors sponsored weekly by the council of churches. Other stations hit at about the same time, but WDAF claimed the first break, beating the regular network flashes by about ten minutes.

Kansas City's two newspapers, the Star and the Journal, held back extras until they could make a creditable showing on the streets. By 7 o'clock both were out -- the Star with four pages, the Journal with eight. By 8 o'clock, the Star had jumped to 16 pages for a second extra edition. (The Star's extras were of its morning paper, the Times).

The Journal carried in the 3-column front page space in which Harry Newman had written an editorial every day since he took over the paper a month ago, Newman's by-lined comment, which began:

"The little yellow man is really yellow.

"Almost 100 years ago this Sunday afternoon an admiral of the U. S. Navy -- reached into the dark drawer of Medievalism and pulled the intellectually and physically dwarfed Nipponese out into the light of civilization and education.

"The cycle seems to have come about again and that same navy -- seems duty bound to put them back into the drawer and into the dark."

Charles V. Stansell, Associated Editor of the Star hurried to the office to write for the second extra edition:

"There can be but one reply to the deliberate dastardly and unprovoked Japanese attack upon the U. S.

"A war fought with the clear knowledge that our government made every effort to achieve a peaceful and honorable settlement of the outstanding problems on the Pacific and that it was unprovoked aggression of which history can offer any record rewarded by one of the most flagrant examples of unprovoked aggression of which history can offer any record.

"There must be no illusions. This is not a war that can be fought with one hand behind our back. It is not going to be a cheap or a painless war. It will be a war with /a seasoned and desperate antagonist, an antagonist, moreover from whom every form of treachery must be expected as a matter of course.

"But whether our losses are small or great, whether the struggle requires months or years, we must make sure of one thing -- that although Japan has struck the first blow, we shall strike the last and the result of that last blow shall be the complete destruction of the Japanese empire. To the end that our children and our children's children may live in a free and decent world."

Although it listened to its radio, quickly bought out extras and flooded newspapers with telephone calls, however, Kansas City took the news more or less in its stride. There were cars on streets, many of them with horns tooting. They arrived downtown and on the country club plaza where colored lights outlined the Spanish type buildings in the spectacular annual Christmas display.

At Loew's Midland Theatre, the manager, John McManus, seized an opportunity in a B picture called "Niagara Falls" when the sound track contained no dialogue and announced to his audience that Japan had declared war he was the only first run theatre manager to do so. The Midland, where "Sundown" was the A picture and the N Newman with "Skylark" reported good houses tonight, perhaps better than average. The Uptown "Swamp Water" and the Orpheum "Look Who's Laughing" decided people were staying home to listen to their radios.

Most conversation about the war, on the streets at least, was good-humored, almost gay with a sense of relief, of "Well, here it is at last." Newsboys yelled, "Gotta whip those Japs" and their customer grinned back at them. Calls to the newspapers indicated, however, that in many a Kansas City home, the bombing of Hawaii held more of sorrow than of adventure. Mothers of sailors on the Oklahoma who had been looking forward to Christmas visits from their soldier sons, called for more information, many of them in tears. Service men themselves wanted to know about the concellation of furloughs, about any orders for reporting to ships or camps.

At the USO club soldiers danced to a juke box, played ping pong and gathered around copies of newspaper extras. They spoke bravely of what "we'll do to those blankety blank Japs" but their interest did not seem particularly deep.

In the afternoon, 1,000 Catholics gathered for the dedication of a De La Salle Academy gymnasium, heard the grim news from their bishop, the very Rev. Edwin Vincent O'Hara. Other Kansas Citians heard further bulletins at a sparsely attended night hockey game between Kansas City and Omaha.

The Southwestern Bell Telephone Co. had no accurate check on call volume, but thought it had risen although not enough to tie up switchboards.

The job co-ordinating all of Kansas City's defense activities will be directed by Rear Admiral Hayne Ellis, retired.

Appointment of Admiral Ellis was announced early tonight by L. P. Cookingham,

Page 4 -- Vaughan, Kansas City

city manager, who with Mayor John B. Gage, conferred with Ellis.

Admiral Ellis will serve as director of Civilian Defense at a salary of $1 a year. The appointment of a director was authorized last week by the city council, which created a municipal defense department. Under the ordinance the mayor will appoint an executive advisory committee of 25 members, which will appoint a large advisory committee including city, state and county officials and representatives of organizations participating in (probably word missing here)... There are expected to be more than 100 members.

Cook, labor and business leaders were unanimous in statements calling for crushing of the Axis.

All utilities and big plants, including North American Aviation, Inc. Bomber plant being built in Kansas City, Kansas, and Remington small arms ammunition plant at Lake City Mo. added guards, took all precautions against sabotage. Police and deputies ordered to stand by.

Wire from Charlton Whitehead, Norfolk, Va. to J. McConaughy - Dec. 8, 1941

After midday-dinner stupor of the majority of Norfolkians, they were kept home by the coldest day of winter, broken at 2:26 p.m. by a brief bulletin over local NBC outlet WTAR, stating that Pearl Harbor had been attacked. Incredulous listeners swamped newspapers and radio, but 10 minutes later NBC news-room confirmed the report. Indignation mixed with fear was most noticeable. On the street corners, where loungers gather to watch the Sunday parade, and in homes, the reaction was "I don't believe it," or "For God's sake why do we always let foreigners get the jump on us," Also heard was the belief that Roosevelt had engineered this so we would be at war, which he wants. Everyone, including Congressman Winder R. Harris, asked, "How could such a raiding force approach without a Navy patrol or at least warning of impending raid."

The first bulletin interrupted Sammy Kaye. The other radio station, WGH, a Mutual outlet, not until 4:20.

Within less than two hours, Chief Police John Woods had rounded up and jailed 14 Japs in Norfolk, all known.

Movies report no bulletins issued, moviegoers not knowing of the war until they got out. However, after 6:30, the Navy's request that men on the delta and the Little report immediately to their ships was announced in all theatres. No falling off of attendance was reported, although the day was poor due to cold. No football or other big crouds were out today.

Brigadier General Rollin H. Tilton, commanding the Harbor Defense of Chesapeake Bay bulletined through WTAR that all officers and men were called to return to their posts. However, late tonight the radio reported that the Third Corps Area Army/rescinding this order. Meanwhile, calls were continuing for all Army men to return. There was much discussion, does this mean Christmas leaves will be cancelled.

Although Commandant of the Fifth Naval District Rear Admiral

Whitehead, Norfolk, Dec. 8, 1941

Manley H. Simons issued an announcement that guards were doubled, he has not called men back. Two ships, the Little and the Delta, however, are recalling their crews. It was rumored they will be sent to the Pacific. There is much wonderment will some of the Atlantic Fleet now here be sent too.

Telephone lines are jammed with calls. Long distance and local calls are very slow, Army and Navy officials burning up the wires, and everyone calling everyone else to tell the latest rumor and news.

The first and only extra was put on the street about 7 o'clock, four pages, published by the Virginian Pilot morning sheet. All carrier boys were recalled from morning and evening papers. The extra was a sell-out within an hour, never reached the suburbs.

The local recruiting office announced that it would remain open all night. Only one man has enlisted so far. He wanted to beat the Japs with his own two hands.

There was much consternation when the night train arrived from New York as no passengers knew of the war until their arrival here.

As a typical Navy town, Norfolk is ready for whatever happens and the concensus is that our Navy can whip the pants off the Japs in a hurry if given a chance. No one seems sorry to see war come, except that they hate to see youngsters killed.

End.

www.ingramcontent.com/pod-product-compliance
Lightning Source LLC
Chambersburg PA
CBHW080049190426

43201CB00035B/2142